I0887334

Creating New Strategies for Cooperative Collection Development

Creating New Strategies for Cooperative Collection Development has been co-published simultaneously as *Collection Management,* Volume 24, Numbers 1/2 and 3/4 2000.

Creating New Strategies for Cooperative Collection Development

Papers from the Aberdeen Woods Conference

Milton T. Wolf
Marjorie E. Bloss
Editors

Creating New Strategies for Cooperative Collection Development has been co-published simultaneously as *Collection Management,* Volume 24, Numbers 1/2 and 3/4 2000.

Routledge
Taylor & Francis Group
New York London

First published by
The Haworth Information Press, 10 Alice Street, Binghamton, NY 13904-1580 USA

Harrington Park Press is an imprint of The Haworth Press, Inc., 10 Alice Street, Binghamton, NY 13904-1580 USA

This edition published 2013 by Routledge

Routledge
Taylor & Francis Group
711 Third Avenue
New York, NY 10017

Routledge
Taylor & Francis Group
2 Park Square, Milton Park
Abingdon, Oxon OX14 4RN

Routledge is an imprint of the Taylor & Francis Group, an informa business

Creating New Strategies for Cooperative Collection Development has been co-published simultaneously as *Collection Management*, Volume 24, Numbers 1/2 and 3/4 2000.

© 2000 by The Haworth Press, Inc. All rights reserved. No part of this work may be reproduced or utilized in any form or by any means, electronic or mechanical, including photocopying, microfilm and recording, or by any information storage and retrieval system, without permission in writing from the publisher.

The development, preparation, and publication of this work has been undertaken with great care. However, the publisher, employees, editors, and agents of The Haworth Press and all imprints of The Haworth Press, Inc., including The Haworth Medical Press® and Pharmaceutical Products Press®, are not responsible for any errors contained herein or for consequences that may ensue from use of materials or information contained in this work. Opinions expressed by the author(s) are not necessarily those of The Haworth Press, Inc.

Cover design by Thomas J. Mayshock Jr.

Library of Congress Cataloging-in-Publication Data

Creating new strategies for cooperative collection development : papers from the Aberdeen Woods conference / Milton T. Wolf, Marjorie E. Bloss, editors.
p. cm.
Discussion papers from the conference "Creating New Strategies for Cooperative Collection Development" hosted by the Center for Research Libraries, November 12-14, 1999.
Co-published simultaneously as Collection management, v. 24, nos. 1-4, 2000.
Includes bibliographical references and index.
ISBN 0-7890-1158-1 (alk. paper)–ISBN 0-7890-1159-X (pbk. : alk. paper)
1. Cooperative collection development (Libraries)–Congresses. 2. Research libraries–Collection development–Congresses. I. Wolf, Milton T. II. Bloss Marjorie E. III. Collection management.
Z687.15 .C74 2000
025.2′1–dc21 00-053962

Creating New Strategies for Cooperative Collection Development

CONTENTS

ABOUT THE EDITORS

Milton T. Wolf, MLS, served as Senior Vice President for Collection Programs at the Center for Research Libraries from February 1998 through November 1999. He was responsible for the management and development of the five major components of CRL's expanding cooperative collection development program for academic and research libraries worldwide. Director of Collection Development at the University of Nevada, Reno, since 1977, he held a variety of staff positions at the libraries of Pennsylvania State University, Wright State University, and the University of North Carolina at Chapel Hill. A Phi Beta Kappa graduate in English from Pennsylvania State University, he obtained a master's in library science from the University of Michigan. His professional activities include extensive professional involvement, published papers, and presentations. He is a well-known consultant to libraries in collection development issues. His interests range widely and often include research and writing involving science fiction.

Marjorie E. Bloss, MLS, is currently Vice President for Library Operations at the Center for Research Libraries. She has held positions in technical services and resource sharing at OCLC, Illinois Institute of Technology, the Rochester (New York) Regional Library Council, and the Rochester Institute of Technology. She received her BA from the University of Rochester and her MLS from Case Western Reserve University. Her professional activities include extensive involvement in the Association for Library Collections and Technical Services of the American Library Association and the International Federation of Library Associations and Institutions. She has written numerous works on serials, union listing, applications of standards on serial holdings statements, and serials cataloging. In 1988, she was the recipient of the ALA/ALCTS Bowker/Ulrich's Serials Librarianship Award.

Introduction

Milton T. Wolf
Marjorie E. Bloss

The foundation for cooperative collection development was laid in the early 1800s, with international exchange programs begun by European universities. A century later conventions for resource sharing, such as union catalogs and interlibrary loan, were established. The mid-20th century saw the introduction of a number of cooperative collection development programs: the Farmington Plan; the Foreign Newspaper Project of the Association for Research Libraries; and the Midwest Inter-Library Center, later known as the Center for Research Libraries. At the end of the 20th century, many new consortia entered the playing field in a variety of configurations. Some found their basis on geographic parameters, others came together as a result of licensing agreements, still others formed ties based on type of library or topical interests.

This significant increase in the number and vitality of consortia in the late 20th century can be attributed to a number of factors. Notably, economic, social, and technological changes have all had their impact on the need to cooperate and work together. In the opinions of many, cooperative collection development is the best hope for rationalizing effective access and ownership strategies given the economic and technological pressures we face today.

Milton Wolf is Senior Vice President (retired) for Collections, and Marjorie E. Bloss is Vice President for Library Operations, The Center for Research Libraries, 6050 South Kenwood Avenue, Chicago, IL 60637-2804 (e-mail: bloss@crlmail.uchicago.edu).

[Haworth co-indexing entry note]: "Introduction." Wolf, Milton T., and Marjorie E. Bloss. Co-published simultaneously in *Collection Management* (The Haworth Information Press, an imprint of The Haworth Press, Inc.) Vol. 24, No. 1/2, 2000, pp. 1-4; and: *Creating New Strategies for Cooperative Collection Development* (ed: Milton T. Wolf and Marjorie E. Bloss) The Haworth Information Press, an imprint of The Haworth Press, Inc., 2000, pp. 1-4. Single or multiple copies of this article are available for a fee from The Haworth Document Delivery Service [1-800-342-9678, 9:00 a.m. - 5:00 p.m. (EST). E-mail address: getinfo@haworthpressinc.com].

© 2000 by The Haworth Press, Inc. All rights reserved.

CONFERENCE GOALS

In order to discuss these changes and evaluate their impact, a major collection development conference devoted to new strategies was held on November 12-14, 1999 at the Aberdeen Woods Conference Center in Atlanta, Georgia. Sponsored by the Center for Research Libraries (CRL), the Association of Research Libraries (ARL), the International Consortium of Library Consortia (ICOLC), and the Research Libraries Group (RLG), the conference was held as part of the 50th year anniversary celebration for the Center for Research Libraries, which operates the nation's oldest cooperative research library.

The purpose of the conference was to assemble a group of knowledgeable, experienced and diverse information professionals involved in the planning and implementation of cooperative collection development programs. One goal of the conference organizers was to determine a new agenda for cooperative collection development in order to increase the benefits currently derived from resource sharing efforts. A further goal was to formulate an agenda so the community could begin to design and implement new strategies for cooperative collection development. Conference goers were able to examine the pros and cons of both centered and decentralized models in order to identify a hybrid model employing the best elements of these approaches.

The conference was divided into three overlapping investigations:

1. *Assessing the Situation:* Looking at cultural, commercial and political issues, such as volume count fixations (quantity vs. quality), faculty and commercial resistance to reforming scholarly communications, publishing monopolies, look-alike research collections, traditional campus cultural impediments, and how some groups have been able to manage them.
2. *Identifying New Opportunities:* How do we build on our traditional cooperative models (large scale centralized like CRL, large scale distributed like ARL/AAU, and regional like ICOLC) to advance new approaches in areas such as archiving, preservation, and digitization? What are the characteristics of successful programs? What case studies/models provide insight? How have they built on lessons from the past? What enabling technologies can assist us? What achievable benefits are appropriate to strive for in the current environment?

3. *Eliminating Borders:* What are the implications/opportunities presented to cooperative collection development by the growing unimportance of national borders and other geographic restraints? Can technologies provide new forums for cooperation? Can we grow new partnerships? How?

This volume contains 18 papers from the conference dealing with these and related themes and topics. The speakers were as diverse as the topics, providing participants with a broad rage of perspectives, insights and ideas.

CONFERENCE AFTERMATH

During the conference, representatives from more than 125 academic and research libraries and library consortia were given time to share information, to mingle with colleagues, and to formulate ideas for how best to handle issues they were facing in their own institutions. Over the course of the weekend, the participants developed a deeper understanding of the potential for greater efforts of cooperative collection development and the essential nature of this activity for the future of academic research. The conference participants defined a number of the needs that should be addressed by the library community to foster the advancement of cooperative collection development, and recommended a series of steps to be taken to insure its future success and expansion.

In order to move forward some of the concerns, participants were asked if they would be willing to volunteer to work on one of the action items. These are in the process of being tallied and prioritized. Committees will be established in the spring of 2000 to move these activities forward.

Additionally, the Center for Research Libraries will undertake two initiatives from the conference. The first is that Beverly Lynch, interim president of CRL, will convene a meeting of the directors of the major national research library organizations–CRL, ARL, RLG, CLIR, DLF, ACRL and possibly OCLC. While conference participants were able to point to a good number of successes in cooperative collection development, they identified a need for greater national leadership, coordination, and advocacy. Bringing the directors of these organizations together will provide a forum for discussing an evolving strategy for working in a more coordinated manner that will help define a national agenda, both with AAU and perhaps with federal agencies.

Second, CRL will work to compile a central website/clearinghouse that will provide links to other web pages dealing with cooperative collection development activities and organizations. The intent is to facilitate ongoing communication among the participants of the regional and subject-based projects and provide assistance to new projects under consideration. The timeframe for availability of this website is mid-2000.

While the conference in and of itself was productive it will be the ability and concerted effort by many of the players to move the agenda forward that will be the most telling sign of its success. The topic was cooperative collective development, but in reality, the emphasis on cooperation goes far beyond collection development.

KEYNOTE ADDRESS

University Libraries as Agents of Change

Myles Brand

I am very happy to be with you this evening to commemorate the 50th anniversary of the Center for Research Libraries.

Anniversaries are special occasions because they give us a chance to take stock of the experiences that have drawn us together and made us what we are. They inspire a renewed appreciation of the values and traditions that have sustained us.

And they prompt us to anticipate how those values, traditions, and experiences will help us meet the challenges of the future.

One of the values that has sustained the Center for Research Libraries over the last fifty years is a bedrock belief in the necessity of teamwork. Teamwork can be a complicated concept, but it is one that we understand very well at Indiana University. Teamwork means working as hard as one can to cultivate individual strengths while at

Myles Brand is President of Indiana University, Bloomington, Indiana.

This keynote address was delivered at the Center for Research Libraries Annual Meeting, November 12, 1999.

[Haworth co-indexing entry note]: "University Libraries as Agents of Change." Brand, Myles. Co-published simultaneously in *Collection Management* (The Haworth Information Press, an imprint of The Haworth Press, Inc.) Vol. 24, No. 1/2, 2000, pp. 5-14; and: *Creating New Strategies for Cooperative Collection Development* (ed: Milton T. Wolf and Marjorie E. Bloss) The Haworth Information Press, an imprint of The Haworth Press, Inc., 2000, pp. 5-14. Single or multiple copies of this article are available for a fee from The Haworth Document Delivery Service [1-800-342-9678, 9:00 a.m. - 5:00 p.m. (EST). E-mail address: getinfo@haworthpressinc.com].

© 2000 by The Haworth Press, Inc. All rights reserved.

the same time furthering the development of the group. It means knowing when to compete and when to cooperate and knowing how to do both with complete dedication.

Let me share with you a story that illustrates this idea. One of the first things anyone thinks about in connection with Indiana University is basketball and Bob Knight. Each year Coach Knight asks one of the world's greatest living cellists–who happens, incidentally, to teach at the IU School of Music–to talk to his basketball team. Janos Starker explains to IU basketball players the importance of tireless practice. He tells them practice is what will give them control of their game. He tells them that if they think they have a tough coach, they ought to sit in on studio sessions with *his* students. Then he tells them that no matter how beautifully a single instrument can play, it takes an orchestra to make a great musical composition come to life, just as it takes teamwork to win games. That is also the guiding principle for cooperative collection development. No matter how strong our individual collections are, in this age of proliferating scholarship, it takes teamwork for us to carry out our mission. It takes national and international teamwork for us for us to provide our scholars and researchers access to the full body of knowledge generated in our era and in past ones. It's a big job, one that is not getting any easier. But it is a job we can accomplish only by working together.

Over its 50-year history, CRL has developed a strong tradition of teamwork. That tradition had its birth in 1940, when 13 presidents from Midwestern universities met to talk about how they might most productively pool the library resources of their individual institutions. From its modest beginnings, CRL has emerged as a truly cooperative nationwide effort of international repute. From the original 13 participants, the Center for Research Libraries now counts among its ranks nearly 100 full members and 34 associate members. In 1949, the cooperative acquisitions program began by recording subscriptions to forty newspapers on microfilm. Today there are over 500,000 records in the CRL Catalog to which member libraries have access. For CRL, access–not acquisition–is the dominant ethos. And that ideology makes available a vast store of global newspapers, international doctoral dissertations, scholarly journals, subject collections, and area studies resources. It provides an abundance of information through electronic databases and adds new meaning to the concept of the library as a treasury of knowledge.

I am proud to represent Indiana University here this evening, as Herman B. Wells did in 1940. Like President Wells, who just celebrated his 97th birthday, I know that the future will bring unimagined changes. I also know that we can be equal to those changes only if we hold fast to the values of cooperation, resourcefulness, and dedication to the scholarly enterprise that prompted our predecessors to join forces 50 years ago.

When President Wells and his colleagues met in 1940 their primary objectives were the same ones as we have today. They were concerned with building solid disciplinary collections, with preservation, and with increased availability of infrequently used materials. While our goals have remained the same, our strategies for achieving them are somewhat different–as they should be. The world Herman Wells and his colleagues faced was very different than one that we live in today.

In 1949, NATO had just been formed. Communist leader Mao Zedong had just established the People's Republic of China. And the magazine *Popular Mechanics* had predicted that "computers in the future may weigh no more than one and a half tons." MIT had just established Whirlwind, the first real-time computer with random-access, magnetic core memory. It was a ponderous device that foreshadowed the sophisticated computers of our era.

In 1949, we were struggling with efficient ways to load and store information. In 1999, we find ourselves struggling to sort and absorb information. As some scholars have suggested, information overload may be the greatest problem we have faced in the twentieth century. It very well may be the most crucial challenge of the next.

When our predecessors met 50 years ago to discuss what would become the CRL, television was just a year old. In fact, Harry Truman's presidential inauguration ceremony was the first one to be nationally televised. It was viewed by an estimated 10 million Americans. The TV viewing audience who saw Truman take the oath of office was greater than the total of all persons witnessing all previous presidential inaugurations. Indeed, more people watched Truman's inauguration than ever before had seen a single event. Just to put that in current perspective, let me tell you that last week more than 13 million people watched *Frasier*. The reach of television gave new meaning to the concept of community and shared experience. More recently, the internet has *virtually* redefined our ability to communicate. And I don't have to tell you what level of impact new technologies are having on university libraries.

In 1949, universities were different places, too. The Servicemen's Readjustment Act of 1944 was in high gear. The GI Bill ushered in an unprecedented period of growth for America's universities. In 1949, our universities were entering the golden age of higher education. They were literally bursting at the seams, doing everything they could to expand classrooms, living spaces, research programs, and libraries. Now, on the cusp of the 21st century, the expansion seems to lie in the volume of scholarly output and disciplinary specialization.

There's a wonderful bumper sticker that says "Change is inevitable; growth is optional." The Center for Research Libraries has a long history of viewing change as an opportunity for growth. First of all, that has meant devising alternatives to the traditional model of collection development–a shift in focus from collection building to collection management. The old paradigm was to build comprehensive collections on site for faculty and students; it didn't matter if most materials were duplicated elsewhere. Bigger was better, and competition, rather than cooperation, was the order of the day for major research libraries. Rightly so, I might add. In programs such as area studies, for instance, collection development was essential for institutional credibility and grant support. The extent of one's collections determined the prestige of one's reputation as a major repository of knowledge.

Yet that model no longer stands for a number of reasons–not least among these are significant budgetary constraints. David Shulenburger, provost of the University of Kansas, has done a fine job of outlining the economic factors that demand a shift in focus. Shulenburger notes that between 1986 and 1996, the consumer price index increased 44 percent. The cost of healthcare increased 84 percent. The cost of monographs increased 62 percent. Scholarly journals rose 148 percent–nearly triple the rate of inflation. These facts make the traditional model of collection building untenable, especially when one considers that library budgets would have to increase by at least 70 percent to maintain the same proportion of monographs and serials as in 1986. Taking into account the proliferation and price inflation of academic publishing, libraries would need acquisitions budgets two and a half times that of their average allocation.

Even a national library, such as the British Library, acknowledges that collecting in all languages, in all subjects, from all parts of the world can no longer be sustained. Yet full-scale, detailed, national and international coordination is not easily achieved. Our most successful efforts have thus far been regional and local in nature. These include such ARL initiatives as the Latin Americanist Research Resources Project, the German Resources Project, the Digital South Asia Library Project and others. I chaired the AAU/ARL task force that developed these global resources projects and found the experience an enlightening one. While the librarians serving on the task force were fully on board with the concept of cooperative collections management, the area studies faculty, by and large, continued to see the crucial issues as ones associated with acquisitions. Our task, then is to foment cultural change in so far as we educate faculty members to revise their ideas about the purpose and function of their libraries.

Among other characteristics, the last decades of the 20th century will be remembered as a time for breaking down borders that divide countries, national economies, and scholarly disciplines. As we develop more global economies and a more global understanding of our world, we must also develop new ways to organize the knowledge we generate. The changing global landscape requires change on our part, and I believe that university research libraries are uniquely well suited to be agents of change in the higher education community.

The great Mahatma Gandhi once wisely said, "You must be the change you wish to see in the world." In the higher education community, that is a long-term proposition. I can tell you from first-hand experience that leading a major research university is like being the captain of an ocean liner: change is slow-moving. Have you ever watched a ship as large as the Queen Mary try to make a starboard turn? Her very size gives one the impression that the ship prefers to maintain a steady course straight ahead rather than deviate in one direction or another. The staff and faculty of a major university exhibit a similar resistance to change. Perhaps this is because the changes in the higher education environment are so gradual that some don't see the need to redirect the course of the institution. Others, who do see the need to react, must do so in cooperation with their peers. Herein lies one of the major challenges for a research library that is acting as an agent of change. We may have crews working against one another at the opposite ends of the ship. Groups of faculty may be isolated from other groups by a number of factors, not the least of which is the old two-cultures paradigm that divides scholars in the arts and humanities from those in the science disciplines. That can make it difficult to effect real change. But while, as I said earlier, research libraries must be the agents of change, and while I firmly believe that institutional leadership in these matters is important, I also believe that we can accomplish our goals only if we galvanize our faculty and staff to address the problems that make the old model of collections development untenable.

As the Pew report issued last year by the ARL and the AAU notes, many in our community perceive the current crisis as the *library's problem*. According to this line of thinking, if university administrators would only allocate enough money to correct the imbalance between the volume of scholarly output and the budgets libraries bring to bear in managing that output, the problem would be solved. Actually, the issue of high-priced journals is one that faculty must resolve. It is faculty who establish the conditions of scholarly discourse, and it is they who can most productively adapt those conditions to the changing environment of electronic publishing. It is they who can alter the reward structure expressed in the habit of mind that requires, say, 32 published articles be included in a tenure portfolio. It is the faculty who must reconsider the tonnage model that pits quantity against quality places an unwarranted burden on research libraries. Faculty have the power to change this as they devise new procedures for electronic publication, peer review, and certification. It is up to us to provide the institutional leadership that motivates them to do so.

There is no singular or clear solution, just as there is not one clear course for a ship to take across the ocean. The course we travel depends on our ultimate destination, on our current coordinates, and on who's piloting the ship.

At IU, I convened a Committee on Scholarly Communications last year to review the current state of scholarly communications, to examine national efforts to change the environment, and to plan a course of action to be undertaken on the campus. In its interim report, the committee wrote that the issues surrounding scholarly communications are many and vary widely among disciplines. Members of this multidisciplinary faculty group, who had spent considerable time discussing the traditions in each discipline, were very surprised at how widely the norms of scholarly publication and the markets for scholarly materials differed among disciplines. Because of these different traditions, the committee did not find that any single "magic bullet" could be used to deflate the prices of journals. Instead they advocated collective actions that would involve colleges and universities working together, the participation of scholarly and professional societies, and collaboration with organizations outside of the academic community.

The committee proposed–and the AAU recently gave its support to–the creation of a national commission on scholarly publishing that would focus national attention on the many substantive issues involved. We are in the planning phases of putting together a conference to be held in the early spring that will serve as a staging ground for forming the National Commission on Scholarly Publishing. The commission will provide a national, ongoing forum for university administrators, publishers, library directors, and others to engage in sustained dialogue about issues of import to university libraries. The commission, for which we will soon be seeking financial support, will add continuity to discussions that are now followed in a somewhat episodic manner. It will also serve the useful role of enabling us to identify which areas of this problem warrant further research.

Recently, AAU and others have endorsed ARL's Scholarly Publishing and Academic Resources Coalition–or SPARC as it is known. The Pew Report called on libraries to "be smart shoppers." Supporting competition among high-priced scientific journals is one way of reducing and containing prices. A competitive market will force the change of the status quo. I was impressed when I learned recently that the new journal, *Organic Letters*, produced by the American Chemical Society in partnership with SPARC, costs one-fourth of a subscription to *Tetrahedron Letters*, a competing publication. In the state of Indiana, where we have a tradition of watching our dollars, Wabash College announced recently that it had canceled its subscription to *Tetrahedron Letters* in favor of the electronic *Organic Letters*. The college made this change with the full approval of its faculty chemists. By eliminating *Tetrahedron Letters*, Wabash College has been able to add thirty-five new journals for ten different departments without any budgetary increase.

The Indiana Committee recognized, as I am sure many members of this audience do as well, the need for "bottom up" change motivated through key influential members of the university community. In this arena, the research library must act as the agent of change by educating faculty about the plethora of important issues posed by the current state of scholarly publishing and the steps faculty can take to address these issues. Groups such as SPARC and the incipient National Commission on Scholarly Publishing will be highly workable vehicles for accomplishing this important goal. I'm proud that Indiana University is a founding member of SPARC.

The good news on this front is that technology facilitates change, but as we all know, technology can be frustrating–involving, as it inevitably does, different interfaces, crashing search engines, remote access, licensing terms, copyright issues, disparities in pricing electronic resources–not to mention budget strains caused by the need to provide electronic resources and paper ones, too. Nevertheless, electronic catalogs and web-based communication enable the cooperative collection development that is our best survival strategy. This is a strategy we have not yet exploited to its full potential. Improved telecommunications, including e-mail, conference calls, and the Internet provide infrastructure for greater possibilities for interlibrary cooperation. Distributed learning also opens new paths of collaborative collection management. As professors teach more in a distributed environment, library resources need to be accessible through professors' web sites. Thus, an investment in technology is also becoming a direct investment in teaching and learning. Such investments are providing the backbone for us to be able to distribute library resources.

Ten years ago, John Howe, a history professor and interim director of libraries at the University of Minnesota, wrote that the library might still be the symbolic heart of a the university, but it was losing its place as a central funding priority. First, information technology was enabling faculty to access scholarly information directly–without library intervention, and money that was being invested to build the technology infrastructure was diverting funds from the library. Second, the decline in arts and sciences and the rise of science and technology programs were eroding the power of disciplines that most directly supported the traditional library. And, third, libraries were not competitive enough in the new, aggressive environment of higher education to be a major player. He concluded that libraries could no longer take it for granted that they had a special status in the university.

I think Howe got it right, but ten years later, with distribution of library materials being so integral to the success of distributed learning, libraries and librarians are becoming key players once again. In addition, faculty need librarians to help educate them about the best values in publications, to suggest alternative publications, and to support their teaching.

My predecessor Herman Wells, whom I mentioned so fondly earlier in my talk, once noted that whoever is talking, no souls are saved after 20 minutes. I think there is a great deal of wisdom in that sentiment. I know we've all had a long day and a fine dinner on top of it. But before I end my remarks this evening, I would like to offer you some advice from my perspective.

My advice to you is to facilitate dialogue with your peers, your constituents, and your administrators. At all costs, maintain and strengthen your contacts with faculty, presidents, provosts. Learn your constituents' needs so that you can avoid the unproductive position of being a passive reactor or a complainer. Make every effort to get the issues on the table, to expand the scope of the conversation about acquisition and cooperative collections management.

In dialogue with your faculty and administrators, pursue those areas where you still need to build unique collections for research, but forge ahead with national and international cooperation. No one will ever build a full collection: economics won't allow it; technologies don't require it. Continue to put your energies into cooperative collections development, no matter how difficult it is. The International Coalition of Library Consortia is a good example of recent cooperative effort. The Coalition continues to be an informal, self-organized group comprised of library consortia that is now expanding to the United Kingdom, Germany, the Netherlands, Australia and other countries. And one of its primary functions is to facilitate dialogue on issues of common interest.

In my talk this evening I have advanced the idea that libraries can be agents of change in the higher education community. In doing so, I do not intend to underestimate the complex and changing world to which libraries must respond. In many ways you are all working in pressure cookers that continue to build up steam as the problems associated with scholarly publishing and technological innovation become more complex.

As AAU board chairman, I look to you to help us devise solutions to the pressing problems facing research libraries today. When I think about the important job that lies ahead of us, I am reminded of the ancient redwood forests that I love to visit in the Pacific Northwest.

There's a fact most people don't know about these beautiful and ancient trees. Despite their impressive size, redwood trees have very small root systems. How then, you might ask, do they reach into the clouds? How do they grow so huge that a car can drive through their hollow trunks? The answer is a simple one: they grow in clumps, and they hold one another up. *Their roots are networked together.* Like the giant redwoods, like the trees in the magnificent redwood forests, we are also intertwined. We can grow; indeed, we can thrive, but only if we do so together. Now more than ever, we must look to the future, rely on our mutual strengths, and share our resources if we are to enter the new millennium with confidence.

Thank you for the important work you do and for the opportunity to speak with you this evening. Like Coach Bobby Knight and Janos Starker, you are distinguishing yourselves by combining unique talents with teamwork–and you are making a difference. I have every confidence that you will continue to do so.

Questions?

COOPERATIVES: APPROVAL PLANS AND CONSORTIA

Designing and Implementing a Consortial Approval Plan: The OhioLINK Experience

Carol Pitts Diedrichs

INTRODUCTION

In a 1993 article on the history of cooperative collection development in the Triangle Research Libraries Network (TRLN), Patricia Dominguez and Luke Swindler define the rationale for success as the achievement of Interlocked collections. "The resulting interdependent collections provide a breadth and depth of coverage that would be impossible for individual institutions to achieve on their own."[1] There is no question that the ever-increasing cost of library materials drives

Carol Pitts Diedrichs is Assistant Director for Technical Services, The Ohio State University Libraries, 1858 Neil Avenue Mall, Columbus, OH 43210-1286 (e-mail: diedrichs.1@osu.edu).

This paper was presented on Nov. 13, 1999 at the CRL "Creating New Strategies for Cooperative Collection Development Conference" in Atlanta.

[Haworth co-indexing entry note]: "Designing and Implementing a Consortial Approval Plan: The OhioLINK Experience." Diedrichs, Carol Pitts. Co-published simultaneously in *Collection Management* (The Haworth Information Press, an imprint of The Haworth Press, Inc.) Vol. 24, No. 1/2, 2000, pp. 15-44; and: *Creating New Strategies for Cooperative Collection Development* (ed: Milton T. Wolf and Marjorie E. Bloss) The Haworth Information Press, an imprint of The Haworth Press, Inc., 2000, pp. 15-44. Single or multiple copies of this article are available for a fee from The Haworth Document Delivery Service [1-800-342-9678, 9:00 a.m. - 5:00 p.m. (EST). E-mail address: getinfo@haworthpressinc.com].

© 2000 by The Haworth Press, Inc. All rights reserved.

libraries to search for ways to extend their buying power and increase the availability of diverse material for their patrons. Dan Hazen argues that a cooperative collection development project must meet one or several of the following criteria (all of which are not necessarily compatible goals):

- Broadening access–acquiring a broader variety of material;
- Containing cost–saving money by reducing redundancy;
- Improving coverage–attempting to ensure complete coverage; and
- Ensuring the exotic–buying material that is not used frequently or at the present time but will be needed in the future.[2]

It is also important for the purposes of this paper to draw a distinction between cooperative collection development and resource sharing. When drawing this distinction, Patricia Bril defines resource sharing as taking advantage of past decisions about what was purchased whether the initial decision was made with sharing in mind or not. In contrast, cooperative collection building is defined as intentional present actions intended to promote cooperative collection building.[3] Shreeves' review of the cooperative collection development literature leads him to two conclusions:

- There is widespread agreement about the factors leading to success.
- Of all the many efforts over the past 50 years, only modest successes can be found.

> How reliable are the success factors identified, if successes to date have been only modest? Are they so rarely found together in sufficient strength and quantity that most efforts are doomed to failure? Or is there a missing critical factor–yet to be clearly identified–which would serve as a catalyst to enable the rest to result in substantive achievement? . . . Finally, how will librarians and scholars know if they achieve success? How is success in cooperative building of collections to be measured?[4]

Based on his experience in Ohio with the OhioLINK consortium, David Kohl cites five landmarks for successful resource sharing: joining a consortium, integrating the catalogs and circulation components, providing physical delivery of print materials, providing electronic delivery of electronic resources, and finally, integrated collection development. "What the OhioLINK experience seems to clearly demonstrate is that coordinated collection development must be the last, not the initial, step in the formation of a superlibrary consortium. Until librarians can demonstrate to patrons that an actual working system is in place that allows them to conveniently, speedily, and reliably get the materials they need from other locations and institutions, it is difficult to make any kind of truly serious case for not just coordinated, but integrated collection development."[5] Thus, true integrated collection development is a second generation of resource sharing which may be more achievable today than ever before.

BACKGROUND

What Is OhioLINK?

Much has been written about the history, founding and goals of OhioLINK.[6] For the purposes of this paper, the About OhioLINK section of the consortium's home page provides the most accurate and up to date summary of its composition and structure. "The Ohio Library and Information Network, OhioLINK, is a consortium of Ohio's college and university libraries and the State Library of Ohio. Serving more than 500,000 students, faculty, and staff at 74 institutions, OhioLINK offers access to more than 24 million library items statewide. OhioLINK also provides access to 67 research databases, including a variety of full-text resources.

OhioLINK offers user-initiated online borrowing through its statewide central catalog. Users have the ability to electronically request items while searching the OhioLINK central catalog. It also provides a delivery service among member institutions to speed exchange of library items. To date, the OhioLINK central catalog contains almost 7 million master records from its 74 institutions, encompassing a spectrum of library material including law, medical and special collections.

OhioLINK serves faculty, students, staff and other researchers at member institutions via campus library systems, campus networks, and the Internet. The system provides access to more than 4,500 simultaneous users at 113 locations, serving more than a half-million patrons. The OhioLINK central catalog is available to outside users through the Internet. However, access to the research databases is restricted to OhioLINK member users (valid patrons at OhioLINK member institutions). OhioLINK's membership includes 17 public universities, 23 community/technical colleges, 33 private colleges and the State Library of Ohio.[7]

Why a Consortial Approval Plan?

OhioLINK's successes–electronic resources including databases, fulltext, electronic journals, image and data files, a central catalog of all member library holdings, and patron initiated borrowing and delivery via private courier–were but one part of the initial mandate for the project dating back to the consortium's founding in the 1980s. Another fundamental tenet was cooperative collection building. Despite its may successes, the consortium still needed to find a way to advance goals for cooperative collection development for traditional materials. Efforts had been made to investigate use of the RLG Conspectus in particular subject areas but the effort involved was considerable with relatively little gain. By 1997, the time had come for some different approach to the issue.

Tom Sanville, Executive Director of OhioLINK, had been tracking various trends within the consortium. When looking at the percent of items held by number of libraries between 1996 and 1999, the percent of titles held in only one library was dropping and the percentage held in more than 5 libraries was growing.[8]

In a 1996 article by Greg Byerly, on average 22.8% of each library's collection was unique when added to the central OhioLINK catalog. This percentage has confirmed one of the original premises behind the consortium's founding–that each of Ohio's universities had unique and diverse holdings.[9]

In a 1995 paper on OhioLINK, Randy Dykhuis concludes that cooperation within OhioLINK will be tempered because more than 60% of the combined collection is held in only 1 library with almost 85% held by fewer than 3 libraries. He concludes that the OhioLINK libraries have already been doing an excellent job of focusing on their individual missions and avoiding unnecessary duplication.[10] However, as the uniqueness of the collection deteriorates, the need to facilitate and encourage cooperation re-emerges. Dykhuis also reveals elsewhere in his paper that his data were compiled before some of the largest libraries in OhioLINK had begun to contribute to the central catalog including Ohio State University, University of Toledo, Kent State University, and Cleveland State University. Once these databases were added, the uniqueness percentage continued to fall. As Table 1 reveals, the percentage of unique titles has continued to decline from a high of 57.1% in 1996 to 55.9% in 1999. In addition, the Database Management and Standards Committee of OhioLINK has sampled the duplication of bibliographic records within OhioLINK. They found that approximately 5% of the titles in the database could actually be considered duplicates of other records in the database. If this 5 percent of records were combined with the correct records, the uniqueness number would likely fall even further.

Much earlier in the early 1980s, Paul Mosher and Marcia Pankake proposed a model in which the total collection development efforts of the ARL libraries would result in a comprehensive national collection among those libraries. "'This approach presumes that the total collecting activity of ARL and other major research libraries achieves, on a national scale, reasonable depth in every area of interest to research in the United States, both in the present and future. It is the total of the collections of research libraries which approaches comprehensiveness' (p. 424)."[11] However, by 1994, there was clear evidence that the range of resources was growing narrower and more homogeneous. In spring 1994, Anna Perrault's landmark research on the shrinking of monograph collections was released. She concluded the following:

> The national collection is shrinking . . . There is an overall 27.76% rate of decline in nonserial imprints from 1985-1989 for the collective resources base of the 72 ARL libraries whose holdings are included in the 1991 edition of the OCLC/AMIGOS Collection Analysis System.
>
> A decline in total number of monographs purchased and proportional declines in number of unique titles indicates that there is a concentration down to a core of titles occurring in U.S. academic libraries. . . . Instead, the 1.14% decline in unique titles for the period under study suggests that the core of titles academic research libraries select in common is increasing, resulting in less diversity in title and subject coverage among those libraries.
>
> The suspicions and fears expressed by the ARL that a drastic reduction is occurring in foreign-language purchasing are borne

> out by the results of the research reported in this article. The number of foreign language imprints experienced an overall 43.33% reduction while English language imprints declined 12.34%. . . . United States research libraries are acquiring a smaller and smaller portion of the world publishing output. The danger is that the unavailability of a diversity of cultural as well as research materials could foster a narrowing of education and inquiry.[12]

Armed with this research and the concern that the OhioLINK collection was becoming too homogenous, Sanville explored the OhioLINK duplication issue in a different manner. He constructed statistics based on the availability of material to meet actual patron requests. First, he found that a large proportion of titles requested by OhioLINK users and also published in the past few years (recent imprints) had 5+ copies available at the time of request. Second, a significant number of requests went unfilled because no copies were available. In October 1998, in just over 10% of requests, no copy was available to fill the request. The number of unfilled requests had grown steadily from 5% in March 1995. In contrast, in October 1998, for approximately 30% of requests, 5 or more copies were held within the consortium. This percentage had grown from 21% in March 1995. When this data was shared with the Library Advisory Council in June 1997 (the primary operational governing body of the consortium composed of library directors), the LAC attributed the growth in the over 5 copies range to the homogeneousness of approval plans. As a result, the Cooperative Information Resources Committee (CIRM) was asked to explore the idea of a consortial approval plan.

TABLE 1. Percentage of Unique Titles Held by OhioLINK Libraries

Year	1 library	2 libraries	3 libraries	4 libraries	5 libraries	5 or more libraries
1999	55.9%	14.0%	7.0%	5.3%	3.5%	14.3%
1998	56.0%	14.0%	7.8%	5.0%	3.4%	13.8%
1997	56.5%	14.8%	7.3%	4.5%	3.3%	13.6%
1996	57.1%	15.9%	7.9%	4.7%	3.3%	11.1%

PROJECT DESIGN

CIRM charged a three member task force to investigate the feasibility of a consortial approval plan. There was clear agreement that the consortium could be doing a better job of purchasing current monographs. In essence, the question was how could OhioLINK improve its buying patterns to purchase fewer duplicates and to acquire more of the material held by no one in the consortium? The task force synthesized the problem into two questions:

- Through cooperation in monograph purchases via approval plan(s) could OhioLINK build a more heterogeneous consortial collection? The project was also intended to assist with firm order purchasing for those consortium members for whom approval plans were not a viable option.
- Would a joint contract allow OhioLINK to collectively purchase more books than OhioLINK libraries currently did?

Preliminary investigation with vendors revealed five areas of concern on the vendors' part:

1. *Volume of business*–Would the volume of business be enough to interest the vendors? Did the consortium have firm commitments for participation or was this strictly exploratory? Would the vendor bid be based on a volume of business which might not materialize?
2. *Potential for phasing of the adoption of the plan or pilot projects*–Would OhioLINK expect to implement 74+ approval plans on the same day within a very short time period of the bid completion? Could the implementation be phased to allow the vendor time to prepare and staff for the operation? Depending on the intentions of the plan, would OhioLINK consider pilot projects to test the more exploratory aspects of the plan?
3. *Possible negative attitudes about the project*–Did OhioLINK already have the buy-in of its consortial members? Did OhioLINK recognize that any attempts to limit the number of copies purchased would have to be based on policy adopted by the consortium to be successful?
4. *Availability of existing data on collection strengths*–Did OhioLINK have existing data on which to build a central profile? If

the vendor was expected to provide this, did OhioLINK recognize the time and effort involved?

5. *RFP and bid requirements*–What exactly would the terms of the RFP and bid requirements be? Was OhioLINK expecting an extraordinary discount as well as development efforts and outstanding service?

Of course, the task force had its own set of issues to be investigated and addressed. As a result of these preliminary discussions with vendors and further discussion within the consortium, the initial task force recommended proceeding based on the following findings:

1. The vendors had the necessary systems available.
2. Those systems would allow libraries to share ordering and approval shipment information.
3. The vendor systems could generate consortial collection development reports.
4. The vendors were interested in developing consortial elements and reports where they did not already exist.
5. Library involvement could be phased in.
6. Measures to limit duplication could be phased in later or could be made voluntary.
7. Sales volume would guarantee a substantial discount.

THE VISION

The next step was to develop a vision of the project which could be used to foster extensive discussion within the consortium. The project envisioned that a contract would be signed by OhioLINK on behalf of all participating libraries with a single vendor for the provision of English language approval plans. A discount based on the size of this contract would be equal to or an improvement over existing approval arrangements. Excellent service would also be an expectation. Libraries not involved in approval plans would be able to place firm orders via the same vendor. Libraries would have access to shelf-ready options, PromptCat services and standing orders plans from the same vendor as desired (but likely at a different, yet consortial, pricing structure). Approval profiles include options to send a book automatically or a notification slip in lieu of the book. Some plans are entirely notification slips and this is an option that might be beneficial to the two year colleges or smaller libraries.

Each local library would control its own approval profile. The profiles would be accessible to all OhioLINK institutions via a Web-based vendor tool. This tool would enable collection managers at each local library to look at their own profiles online as well as those of their colleagues in other OhioLINK libraries. Staff could search, view a list of books that matches their profile and see what action was taken for their library and other OhioLINK libraries on each title, e.g., received as book, notification slip, etc. In one possible scenario, forthcoming titles would also be pre-profiled by the vendor to determine probable action. This information on action expected could appear in the database as soon as a title was identified for inclusion on the approval system (prior to publication). Collection managers would be able to review titles and mark for shipment on approval. Staff would be able to place firm orders online and that data could be transferred electronically into the Innovative Interfaces system.

The system would keep track of the number of copies of each title profiled for or ordered by OhioLINK libraries. As a result of this calculation, the user could be alerted if their order surpassed a pre-defined threshold for copies but would not be prevented from placing the order or approval shipment flag. The system would provide collection management reports as another tool for cooperative collection development endeavors. These reports could be used to identify overlaps or gaps among OhioLINK libraries' profiles or materials shipped. As a result, profiles could be modified to address areas of intense need, to fill gaps or to reduce unnecessary overlap.

Based on this vision, the consortium accepted the recommendation to proceed. An expanded task force developed an ambitious timeline. In essence, in an 8-month period (between December 1997 and August 1998), an RFP was developed, reviewed, bid, and awarded. Focus groups were held to discuss barriers to success and review the RFP. The RFP was released and bids reviewed by the task force. Open meetings were held to review the leading bids. Consensus was built to support the project and member libraries were surveyed to determine their preliminary interest in participating in the project. In August 1998, a recommendation on vendor was made to the LAC and the contract was negotiated for implementation with shipments in January 1999.

BARRIERS

In the early stages of the project evaluation, the original three member task force and the OhioLINK staff spent considerable time and effort meeting with prospective vendors to see if the plan design was a viable idea. As a result, the thinking of those five individuals (Tom Sanville and Anne Gilliland from OhioLINK, Carol Diedrichs from Ohio State University, Linda Brown from Bowling Green State University, and Kent Mulliner of Ohio University) was considerably ahead of others who had not been privy to those initial conversations. One of the key pieces of advice that Sanville provided to the task force was to consult with a wide range of the stakeholders in the process to identify as many of the perceived barriers to success as possible. Only then would the task force be able to determine if those barriers could be eliminated to the satisfaction of the consortium so that the project could proceed.

One of the key points of discussion in most of the professional literature on cooperative collection development is an explication of the barriers to success. Two of the most critical potential barriers to this particular project were commitment to the project and infrastructure support.

Commitment to the Project

To be successful, commitment to a cooperative project must come from all levels within the consortium and individual institutions. At the most basic level, the consortium and its leadership must believe that the project is important. Clearly, for OhioLINK since the request to explore this option had come from the Library Advisory Council, the directors of the individual libraries were supportive of the idea. Although the front line management of the consortium occurs via the LAC, the Governing Board of OhioLINK is staffed by university administrators under the jurisdiction of the Ohio Board of Regents which governs all of higher education and is the funding authority for OhioLINK. Since one of the founding tenets of OhioLINK was cooperative collection development, the groundwork was already in place to advance this agenda. The consortium's commitment to cooperative collection development did not mean that individual library budgets would be cut as a result but rather that the aggregate buying power of the consortium and the individual institutions would be increased. The ability to advance this agenda was also eased by the fact that the individual participants would be funding the approval plan from their own materials budgets rather than through central funding. OhioLINK provided funding to overcome some barriers to the project such as the software for the III system which makes the transfer of data simpler.

In many ways, this high level support and commitment was the easiest to attain since it occurs at the idea and principle level. Commitment from the individual libraries and, in particular, the faculty and selectors was more complicated. The early focus sessions identified some misunderstandings that could be overcome easily by rewriting the vision so that it dealt with these concerns. As a result, a second section of the vision was written, titled: "What it is and what it isn't." The key misunderstandings which needed to be clarified follow:

- participation would be entirely voluntary;
- the discount would be excellent but the selection of a vendor would also be determined based on service;
- each library would control its own profile;
- each library could continue to make independent selection and return decisions;
- no library would be prevented from buying anything it required for its collection; outsourcing of cataloging was not required; and
- there was no mandate to make titles purchased through the plan circulating copies.

These clarifications were in concert with success factors that others have identified. For example, in a presentation made at the 1997 ALA Annual Conference, Tony Ferguson updated and elaborated on a series of success factors that Robert Downs and Harvie Branscomb[13] articulated in founding the Triangle Research Libraries Network. In particular, he confirmed a perception the task force had for this project that "forced collaboration still fails. It is best to allow members of a cooperative to selectively participate . . . just as it was wise in the past to make sure that any agreement to purchase certain materials for the cooperative would not restrict partners from buying whatever additional books and journals they wished for their own patrons."[14] These revisions to the OhioLINK vision eased what concerns existed with the individual libraries and, in some cases, their faculty so that the project could proceed. However, in order to take the project to the stage where selector decisions are impacted and influenced by the decisions of colleagues around the state, new incentives may be required.

Shreeves discusses another aspect of building support and commitment. "An often overlooked function of leadership here is the role of university and library leaders in selling the concept of resources sharing and shared collection building on campus, especially to faculty and other researchers. To accept reliance on other libraries' resources demands cultural changes among faculty, who must give up cherished notions about the self-sufficient collection, browsing, and immediate access. Leadership is required not only to persuade library staff of the merits, or necessity, of cooperation, but also to ensure that the message is delivered to the rest of the academic audience."[15] OhioLINK held focus sessions with faculty in the early stages of the consortium to deal with this issue of sharing resources across the state. Inevitably, the faculty at the smaller institutions were convinced that the larger institutions, particularly Ohio State, would borrow all of their material leaving the shelves bare. In contrast, faculty at the larger institutions were convinced that the smaller institutions would borrow all of the research, unique material from their libraries making that material unavailable when they needed it. Of course, neither of these expectations has eventuated. Instead, most faculty successfully request material and have it delivered to their offices regardless of where in the state it resides. Again, because of the success of the delivery mechanism, the current approval plan project is of little concern to most faculty. However, the task force still needs to continue working with front line collection managers who still perceive their role to be anticipating what faculty need and have it readily available on the shelf at the home institution.

Infrastructure Support

OhioLINK has spent considerable time, money and energy developing the infrastructure to support cooperative collection development. Having a single integrated library system with a union catalog capable of user-initiated borrowing is the first step in providing adequate delivery mechanisms to support cooperative collection delivery. One of the first funding priorities of the consortium was also retrospective conversion of library holdings not in machine-readable form. There is no question that individual institutions such as Ohio State would have been hard pressed to find the money to complete this conversion without OhioLINK. And yet, the idea of cooperative collection development cannot fully proceed without full conversion. In addition, the union catalog displays up-to-the-minute circulation status of material so that the patron knows when making a request whether the material is available. The system has also been refined to balance the borrowing and lending activity so that all institutions share in the volume of requests generated. Second, the statewide courier system ensures that material reaches individual users quickly. " . . . repeated studies (unpublished OhioLINK internal studies) have shown that almost half (41-44 percent) of the requested materials are delivered within forty-eight hours while almost three-quarters (71-75 percent) are delivered within three days. Approximately 12 percent of the materials cannot be delivered for various reasons, primary among them: items missing from the shelves which the record lists as available. System enhancements already underway allowing local libraries to easily pass on such requests to other holding libraries are expected to reduce the no-fill rate to less than 5 percent."[16] With this structure (or physical proximity as in TRLN), relying on the collections of others becomes possible and reasonable. Without this effective delivery mechanism, cooperative collection development may be perceived to be too difficult and time-consuming.

Other Barriers

At least six other barriers have been identified in the literature as significant issues for consideration when implementing cooperative collection development projects.

Turf Protectionism

Richard Wood defines one barrier as "turf protectionism, or a desire to be self-sufficient."[17] Certainly, the Association of Research Libraries and individual libraries are struggling with the current environment which measures success often solely on the size of collections. Electronic resources are bringing this issue to the forefront but no easy solutions have been found. Until new mechanisms can be identified to measure success, libraries will have to cope with these conflicting messages. Budget realities, however, are a compelling mandate to provide better access and service often on reduced budgets. Because of the well founded statewide commitment to OhioLINK particularly at the library and university administration levels, this is not a serious issue for OhioLINK. However, for more loosely constructed consortia, it may be an important issue. It may also be a more critical issue on the local campus with individual selectors who work on the front lines with faculty members who still want their local library to serve all of their research needs.

Following a vigorous discussion on the success of cooperative collection development for electronic resources, Donna Heady reveals a nuance of this barrier in her summary of the question and answer period of a program held at the 1995 ALA Annual Conference aptly named "Cooperation Works! Successful Models of Cooperative Collection Development." "Questions at the end of the program focused on the difficulties of translating the experiences described for sharing electronic resources into cooperative collection development for monographs. The major point discussed was that cooperation is a more difficult process when a decision must be made about which library will house the resources, thereby allowing that library easier access, than when a decision to share allows equal access to all, as is the case with electronic resources."[18] At various times within OhioLINK, it has even been suggested that the book be left at the institution borrowing it rather than returning it to its owner. There are certainly barriers to this suggestion, but it is also easy to see the merits in time and expense saved.

Expense of Loaning Rather than Purchasing

Patricia Bril identifies the expense of loaning as another potential barrier. She cites a 1985 article by Joel Rutstein noting that few libraries experience interlibrary loan rates above 1 per cent of their total circulation figures.[19] "If resource sharing is pursued on a much grander scale in future, this percentage could increase dramatically. Libraries must then face the problem of determining when it is actually less expensive to purchase an item than provide access to it."[20] In 1996, Sanville compared the $40 average cost of purchasing a book (not including the cost of processing and cataloging) with OhioLINK's $8 per unit cost for resource sharing. Only 40 cents of that $8 cost is for inter-library transportation costs. Over half of the cost is in local library retrieval and circulation with about $3 or less in costs directly attributable to the OhioLINK central program's hardware, software and staff.[21] David Kohl (University of Cincinnati) revealed that in the mid-1990s, UC's OhioLINK circulations amounted to over 10 percent of UC's total circulation activity.[22] He anticipated the likely increase in that percentage in the late 1990s as more institutions were added to OhioLINK.

Rigidity of Definition

In the introductory materials for ARL's August 1998 SPEC Kit, "Collaborative Collection Management Programs in ARL Libraries," inclusion in the survey was confined to programs which could meet the following definition: "a formal collaborative collections management (CCM) program was defined as one for which there were written agreements, contracts, or other documents outlining the commitments and responsibilities of the participants."[23] Scientific surveys require concise definition for credibility but this very rigidity may constrain thinking about how to advance the cooperative collection development agenda. Certainly, OhioLINK has written agreements and documents which govern participation in the consortium and there is a contract with YBP for the provision of the approval project. However, individual participating libraries have no specific contract or documents which govern their participation in this particular program and thus, the OhioLINK approval project might not qualify for inclusion in the ARL survey. OhioLINK has intentionally not required elaborate documentation to participate in the approval plan project in order to overcome concerns about individual library autonomy in making vendor decisions. The task force continues to educate and build the components of the system so that participation will be compelling on its own merits rather than coerced.

Budget Issues

There are two primary areas where budget can be a barrier to successful cooperative collection development. Where a consortium has no central funding, individual libraries must contribute to support any initiative often in competition with local initiatives. Reaching consensus in this environment particularly for book materials can be a challenge. The second issue is the potential for a difference in budget cycles which makes for awkward if not impossible sharing of costs. Again, the design of the OhioLINK approval project makes these barriers moot. Each library controls its own approval profile, the funding of that profile and the timing of its participation in the project. The state institutions in OhioLINK share a common fiscal year (July 1 to June 30). Approval profiles often run January 1 through December 31 to coincide with publisher imprint years. Thus, individual libraries have the lead time to plan for a change in vendor and the budget support for that change. Because the aggregate purchasing power of the initial participants in the plan was great enough to ensure a strong discount, most of the larger participating libraries were able to match the discount that they had achieved on their own or saw some improvement in their discount under the new plan. However, most of the smaller institutions saw a considerable improvement in discount as a result of their participation in the project.

Strained Consensus

Cooperative collection development projects can encounter difficulties if the participating institutions serve varying user populations so that consensus is difficult to reach. This can be particularly true when selecting electronic resources, some of which are of most utility to research institutions while others are most useful to undergraduates. In a consortium like the CIC, consensus is easier to reach because the nature of the institutions is very similar. For OhioLINK. the user base covers two year community and technical colleges as well as ARL libraries. Thus, electronic resources have focused on those which support the greatest number of institutions leaving the research libraries with freed resources to purchase databases of lesser use to others in the consortium–a true win/win situation for all involved.

Reaching consensus on the vendor to be selected for the OhioLINK approval plan project was much easier to achieve because all of the institutions in OhioLINK serve higher education in some form. Thus, the consortium was looking for a scholarly approval vendor who could provide a substantial discount, excellent service, and an automated system which could support cooperative collection development. Also, because all OhioLINK libraries used III systems, the interface issues were modest. In February 1998, the approval plan task force conducted a survey to collect data from OhioLINK libraries regarding current approval expenditures, receipts, discounts, vendors and interest in participating in the project. A number of libraries expressed interest in participating in the project depending upon the vendor selected. As the task force expected, some individual libraries were reluctant to sign on to the project until the vendor was determined. However, a number of other institutions (University of Akron, Bowling Green State University, University of Cincinnati, Miami University, Ohio State University Libraries, and Shawnee State University) were willing to commit to the project regardless of the vendor selected. It was on the basis of these institutions that the RFP went forward. The task force also had full confidence that once the vendor was selected others would come on board quickly and that has, indeed, proven true.

Turnover in Membership

A possible barrier to cooperative collection development is turnover in membership which is more common in loosely constructed consortia. Consortia which come together for the sole purchase of aggregated buying power may experience considerable turnover in membership which will inhibit projects which require a long-term commitment for success. A project such as OhioLINK's approval plan project is a multi-year project whose fruits will only be seen after many years. Certainly, there is a quick payoff for many libraries in the improved discount immediately available. But, the goals of the cooperative collection development portion will be seen only if libraries maintain their commitment over many years. As a centrally funded and state-mandated consortium, OhioLINK members have already established their long-term commitment to the overall project. The approval plan project is still vulnerable to a change in participants if the plan and vendor do not work as expected. However, early experience has seen only growth in participation rather than any withdrawal from the plan. And. the task force included an item in its timeline: Summer 1999, review current satisfaction with approval plan. This will enable the task force to identify any dissatisfaction early and attempt to remedy it as quickly as possible to avoid withdrawal from the project. The only other aspect of this issue which OhioLINK must deal with is the addition of new OhioLINK members on a regular basis. These libraries must be brought up to speed on the history of various projects, their goals, and the member agreements.

CHARACTERISTICS OF SUCCESS

It is almost impossible to talk about barriers to success without also talking about how those barriers were and can be overcome. However, in addition to the information in the previous section, the literature of cooperative collection development has articulated a number of characteristics of success in cooperative collection development (CCD) projects. In particular, Patricia Dominguez and Luke Swindler identified seven major factors which promote successful CCD.[24]

Propitious Circumstances

This is defined as a need for library resources without adequate funds to acquire them. One of the founding principles of OhioLINK was CCD; the approval plan project was the logical extension of a consortium which had created solutions to identifying and delivering resources within the consortium and had taken an aggressive stance in acquiring electronic resources. With the several years worth of data about the consortium's ability to fill requests for material, there was a clear need to improve the statistics for material which could not be delivered and to decrease the ownership of too many multiple copies.

Visionary and Committed Individuals

From its earliest days, OhioLINK has enjoyed the sort of leadership any group would envy. The Ohio Board of Regents shepherded the project through its initial stages of funding with the Ohio Legislature. Individuals such as Don Tolliver and Greg Byerly (Kent State), William J. Studer (Ohio State) and now executive director, Tom Sanville, provided the vision and leadership in the early, most critical stages of the project. The core 18 institutions have invested heavily in the project both financially and through use of their staff resources. Decision making has been highly collaborative resulting in mutual dependence of the consortial offices and its member libraries. The approval project plan has been led by a series of committed individuals who were willing to commit their institutions to the project early, to work diligently to build consensus and support for the project and eliminate barriers. In turn, the approval vendors contributed ideas and time to the initial phases of the project. The project is now well served by the leadership and vision of the vendor ultimately selected, Yankee Book Peddler, as we jointly develop the plan and the tools needed to advance the goals of the project.

Supportive Organizational Structures

OhioLINK has a highly collaborative decision-making process through its standing committees. This particular project was developed by a task force formed by the Cooperative Information Resources Management Committee (CIRM) but also included participation from the Database Management and Standards Committee (DMSC) which represented the technical services aspects of the project. Through this collaboration the task force was able to consider and address the goals of collection development in the context of the issues presented by the acquisitions professionals. The vendors were also generous with their time and expertise. In the early stages of the project, several vendors were invited to the OhioLINK offices for a brainstorming session. The vendors spoke candidly and presented novel and agenda-stretching alternatives to consider. In negotiating the initial contract with YBP, YBP was as anxious as OhioLINK to enter into a joint development process which would initially deliver a standard approval plan to the participants but would also develop a set of enhancements to the system which furthered its CCD goals.

Appropriate Staff Participation at the Operational Level

As always, the OhioLINK institutions were generous in the amount of time and energy their individual librarians committed to participation on the task force, in focus groups, and in open vendor sessions to help select the vendor. Once the plan was in full operation with at least the original participating libraries, YBP and the task force (now renamed the Collection Building Task Force to better reflect the full range of its goals) held a brainstorming session in May 1999 with frontline selectors to determine ways in which the vendor's GOBI system could be enhanced to provide them with the information needed to make better informed selection decisions. The project is now at a critical stage of ensuring that the system performs in such a way that it supports the primary agenda. All of the infrastructure issues have been addressed, now changes in individual selector behavior must be encouraged for the goals of the project to ensue.

Bibliographic and Physical Accessibility to Collections

In 1997, Gay Dannelly (Assistant Director for Collections at Ohio State) was already seeing changes in behavior: "Although the project is still very young, the influence of OhioLINK in the local selection process is becoming clear. Large, expensive purchases are regularly reviewed at the local institution with the holdings of the state in mind. Decisions to purchase such materials are beginning to be made in concert with institutions who hold complementary or supplementary collections. While this process is tentative at present, it is becoming more a part of the purchase decisions process at many of the member institutions, and it is certainly part of the process at the administrative level. The ability to see readily what other institutions hold certainly changes the selection process, as does the ability to count on the actual provision of the materials to the patron at a location remote from the owning library."[25]

The task force wanted to build on this obvious use (expensive purchases) where the extra effort of looking at the central catalog was worth the potential dollars saved. From the earliest days, the OhioLINK central catalog has included on-order records to encourage cooperative collection development. However, for item by item book selection searching the central catalog was less effective and not convenient. Instead, the current project puts this information together in the vendor's database at an earlier point–either for shipment on approval or placement of the firm order. In addition, some libraries such as Ohio State are using the features of the YBP system to allow selectors to tag titles for order in YBP's system as a part of traditional selection rather than submitting order requests into the III system. The individual selector is allowed to search and construct reports in GOBI for review, select the title for purchase while also being able to see if the title had been shipped on approval as well as how the title had been ordered or treated on approval for all participating OhioLINK libraries. At some stage, the task force hopes to select a threshold of orders which would serve as an alert. For example, if an individual selector tagged a title for order and that was the fifth title tagged for purchase (or sent on approval), an alert would be displayed for the selector indicating that information. Selectors would be educated about the goals of CCD so that in these circumstances they could reconsider whether they should actually purchase the fifth copy or decide to rely on the other copies in the state. During the RFP process and the vendor open sessions one bidder, Academic Book Center, suggested one strategy for reinforcing or rewarding such behavior. In the Bonus Program suggested by Academic Book Center, each library would deposit a portion of its book buying funds in a central pool. If a library purchased a copy of a book which surpassed the OhioLINK pre-defined threshold, they would accumulate points. On a regular basis, the central pool of funds would be distributed to individual libraries with those libraries with the fewest points receiving the most funds. Libraries would be able to purchase whatever they saw fit but libraries that bought fewer additional copies would receive extra money to broaden their collections.[26] Again, Gay Dannelly has articulated the importance of this aspect of the project: "The most important enabling factor, however, is to convince the selectors and the faculty that academic institutions must recognize mutual dependence as a normal part of the academic process and a survival mechanism in the shrinking higher education economy. In addition, the library reward system should recognize and provide incentives to selectors who participate in cooperative projects at the behest of their libraries."[27]

Outside Funding

In this particular case, outside funding is not a compelling factor since the libraries will continue to use the funds they have always devoted to approval plans and firm orders. However, for libraries where the new discount is a considerable improvement, their buying power has been enhanced. OhioLINK has also used its central funding to overcome barriers for individual libraries. Where III approval loaders were needed to move bibliographic records and orders from GOBI to the local system to improve participation in the system, OhioLINK has funded those purchases. Should OhioLINK adopt some incentive program the funding for that could come either from the central system or through a cost-sharing among the participants.

History of Successful Cooperation

Cooperation in Ohio dates back many, many years including the initial founding of the *OHIO* College Library Center (now OCLC) by Ohio public and private libraries. OhioLINK has resolved problems which, on the surface, seem simple but which can become deal-breakers. For example, the approval contract is signed and administered at the OhioLINK level; however, the actual payment of invoices for approval shipments will be made by the individual accounting offices on the individual campuses. Early in its development, OhioLINK recognized this potential problem and worked with the individual campuses to determine how best to handle these central contracts. Today, contracts signed by OhioLINK on behalf of all libraries are recognized by the purchasing bodies on each campus.

Other Success Factors

Two additional success factors were articulated by Pat Iannuzzi at a 1997 program on consortial licensing of digital resources at the ALA Annual Conference: marketplace clout and the willingness to say "No" to a bad deal. Although mentioned by Iannuzzi in the context of consortial licensing for digital resources, these were certainly factors in the success of the OhioLINK approval plan project. In particular, the consortium recognized that it had the marketplace clout to make this a viable proposition for a vendor even though there were no economies of scale in the initial design of the project. This clout ensures OhioLINK of the opportunity to influence the development of the vendor's database system to facilitate the project. Consortia are a hot ticket in the marketplace at the moment, particularly for digital resources. All of the vendors involved in this project recognized that the future might hold consortial deals for print materials as well. OhioLINK's reputation as a risk-taking consortium led the vendors to believe that whatever OhioLINK was investigating might well be the harbinger of the future.

The second factor–the willingness to say "No" to a bad deal–is another hallmark of the way OhioLINK does business. At the same time that the approval idea was being investigated, a second task force was investigating the viability of bidding for a central serials vendor. In contrast, that task force found few reasons to proceed with that agenda and many reasons to abandon it at this time. Once again, OhioLINK institutions made an objective analysis of two ideas and were willing to proceed with one while recognizing the limitations of another.

CHANGES IN PHILOSOPHY

Finally, both Downs and Branscomb and Dominguez and Swindler concur that one major success factor is restricting cooperation to material needed for graduate and research activities.[28,29] This may be one area where the OhioLINK project flies in the face of traditional cooperative collection development models. Instead, this model focuses on making more judicious choices of all materials purchased focusing particularly on English language, recent imprints, often used by undergraduates. As monograph budgets have shrunk, libraries have maintained their commitment to approval plans which bring in the mainstream material. In this environment, statistics reveal that collections have become more homogeneous. The OhioLINK project by design strives to make collections more heterogeneous. Again, it is the success of the delivery mechanism which may support this change in philosophy.

Shreeves confirms that "there is, however, widespread belief that cooperation in building collections can significantly improve the quality of library service by broadening and deepening the range of materials collectively available. Libraries–so the argument goes–can increase the portion of the information universe maintained within the national (or state or regional) collection through a planned and conscious division of labor in building collections. Thereby, users will have access to a collectively richer whole than if that collection had been developed purely in response to local imperatives. . . . A fairly standard model for cooperative collection development in the print environment divides the information universe into 'core' and 'peripheral' materials. A research library has a responsibility to maintain on-site a 'core' collection that serves immediate needs, especially those of its undergraduates. At the same time it will develop collections of 'peripheral' material in selected areas that respond to local priorities but also serve consortial needs. This collection, in turn, is backed up by the collections of consortial partners built through distributed responsibility for peripheral materials in complementary fields. Defining what 'core' and 'peripheral' really mean has always been one of the stumbling blocks to successful cooperative projects." Again, the OhioLINK Project flies in the face of this traditional model. These stumbling blocks have been eliminated by jumping forward to skip the process of defining who will collect what, to identifying, instead, what has been missed completely and purchase that material. OhioLINK has not yet taken the step to deal with the issue of purchasing the missing material, but it is easy to imagine that as the next potential step in the process particularly where central funding might be used for that purpose.

ACHIEVABLE BENEFITS AND CURRENT STATUS

As mentioned earlier, the OhioLINK Approval Plan Project is now at the threshold of success; the infrastructure is in place or developing quickly to support true cooperative collection development for print materials. What achievable benefits can be expected?

Development Agenda with YBP

At the point YBP was selected as the vendor for the OhioLINK Project, they had already developed a series of reports designed to evaluate consortial book purchases. In one series of reports, a consortium can compare the coverage of their approval plans by specific publishers and LC sub-class. For example, one report–approval presses with book coverage for at least one plan–lists a series of publishers/imprints and how that publisher is treated by each library in the consortium, whether they are receiving books, slips or nothing for titles from that publisher. A similar report can be constructed based on LC sub-class or series treatment to identify areas of significant overlap as well as underrepresented areas. OhioLINK expected to be able to take this type of report and compare it to LC sub-class reports sorted by library and imprint year generated from the central catalog to determine areas of weakness.

YBP also had a report which they call a supra profile which was developed to help a consortium evaluate its goals. For example, if the consortium had a goal among its libraries to collect at least 70 percent of the English-language books distributed in the U.S., this report would help determine whether the goal had been met. The profile shows the percentage covered by individual libraries within the consortium and then by the consortium as a whole. The combined profile takes into account the overlap so that you can determine whether as a group you have reached such a goal as collecting 70 percent within a subject. Ideally, the goal would be met by the consortium but would not be possible by any single library alone. By engaging in a joint development agenda with YBP, OhioLINK expects to develop a system which will result in reducing the level of current duplication within the consortium and to also collect that material not currently being made available.

Profile Comparisons

Blackwell Book Services' Collection Manager System has a well developed component which will permit individual selectors to compare their profiles to others on the system. OhioLINK would like to see features such as this developed within the GOBI system so that individual selectors could compare their profiles with colleagues working in the same subject fields in OhioLINK. At a higher administrative level, all of the profiles in a particular discipline could be compared by the collection development officers and their subject specialists to see if entire areas within a subject were being excluded by everyone participating in the project.

Enhancement of Approval Slips with OhioLINK Information

It was clear in the focus groups conducted that individual selectors continue to make active use of the printed notification slips provided by approval vendors. Because of the chronic understaffing of most libraries, it is not uncommon for much collection development work to be done at home in front of the TV with a stack of notification slips. Recognizing the reality of this approach to collection development, the approval project moved a step beyond having the information about what colleagues were doing available only in the online system. The YBP notification slips, as well as the slips which appear in shipped approval books, have been enhanced to include information about treatment of titles for OhioLINK libraries. Each slip now includes a notation such as OL: 1/5. This note indicates that at the point the slip was printed, 1 OhioLINK library would be receiving this book on approval and 5 would receive slips. Although there was no room on the slip to add the symbols for the libraries, this information is intended to provide an alert to the selector that they might want to check the system for further information if the number of copies known to be going to OhioLINK libraries might affect their decision to purchase. Some smaller institutions also saw a use for this information on the slip because the slips are sent to faculty members for input on selection decisions.

CONSORTIA-SPECIFIC ISSUES

There are also a few issues related to this type of cooperation which may be specific to consortia such as OhioLINK.

Impact on the Vendor

Is this a viable economic model for a vendor? Daniel Halloran, President of Academic Book Center, speculates that the model is viable only because of the promise of a certain volume of business for a period of time. "Consortia participants are unlikely to reduce their total number of book purchases (good news), but there are no operational economies of scale for the book vendor when he enters into a contract with a consortium (bad news). He still must work with each library individually to bill and ship materials. So, for the book vendor, the attraction of a consortial contract may be the assurance of volume business over some period of time. For the consortium, it's the expectation of standardized discounts (at the most favorable rate) for all members, as well as shared access to purchase information."[30]

Uniqueness of OhioLINK

Halloran goes on to speculate on the uniqueness of the OhioLINK consortium as a critical factor: "The OhioLINK statewide approval plan, awarded to YBP, was the first consortia contract to address resources sharing and cooperative buying of books. However, the OhioLINK contract may be unique because OhioLINK is unique. The consortium shares a common integrated library system, has a sophisticated interlibrary lending infrastructure, and represents a highly diverse group of libraries. The OhioLINK contract is in its initial stages. We'll all be watching as it develops and we await its success or failure with interest. In the meantime, we know that other consortia are beginning to look closely at their relationships with book vendors."[31] Indeed, it is impossible to know at this stage whether the unique aspects of the OhioLINK consortium make this a viable model only for OhioLINK or whether the model can be extended to other consortia with different structures. Although Halloran clearly expresses some skepticism, John Berry paints a more glowing assessment of Ohio's libraries in an editorial titled "A Glimpse of the Future in Ohio":

> I saw the future in Ohio. It was only a glimpse. and it left plenty of room for many other new models and styles. Still, if you want to watch academic and public librarians hard at work creating the library of the future, be sure to take a close look at Ohio.

Berry goes on to talk about a variety of things including how public libraries are funded in Ohio, a joint branch of the Columbus Metropolitan Library and the Worthington Public Library, OPLIN (the consortium for the public libraries in Ohio modeled on OhioLINK), and OhioLINK's licensing contract for Elsevier titles:

> Sure, there are potential problems with all of these amazing innovations, but that's why we invented terms like 'risk-taker.' Rather than wait for the future to be imposed upon them, Ohio's librarians have boldly ventured out to create that future.[32]

Survival of the Print Environment

It has certainly been suggested that cooperative collection development projects might not be worth doing because the print environment may not survive long enough to make them worthwhile. Shreeves likens this argument to that "sometimes made by campus planners that new library buildings will never again be necessary because of the shift to digital resources."[33] Again, the OhioLINK Approval Plan Project takes a broader brush stroke of attempting to limit excessive duplicate copies and to focus on purchasing items previously unavailable in any library. In this environment less effort would be involved to advance this agenda over earlier more labor intensive collection development approaches. In addition, OhioLINK has already agreed to test the netLibrary product for the supply of scholarly electronic books to libraries. "This service allows library patrons to search e-books online, view their full-text content, and check them out by downloading them to PCs using netLibrary client software it distributes at no charge."[34] The Collection Building Task Force has already been asked to consider how this product might interface with its goals and plans for the consortial approval plan.

CONCLUSION

In an article about OhioLINK, David Kohl notes that "the nature of today's cooperation is a much more highly integrated operation where key central functions of the coöperating libraries are linked. The result is a blurring of the independent self-contained nature of the individual libraries, as individual institutions are transformed into distinctive elements of a superlibrary information mosaic."[35] The OhioLINK approval plan project takes the consortium one step closer to this superlibrary concept.

In conclusion, Mary Moore ends her article on Washington State's cooperative collection development project with this insightful injunction to all librarians engaged in such endeavors:

> We know that it is not possession of materials that matters, but rather access to materials that is important. We know that sharing of what we do have is vital to our present and future success. We know that the average information customer doesn't care where the information comes from just as long as it is easy and convenient to get. When are we going to make that great paradigm shift that will allow us to start acting upon that which we profess to know?[36]

NOTES

1. Dominguez, Patricia Buck and Luke Swindler. "Cooperative Collection Development at the Research Triangle University Libraries: A Model for the Nation." *College & Research Libraries* 54 (November 1993): 485.

2. Hazen, Dan C. "Cooperative Collection Development: Compelling Theory, Inconsequential Results?" In *Collection Management for the 21st Century,* edited by G.E. Gorman and Ruth H. Miller. Westport, CT: Greenwood Press, 1997, p. 264.

3. Bril, Patricia. "Cooperative Collection Development: Progress from Apotheosis to Reality." In *Collection Management in Academic Libraries,* edited by Clare Jenkins and Mary Morley. Aldershot, Hants, England: Gower, 1991, p. 236.

4. Shreeves, Edward. "Is there a Future for Cooperative Collection Development in the Digital Age?" *Library Trends* 45 (Winter 1997): 378.

5. Kohl, David F. "Resource Sharing in a Changing Ohio Environment." *Library Trends* 45 (Winter 1997): 445.

6. Potter, William Gray. "Recent Trends in Statewide Academic Library Consortia." *Library Trends* 45 (Winter 1997): 416-434; Dannelly, Gay N. "Cooperation Is the Future of Collection Management and Development: OhioLINK and CIC." In *Collection Management for the 21st Century,* edited by G.E. Gorman and Ruth H. Miller. Westport, CT: Greenwood Press, 1997, p. 249-262; Kohl, David F. "Resource Sharing in a Changing Ohio Environment." *Library Trends* 45 (Winter 1997): 435-447; Dykhuis, Randy W. "OhioLINK: Vision, Money, and Technology." *Computers in Libraries* 15 (February 1995): 16-21; Kohl, David F. "OhioLINK: Plugging into Progress." *Library Journal* 118 (October l, 1993): 42-46; Byerly, Greg. "Ohio: Library and Information Networks," *Library Hi Tech* 14(1996): 245-253.

7. *http://www.ohiolink.edu/about/what-is-ol.html*

8. Expectations Fulfilled, Expectations Yet to Keep. Columbus, OH: OhioLINK, 1996; Snapshot 1998: OhioLINK, Six Years of Serving Ohio Higher Education. Columbus, OH: OhioLINK, 1998.

9. Byerly, Greg. "Ohio: Library and Information Networks," *Library Hi Tech* 14 (1996): 247.

10. Dykhuis, Randy W. "OhioLINK: Vision, Money, and Technology." *Computers in Libraries* 15 (February 1995): 20.

11. Shreeves, Edward. "Is there a Future for Cooperative Collection Development in the Digital Age?" *Library Trends* 45 (Winter 1997): 377; Mosher, Paul H. and Marcia Pankake. "A Guide to Coordinated and Cooperative Collection Development." *Library Resources & Technical Services* 27 (1983): 417-431.

12. Perrault, Anna H. "The Shrinking National Collection: A Study of the Effects of the Diversion of Funds from Monographs to Serials on the Monograph Collections of Research Libraries." *Library Acquisitions: Practice & Theory* 18 (Spring 1994): 15-16.

13. Downs, Robert B. and Harvie Branscomb. "A Venture in University Library Cooperation," *Library Journal* 60 (Nov. 15,1935): 877-879; Branscomb, Harvie and Robert B. Downs. "A Plan for University Library Cooperation," *School and Society* 42 (July 13, 1935): 64-66.

14. Alleman, Steve. "Consortial Licensing of Digital Resources: Implications for Cooperative Collection Development: A Program Sponsored by the ALCTS CMDS Education for Collection Development Committee." *Library Acquisitions: Practice & Theory* 21 (Winter 1997): 510.

15. Shreeves, Edward. "Is there a Future for Cooperative Collection Development in the Digital Age?" *Library Trends* 45 (Winter 1997): 380.

16. Kohl, David F. "Resource Sharing in a Changing Ohio Environment." *Library Trends* 45 (Winter 1997): 439.

17. Wood, Richard J. "The Axioms, Barriers, and Components of Cooperative Collection Development." In *Collection Management for the 21st Century,* edited by G.E. Gorman and Ruth H. Miller. Westport, CT: Greenwood Press, 1997, p. 235.

18. Heady, Donna M. "Cooperation Works! Successful Models of Cooperative Collection Development: Report of a Program." *Library Acquisitions: Practice & Theory* 20 (Summer 1996): 192.

19. Rutstein, Joel S. "National and Local Resource Sharing: Issues in Cooperative Collection Development," *Collection Management* 7 (Summer 1985), p. 6.

20. Bril, Patricia. "Cooperative Collection Development: Progress from Apotheosis to Reality." In *Collection Management in Academic Libraries*, edited by Clare Jenkins and Mary Morley. Aldershot, Hants, England: Gower, 1991, p. 254.

21. Expectations Fulfilled, Expectations Yet to Keep. Columbus, OH: OhioLINK, 1996, p. 13-14.

22. Kohl, David F. "Resource Sharing in a Changing Ohio Environment." *Library Trends* 45 (Winter 1997): 439.

23. Collaborative Collections Management Programs in ARL Libraries. SPEC Kit 235, August 1998, p. 1.

24. Dominguez, Patricia Buck and Luke Swindler. "Cooperative Collection Development at the Research Triangle University Libraries: A Model for the Nation." *College & Research Libraries* 54 (November 1993): 487-488.

25. Dannelly, Gay N. "Cooperation Is the Future of Collection Management and Development: OhioLINK and CIC." In *Collection Management for the 21st Century*, edited by G.E. Gorman and Ruth H. Miller. Westport, CT: Greenwood Press, 1997, p. 257.

26. Academic Book Center Request for Proposal.

27. Dannelly, Gay N. "Cooperation Is the Future of Collection Management and Development: OhioLINK and CIC." In *Collection Management for the 21st Century* edited by G.E. Gorman and Ruth H. Miller. Westport, CT: Greenwood Press, 1997, p. 260-261.

28. Downs, Robert B. "American Library Cooperation in Review." *College & Research Libraries* 6 (1945): 415; Dominguez, Patricia Buck and Luke Swindler. "Cooperative Collection Development at the Research Triangle University Libraries: A Model for the Nation." *College & Research Libraries* 54 (November 1993): 486.

29. Book Peddler web page, www.ybp.com

30. Halloran, Daniel P. "1998 From a Book Vendor's Perspective." *Against the Grain* 11 (February 1999): 30.

31. Halloran, Daniel P. "1998 From a Book Vendor's Perspective." *Against the Grain* 11 (February 1999): 30.

32. Berry, John N. III. "A Glimpse of the Future in Ohio." *Library Journal* 122 (June 15, 1997): 6.

33. Shreeves, Edward. "Is there a Future for Cooperative Collection Development in the Digital Age?" *Library Trends* 45 (Winter 1997): 387.

34. Dorman, David. "E-Book Vendor Debuts." *American Libraries* 30 (April 1999): 90.

35. Kohl, David F. "Resource Sharing in a Changing Ohio Environment." *Library Trends* 45 (Winter 1997): 437.

36. Moore, Mary Y. "Washington State's Cooperative Collection Development Project." *Journal of Interlibrary Loan & Information Supply* 2 (1992): 37-38.

Making the Common Uncommon? Examining Consortial Approval Plan Cooperation

Kim Armstrong
Bob Nardini

INTRODUCTION

Approval plans and cooperative collection development, as topics in the library literature, are like two long parallel lines. They are long lines, because librarians have been writing about these topics for decades. And they are parallel, because the lines do not cross. This is odd, because the literature of approval plans, after an early debate about whether they would or should survive, has since the 1980s largely been an exploration of how to make what has become for libraries a successful and widespread practice, yet more successful and widespread.[1]

In contrast, the literature of cooperative collection development, as one survey of the field put it, has by and large taken a "skeptical if not cynical perspective," with the relatively few success stories to be found in high-profile national, state, or regional projects.[2] According to a 1998 ARL SPEC Kit on collaborative collections management, electronic resources, serials, and area studies materials all were far more active areas of cooperation than were domestic monographs.[3]

Kim Armstrong is Program Officer, Triangle Research Libraries Network.
Bob Nardini is Vice President and Head Bibliographer, Yankee Book Peddler.

[Haworth co-indexing entry note]: "Making the Common Uncommon? Examining Consortial Approval Plan Cooperation." Armstrong, Kim, and Bob Nardini. Co-published simultaneously in *Collection Management* (The Haworth Information Press, an imprint of The Haworth Press, Inc.) Vol. 24, No. 1/2, 2000, pp. 45-55; and: *Creating New Strategies for Cooperative Collection Development* (ed: Milton T. Wolf and Marjorie E. Bloss) The Haworth Information Press, an imprint of The Haworth Press, Inc., 2000, pp. 45-55. Single or multiple copies of this article are available for a fee from The Haworth Document Delivery Service [1-800-342-9678, 9:00 a.m. - 5:00 p.m. (EST). E-mail address: getinfo@haworthpressinc.com].

© 2000 by The Haworth Press, Inc. All rights reserved.

Why haven't libraries attempted cooperative approval plans? In some ways the two ideas would seem an ideal marriage. Every approval plan has a formal written profile, a statement of subject interests that might help to blueprint a coordinated arrangement. Vendor databases, the best of which ten years ago were available only as microfiche sets, have grown in sophistication to the point that librarians today could use them in tandem with their own integrated library systems, bibliographic utilities, World Wide Web resources, and e-mail, to have at their desktops a good system for the day-to-day, title-level and macro-level management of a cooperative approval plan. Many consortia already have in place efficient document delivery mechanisms, another necessary prerequisite for the sharing of monographs.

The incentives to cooperate are difficult to ignore, as serials inflation has continued to erode monographs budgets, and as the problem of housing growing collections has made space a major issue for many ARL and other libraries. Two or more libraries attempting to pool money, staff, and other resources in order to run a single, shared approval plan would, of course, encounter significant resistance on a variety of fronts. But the mere coordination of separate approval plans would seem a simpler far more achievable organizational feat.

Would it make sense for TRLN libraries to receive fewer approval plan titles in common, and so to make their respective collections more uncommon?

THE TRIANGLE RESEARCH LIBRARIES NETWORK

The Triangle Research Libraries Network is a cooperative endeavor of four geographically-close institutions and their libraries.[4] The consortium has its beginnings in 1935 when Duke University and the University of North Carolina at Chapel Hill issued "A Program of Cooperation," intended to be a framework for building coordinated library collections at the two universities. In 1977 North Carolina State University formally joined the group, then known as the Triangle Universities Library Cooperation Committee. North Carolina Central University joined in 1994, when a revised Memorandum of Understanding was signed by the chancellors/presidents of the four institutions.

Duke University, North Carolina State University, and UNC Chapel

Hill are all Research I universities and members of the Association of Research Libraries. Collectively the TRLN libraries annually spend approximately $27 million on library materials.

The consortium operates, historically and currently, under the principle of using available library resources in a coordinated approach to increase the research material available to library users at participating institutions. The four libraries have collection agreements in place that cover area studies, government documents, newspapers, major microform sets, serials, and southern Americana, and other areas. Recent cooperative efforts have expanded to purchases in the electronic environment and the licensing of online access. Cooperative collection development is reviewed and advanced through formal and informal means. A committee structure exists within TRLN, charged with planning and coordinating activity in information resources. Perhaps equally important is the day-by-day informal collaboration that occurs among TRLN bibliographers.

APPROVAL PLANS OF TRLN MEMBERS

Three of the four members of TRLN have major domestic approval plans in place with Yankee Book Peddler (YBP), a vendor located in Contoocook, New Hampshire. Duke University's YBP approval plan includes all libraries on campus except Business, Medical Center, and Law. North Carolina State University's approval plan, during the period of time included in this study, covered the main library and the branch Design library, but not Veterinary Science. The approval plan at the University of North Carolina at Chapel Hill included all major libraries at UNC-CH except Health Sciences and Law. North Carolina Central University has no approval plans in place with YBP or any other vendor.

During the 1997-1998 YBP fiscal year, when the company's total universe of approval plan titles was 45,671, the volume of automatic approval plan shipments was similar for the three libraries, 8,835 for one, 10,583 for another, and 10,961 for the third. Duke, NCSU, and UNC-CH have never coordinated their approval plans. Each has always operated independently of the others.

The three approval plans all developed in a similar way. Each was begun in the mid-to-late 1970s or early 1980s, when many large academic libraries across the country either started approval plans for the first time or began approval plans with a new vendor following the demise of the Richard Abel Company in 1974. Duke, NCSU, and UNC-CH, as was often the pattern with peer libraries, all began approval plans which included coverage for university presses but not for other types of publishers. Subject scope, in all three cases, was very broad.

While the details have been different, the pattern of change over the years in these three approval plans has been the same. Each institution. while maintaining coverage of university presses, has gradually but steadily added approval plan coverage for other types of publishers.

Duke proceeded subject area by subject area, beginning with history and religion. Other areas of the social sciences and humanities followed, and science and engineering coverage followed next. As each new subject area joined the expanded approval plan, appropriate publisher coverage was added for trade, commercial scholarly, sci/tech, small press, and other publishers beyond the original university press base. In comparison to Duke's very broad university press subject profile, however, the newer coverage for other publisher types has often been more restrictive.

NCSU, reflecting the institution's historic strength, first supplemented its university press coverage with a select group of publishers primarily active in science and engineering. Publishers to support social science and humanities programs were added later, along with more sci/tech publishers. NCSU, unlike Duke, has chosen to maintain the same subject profile for all publisher types. The NCSU profile, for both university presses and other publishers, restricts some subject areas within the social sciences and humanities, but is quite open in the sciences and engineering.

UNC-CH expanded its university press base first with a small group of museum publishers; followed by a select group of leading commercial social science publishers; then a list of significant association publishers; next a much broadened social science publisher base, alongside new coverage in the humanities for a wide base of publishers; and separate additional coverage for a select list of commercial publishers of books in music. The subject profiles established for trade and other publishers at UNC-CH have been somewhat more restrictive than the library's broad university press coverage. The UNC-CH approval plan, in comparison to Duke and NCSU, is much more restrictive toward science and engineering, subject areas where UNC-CH coverage has remained focused only upon university presses.

While the overall pattern of development for these three TRLN libraries has been similar, the components of approval plan structure have been quite various. Not only in subject emphasis, but also in the extent of supplementary notification slip coverage; in the treatment of continuation titles and titles in series; in specifications for country of origin, binding preference, and other non-subject parameters for categories like list price, conference proceedings, textbooks, reference works, and translations; in the configuration of subject sub-profiles and billing and shipping sub-accounts; and in arrangements for electronic cataloging and other records, the approval plans at Duke, NCSU, and UNC-CH reflect in a hundred ways the unique histories and organizations of these three TRLN institutions, as well as the personal preferences of the many librarians who have been involved with these three approval plans.

THE STUDY

The following questions formed the basis of this study:

- How much overlap in approval plan shipments did TRLN libraries experience?
- Were the titles not acquired on approval acquired by other methods?
- What level of use, as measured by circulation, did all of the titles acquired receive?
- Could low-circulation titles be placed in working categories?
- What savings might the libraries have achieved if their approval plan profiles had been formally coordinated?
- How many titles not acquired by any partner library would have been valuable additions to the shared TRLN universe of titles?

QUESTIONS ABOUT COOPERATION

All of the familiar barriers to cooperative collection development in general have played their part in preventing libraries from cooperating on approval plans: institutional politics and competition; lack of confidence and trust between potential partners; the difficulties of coordinating and managing a distance arrangement; and the powerful barriers of culture and inertia.

Other barriers are more specific to an approval plan environment. One of the oldest arguments in favor of approval plans has been that they make it easier to acquire core materials. If approval plans indeed focus on a "core," then sharing would seem out of the question. Would it make any sense to devise a cooperative arrangement for titles known to be in high demand by local users at each cooperating library?

Next, why add a layer of complexity to an already complex process? Don't libraries working independently of one another establish approval plan profiles that in fact achieve a measure of coordination anyway, simply by reflecting the libraries' respective strengths and priorities?

However the most important question would be–what to share? The assumption in any cooperative approval plan would be that individual libraries would agree not to own certain titles that they otherwise would have acquired. Two possible benefits, which could be achieved independently or in combination with one another, would justify the sacrifice. One would be to broaden the overall universe of titles, with partners bypassing some titles for their own collection, but buying others that normally wouldn't have been acquired by any cooperating library. The other would be to divert money away from the approval plan, toward other lines in the materials budget or other library budget.

In order to realize either of these benefits, partners must first identify groups of monographs where it would make sense to allocate primary responsibility to one partner library. Necessarily working within the vendor's approval plan system of categories, could librarians implement their own definitions of which titles would be "core," desirable for multiple locations to own, and which would be peripheral, and so allocated to one location or another?

Finally, what of the vendor? When partnerships between libraries are difficult to establish and maintain in the first place, would this new party be competent enough and stable enough to carry out library specifications? Is it in the vendor's interest to carry them out in the first place? A successful shared arrangement for purchasing new books might, after all, lower the libraries' overall level of book purchasing. If that did not happen, what would instead likely occur is the overall purchase of fewer copies per title of a greater number of unique book titles, a less attractive profit equation for the vendor than the uncoordinated purchase of more copies of fewer unique titles.

Even if all problems were solved and all questions answered, the value of jointly owning more peripheral books would then have to be weighed against the effort of maintaining a cooperative program. That, obviously, would not be an easy question to answer. This paper doesn't attempt to answer it; nor do we think, as vendor and consortium program officer, that we have the standing even to try. Instead, we hope that our data and analysis will provide a framework to make it possible for librarians to approach and perhaps answer it from their own points of view.

DATA GATHERING

This study is based upon eight lists of titles. A YBP bibliographer queried the company's system to produce lists of titles shipped on approval to the three TRLN libraries with approval plans in four subject areas during the six-month period January 1997 through June 1997. The four subject lists showed whether each title was shipped on approval to one, to two, or to all three TRLN libraries during these months. The lists were sorted alphabetically by title, so that simultaneously published hardcover/paperback editions were listed consecutively and so could be accounted for as one bibliographic entity. The lists recorded automatic approval shipments only. Firm orders, notification slip orders, and standing orders were ignored.

The four subject areas were defined by four Library of Congress classification system classes and subclasses: F History, HD Economics, PN Literature, and QD Chemistry. These four areas were chosen because they are covered by virtually all academic library approval plan profiles, and represent the sciences, social sciences, and humanities. In comparison to many other LC subclasses, they also contain a variety of discrete subject areas that often result in more detailed approval plan profiles.

(The profiles for all three TRLN libraries are written under the LC system, although Duke's collection is organized under the Dewey Decimal classification system.)

The remaining four lists showed titles offered by YBP's approval plan program during these six months in the four subject areas, but shipped on approval to none of the TRLN libraries.

DATA HANDLING

With the data in hand, TRLN sought to answer three questions. How much overlap was there on the approval titles? How often did overlapping titles circulate? Did YBP treat other titles that would be candidates for purchase with money saved from any reduced duplication?

To determine the amount of overlap, the four lists of titles shipped on approval to TRLN libraries were searched in the online catalogs of each institution. TRLN libraries all use the DRA system. The searches yielded a clearer picture of actual title duplication, since copies acquired through YBP slip, firm, or standing orders, or from other vendors or through gifts, were added to the list. The lists were merged and a comprehensive list of duplicate titles in the libraries created for each of the four subject lists from YBP.

The next step was to determine circulation activity. Circulation counts were a combination of first-time circulation, renewals, and reserve uses. Using the CIRCLE (Circulation subsystem of DRA) records for the institutions, each title was searched and the number of circulations recorded. The potential circulation period for each title would be somewhat different, because they were shipped by YBP at weekly intervals during the January-June 1997 period, and then cataloged and entered into the online catalogs under the differing work cycles of the three institutions. TRLN searching took place during the March and April 1999, so all titles had a period of at least 19 months and as many as 27 months in which to circulate.

The last step for TRLN was to review the lists provided by YBP of titles offered between January and June 1997 but not shipped to any TRLN library. All of these titles were also searched in the DRA catalogs and in GobiTween, a feature of YBP's GOBI database (Global Online Bibliographic Information). GobiTween allows librarians at separate institutions to view activity on a given title between YBP and the library's consortial partners. Some activity was reflected in GobiTween before becoming accessible in the online catalogs of the libraries, such as records for books shipped by YBP but not yet received by the library, and books ordered by a library but not yet shipped by YBP.

TRLN then eliminated from the "not shipped" list any titles that had subsequently been purchased by TRLN libraries. The remaining titles were analyzed as candidates for purchase.

How much overlap did TRLN Libraries see in their YBP approval plan shipments?

Table 1 shows that automatic approval plan shipments across the four subject areas resulted in modest levels of overlap among the three TRLN members. Only 14% of approval titles shipped to any TRLN library were also shipped to all three, with the highest percentage in PN Literature, where 32% of titles shipped fell into that category. Three-library overlap for the other subject areas ranged from 0% in F History to 9% in HD Economics, and only 149 titles in all were shipped automatically to Duke, NCSU, and UNC-CH. The highest percentage of titles shipped to two libraries was 62%, the result in F History, with the other subject areas ranging from 23% to 31%. The percentage of titles shipped to two libraries, 36%, was well below that for titles shipped to only one, 50%.[5] The percentage of titles shipped to only one library showed a high of 72% in QD Chemistry and a low of 37% in PN Literature.

What effect did subsequent purchases have on the overlap resulting from approval plans?

The overlap pattern shown in Table 2, where notification slip orders, firm orders, standing orders, and gifts are considered, reverses the pattern of Table 1. The percentage of titles held by only one library, 50% following approval plan shipments, fell to 11% after other types of purchases. Titles held by all three TRLN libraries, 14%

TABLE 1. Overlap Among Titles Shipped on Approval to TRLN Libraries

	F History	HD Economics	PN Literature	QD Chemistry	Total
Titles shipped to 1 library	68 (38%)	257 (60%)	124 (37%)	76 (72%)	525 (50%)
Titles shipped to 2 libraries	111 (62%)	134 (31%)	103 (31%)	25 (23%)	373 (36%)
Titles shipped to 3 libraries	0 (0%)	38 (9%)	106 (32%)	5 (5%)	149 (14%)
Total titles shipped	179	429	333	106	1,047

due to approval plan shipments, rose to 64%. The change is most dramatic in F History, where approval plan shipments placed no titles in all three libraries. Yet Table 2 shows that all three libraries in fact acquired 72% of the titles in F, while only 10% were held in the end by just one TRLN library. The pattern was similar in the other three subject areas, with QD Chemistry showing the lowest amount of overlap, with 41% of the titles in all three libraries, 34% in two, and 25% in only one library.

These results run contrary to the opinion held by some librarians, that is, that approval plans homogenize library collections.[6] In the case of the TRLN libraries, the relative uniqueness resulting from approval plan shipments in fact was largely erased by discretionary purchases.

How frequently did approval plan titles circulate in the three TRLN libraries?

Table 3 shows that 83% of the titles circulated at least once, while 17% did not circulate. TRLN users placed the highest demands upon QD Chemistry titles, where only 3% did not circulate and 22% circulated in all three TRLN libraries. Patterns for the other subject areas were quite similar to one another, with titles circulating in one library ranging between 34% to 36%, titles circulating in two libraries between 27% and 29%, and titles circulating in all three libraries between 13% and 21%. All in all, 46% of the approval titles circulated in two or three TRLN libraries, while 54% circulated either once or not at all.

A small number of titles, 4% of the whole, circulated at a very high rate, three times or more in each of the three TRLN libraries.

It was no surprise that some of these titles focused on popular culture, such as *Architects of the Web: 1,000 Days that Built the Future of Business* (Wiley), and *Gen X TV: The Brady Bunch to Melrose*

TABLE 2. Modified TRLN Overlap
(After slip orders, firm orders, standing orders, gifts)

	F History	HD Economics	PN Literature	QD Chemistry	Total
Titles in 1 library	17 (10%)	45 (10%)	28 (8%)	27 (25%)	117 (11%)
Titles in 2 libraries	33 (18%)	124 (29%)	69 (21%)	36 (34%)	262 (25%)
Titles in 3 libraries	129 (72%)	260 (61%)	236 (71%)	43 (41%)	668 (64%)
Total titles shipped	179	429	333	106	1,047

TABLE 3. Circulation Activity

	F History	HD Economics	PN Literature	QD Chemistry	Total
Titles with no circulation in any library	31 (17%)	86 (20%)	61 (18%)	3 (3%)	181 (17%)
Titles with circulation in only 1 library	64 (36%)	165 (39%)	114 (34%)	44 (42%)	387 (37%)
Titles with circulation in 2 libraries	51 (29%)	121 (28%)	87 (27%)	36 (33%)	295 (28%)
Titles with circulation in all 3 libraries	33 (18%)	57 (13%)	71 (21%)	23 (22%)	184 (18%)
Total titles	179	429	333	106	1,047

TABLE 4. High-Circulation Titles

	F History	HD Economics	PN Literature	QD Chemistry	Total
Titles with at least 3 circulations in each library	4 (2%)	22 (5%)	9 (3%)	10 (9%)	45 (4%)

Place (Syracuse). Or, that certain titles in southern history were in high demand, for example, *Devil's Lane: Sex and Race in the Early South* (Oxford), and *Rising Tide: The Great Mississippi Flood of 1927 and How It Changed America* (Simon & Schuster).

High circulation for two other titles, though, suggested that study and research were taking place throughout TPLN in an area which might on its own seem esoteric: *Coffee and Power: Revolution and the Rise of Democracy in Central America* (Harvard), and *Open-Economy Politics: The Political Economy of the World Coffee Trade* (Princeton). Among QD Chemistry titles, where 9% circulated heavily, Oxford was the predominant publisher, with titles such as *Circular Dichroism and Linear Dichroism and Introduction to Hydrogen Bonding.*

Collaborative Purchasing: A Model for Financially Straitened Times

Steve O'Connor
Stephen Pugh

> Fiscal pragmatism can balance the books in the same way as a trained seal can balance a beach ball, but it is plainly not able to simultaneously keep in balance the needs and demands of society.[1]

> . . . the future can and should be more a matter of choice than of destiny.[2]

The importance of this paper lies in the importance of collections to the intellectual life of Universities and indeed a Nation. This paper commences in a review of past and present collecting practices in a country/society that is homogeneous. The paper climaxes in proposals to address the crisis in collecting. The model for this paper is the country of Australia. It is large geographically, it is diverse in population terms, high on technology take-up and a outward-looking country hungry for ideas to balance those which it develops itself.

Steve O'Connor is Chief Executive Officer, CAVAL Ltd., 4 Park Drive, Bundoora, Victoria, Australia 3083 (e-mail: Steve.O'Connor@caval.edu.au).

Stephen Pugh is Vice President, Collection Management and Development Group, YBP Library Services, 999 Maple Street, Contoocook, NH 03229 USA (e-mail: spugh@ybp.com).

The authors wish to acknowledge Gary Shirk for his conceptual framework of shared profiling.

[Haworth co-indexing entry note]: "Collaborative Purchasing: A Model for Financially Straitened Times." O'Connor, Steve, and Stephen Pugh. Co-published simultaneously in *Collection Management* (The Haworth Information Press, an imprint of The Haworth Press, Inc.) Vol. 24, No. 1/2, 2000, pp. 57-77; and: *Creating New Strategies for Cooperative Collection Development* (ed: Milton T. Wolf and Marjorie E. Bloss) The Haworth Information Press, an imprint of The Haworth Press, Inc., 2000, pp. 57-77. Single or multiple copies of this article are available for a fee from The Haworth Document Delivery Service [1-800-342-9678, 9:00 a.m. - 5:00 p.m. (EST). E-mail address: getinfo@haworthpressinc.com].

© 2000 by The Haworth Press, Inc. All rights reserved.

To understand the thesis of this paper it is useful to draw a picture of what the situation has been, and what it is now.

Australia currently has a population of around 20 million persons living primarily by the rather extensive coastline. To clarify this, it is truer to say that about half the population live in the capital cities of Sydney and Melbourne. The other capital cities would attract a further 25% leaving the remainder of the population strewn up the Eastern seaboard and everywhere else. The Shire of Wimmera, for example, in western Victoria, covers an area of 38,000 square kilometers with only a population of 50,000. It is a declining population that is hungry for reading material and therefore there are huge operational and logistical difficulties in mounting such a library service. There are even wider and more complex political and organisational problems gaining a sufficient collection and staff to address their information need.

As a means of comparison it is worthwhile understanding that the landmass of Australia is as large as that of continental USA, but that the population is smaller than California or Canada. The Higher Education system in Australia extends to some 38 Universities and 650,000 students from the very largest Universities with student populations of 30,000 plus to the smallest with but a few thousand students. Australia has a Federal system of public universities that are Federally funded but founded under State legislation. Increasingly these Universities are required to generate substantial amounts of income from their own activities. The Universities jealously guard their independence from government in the disbursement of funds within the University. The extent to which they fund their own library depends largely on historical factors but is certainly based on their own institutional judgement of need. On the whole librarians favour cooperative behaviors even though it is said that the institutions are increasingly in competition with each other for student numbers and research funds. There is always a great deal of pride in one's own library and the library can be a source of competitive strength for the institution in its drive to attract the better students. In this circumstance the librarians find themselves supporting their own teaching, research and scholarship programs with no other resource capacity for other worthwhile ambitions. The question is: How can any of the larger, let alone the smaller, libraries survive and provide an effective service?

It is well to recognise that the smaller academic libraries might be able to work more effectively with the larger "sandstone" universities with regard to consortial or cooperative purchasing. While they account hr a much smaller percentage of purchases, the younger city and regional universities are the fastest growing sector m tertiary education. The University of the Year in Australia was Deakin University and the University Achiever of the Year was Wollongong University. Both of these Universities are located well outside the boundaries of the cities. They are also ambitious and flexible with a strong market orientation.

On a wider analysis the percentage of overseas English language books being purchased for any libraries across Australia has been falling steadily from 1975 through 1995. Table 1 and Graph 1 indicate that this percentage of collected material has fallen from 68% in 1975 to 55% in 1995. This data has been provided from the analysis of the National Bibliographic Database, KINETICA, which operates from the National Library of Australia and to which all significant Australian libraries contribute their bibliographic data. It can be credibly ascertained that this percentage has fallen to less than 50% as we conclude the 1990s.

The number of monographs collected by the University Libraries across Australia had been steadily rising until it peaked at 840,000 in 1997. In 1998, however, the collected number fell to 765,000. This data must be set in the context of increasing rates of publication worldwide and shrinking library budgets. The situation in Australia is compounded by the position of the Australia dollar relative to the Pound Sterling and the US Dollar (see Graphs 2 and 3 and note 3).

The falling dollar caused a major crisis for Australian university libraries in the last fiscal year, forcing them to cancel, nearly A$7 million in subscriptions to overseas publications. In fact, in the last five years, Australian universities faced a triple-whammy of funding cuts, a rise in the cost of serials, and the weak dollar. Cumulative budget cuts of over 20% during this period placed Australia's expenditure on tertiary education in the bottom one-third of OECD countries. In 1999, the ruling Coalition government promised another 10% cut in funding for all library purchases in the new fiscal year.

On the positive side, the federal government indicates in its most recent *Higher Education Funding Report* that funding for universities will stabilize in fiscal year 2001. In practice, this will restore federal funds to their 1993 levels. Overall, funds available to the university sector are expected to rise slightly because of increased private fund-

TABLE 1. NBD Data Table for English Language Monographs Published Overseas, 1975-1995[4]

Year	Records on the NBD	Titles Held by Australia	Percent Held
1975	95364	64585	67.73
1976	84310	54390	64.51
1977	85932	54880	63.87
1978	86063	54724	63.59
1979	83452	53684	64.33
1980	82434	53179	64.51
1981	76124	48260	63.40
1982	79370	49514	62.38
1983	78820	49409	62.69
1984	80973	50019	61.77
1985	86031	50834	59.09
1986	89835	51125	56.91
1987	91919	54947	59.78
1988	92855	54996	59.23
1989	99321	57663	58.06
1990	104683	59209	56.56
1991	106936	58280	54.50
1992	113016	60570	53.59
1993	113062	59706	52.81
1994	107955	57625	53.38
1995	98767	54502	55.18
Totals	**1,937,222**	**1,152,101**	**59.47**

ing, growing income from fees and charges, and greater HECS loans (for fully funded undergraduate places). Universities that stand the most to gain are the regional and new universities.

Collectively, the Australian University Libraries have an annual bibliographic budget in the order of AUS$130 million for books and serials. This is not insignificant. The State Libraries and the National Library concentrate their efforts predominantly on Australia and the wider support of the extensive public library networks in their states. There is not, however, coordination of how the collections are built. This statement is made regardless of how the term 'collections' is defined. The development of a strong collection across the university libraries is entirely haphazard. In the 1960s and 1970s, when the percentage of national published output achieved was high, this did not matter. With the percentage now being less than 50%, the situation is a matter of some concern. In addition, the number of monographs being purchased for Australian University Libraries is now declining sharply and the number of inter-loans of monographs is also declining.

GRAPH 1. Percentage of Australian Holdings of English Language Monographs Published Overseas 1975-1995

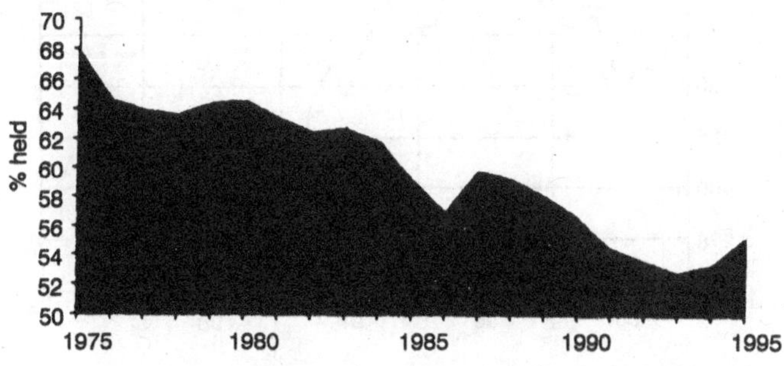

GRAPH 2. Monthly Average Exchange Rates: U.S. Dollars per Australian Dollar

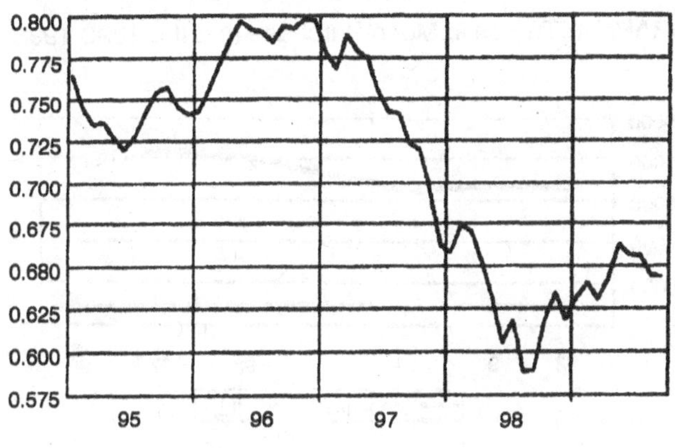

(See Table 2 and Graph 4.) The decline in interlibrary loans could be largely due to budgetary pressure to pass ILL charges onto academic departments, to the available time for academic research and to a decline in postgraduate research student numbers.

Australia has seen its share of subject collecting schemes over the years in universities and public libraries. Most of these have now failed. These schemes involved libraries collecting in very broad areas (e.g., South East Asia). What they collected and how they collected was entirely up to them. There were no reporting devices. There was a

GRAPH 3. Monthly Average Exchange Rates: British Pounds per Australian Dollar

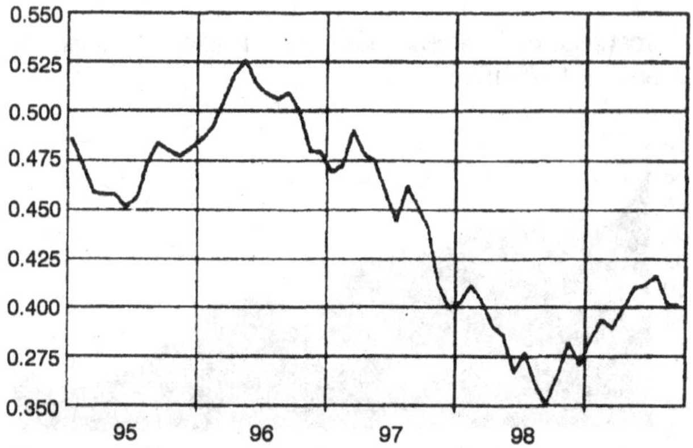

Currency graphs © 1999 by Prof. Werner Antweiler, University of British Columbia, Vancouver, BC, Canada. Time periods shown in diagram: 1/Jan/ 1995-3/Sep/1999.

GRAPH 4. Trends in Mono Purchase and ILL 1992-1998

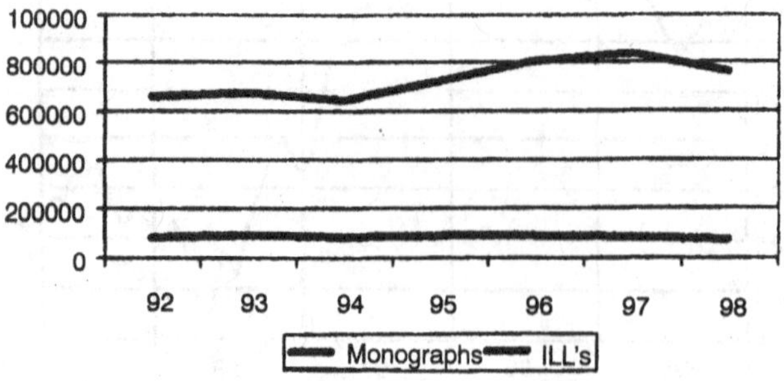

TABLE 2. CAUL Statistics 1994 to 1998

Period	Monographs			Serials		
	Value	Volume	Ave. per Title	Value	Volume	Ave. per Serial
1994	$38,518,791	625,808	$61.55	$57,721,985	200,666	$287.65
1995	$45,606,070	557,871	$81.75	$65,692,123	194,639	$337.51
1996	$52,276,156	904,292	$57.81	$77,557,211	255,836	$303.15
1997	$48,984,406	791,296	$61.90	$50,047,078	143,971	$347.61
1998	$40,786,168	713,056	$57.20	$54,835,331	112,974	$485.38

Source: CAUL Statistics 1994 to 1998 for both serials and monographs (*www.anu.edu.edu.au/caul/stats*). The figures have been adjusted to reflect gaps in the data collection.

significant debate developed in the late 1980s to explore the potential of the 'Distributed National Collection.' This debate was largely led by Eric Wainwright. The notion was to develop collecting strengths across the country's libraries using the Conspectus methodology. The Conspectus approach was strongly taken up by libraries illustrating where their existing collections had strengths measured relative to the published output of particular disciplines. The conspectus collecting levels were then maintained on a database within the National Library of Australia. Unfortunately the conspectus work has never been translated into the reality of a Distributed National Collection due to a variety of factors. Most of these reasons would be to do with institutional imperatives, inevitably these imperatives lay elsewhere. Another significant factor was the lack of incentive to engage in the DNC. The Libraries found it difficult to decide who should collect at a research level in each discipline, especially when their academics could scarcely see the purpose of the macro exercise. In this factor lies the substantive reasons: the DNC did not have academic champions nor did it have driving funds. It did not convince the minds and intellects of our academics that there was an emerging problem or that the libraries had the access and delivery mechanisms to ensure that each academic program would never be disadvantaged. The DNC was not proven to be flawed but the execution of the scheme was. Perhaps it was also an idea before its time.

Debates such as this do not readily or wholly go away. The University Libraries in Australia predominantly are now engaged in a major study called JANUS, named after the Greek God of Gateways. JANUS is focussed on collecting but specifically on creating a business decision model. The business decision model is being developed to enable effective collecting to support national research priorities. The shape of the model is yet to firmly emerge but is seen as groups of libraries supporting particular discipline areas and receiving Federal funds to assist them in this activity. The funds, however, are not expected to be long-term.

The problem can be summarised in the following manner:

- There is a growing budgetary difficulty supporting effective collecting across the country;
- There is a falling percentage of English language published material being collected. This is even truer for serials than for monographs;
- There have been very worthwhile schemes developed such as the DNC and JANUS to address the problem but these have floundered thus far without academic support, developmental resources and conflicting institutional priorities.

It is true to say that models of collection building beyond the perimeter of individual institutions have been absent from the Australian Library scene. Library cooperation has concentrated almost exclusively on models of access and delivery. Australia has long had tools to identify which monograph or serial titles have been held in Australia culminating with the Australian Bibliographic Network (ABN) and now KINETICA.[5] In these ways it has been readily possible to know where to obtain an item or copy. The Inter-library lending system ensured that delivery could and still does occur.

With the implementation of the LIDDAS[6] software across most of the major libraries early next year, nominated users will be able to request material in an 'unmediated' fashion. This will heighten pressure on libraries as groups to address the dual issues of service guarantees and also collecting guarantees.

The national 'design' for collecting has been random and haphazard. If there was design in the higher education system it related to the courses taught at various educational institutions around the country. This has become more complicated in recent days, as institutions have found themselves in competition with each other for student enrollments. The existence of a collection across the nation came about through the sheer sue of the bibliographic purchasing across the country and the statistical inevitability that many of the world's publishing output would eventually find their way onto the shelves of one of our libraries. As has been demonstrated already the percentage of readily accessible monographic materials in Australia is most likely below 50% measured on an annual basis. Some colleges would argue that this is a matter of little concern in that we can either retrieve the material from another library located in the country of origin of the published material or wait until an entrepreneurial company decides to offer such a retrieval service. It is dangerous to believe that either option is viable considering the need for the library community to establish strategies that both display accountability and sustainability. A nation has a right to know that the best of the world's information is readily at hand.

COLLECTION MANAGEMENT STRUCTURES/PROFILING

To combat the random and haphazard nature of collection building and to establish, perhaps unconsciously, strategies that display accountability and sustainability, some Australian libraries now employ collection development tools such as vendor approval plans. Long recognised in the US as effective organizing mechanisms for core collection building, approval profiles offer Australian libraries the means to:

- Measure collections and acquisitions across a broad spectrum of relevant indices (including classification schemes, publishers, non-subject parameters, aspects, etc.)
- Through regular reporting and joint analysis with the vendor, make prescriptive changes to the profile in support of collection development goals.

The design of the profiling methodology may belong to the vendor, but it is the instructions from those in the library or university responsible for selection that inform that methodology and control its results. The profile is a de-selection tool. In any given year, there are approximately 50,000 scholarly and academic monographs published in English from thousands of imprints worldwide. Its basic task is to intelligently and precisely reduce that number to one that provides the most appropriate material without going over the library's budget.

The approval methodologies from every vendor share some basic elements. Monographs "treated" or profiled by the vendor arc compared against each library's profile. This process will yield one of three results for each profile:

- The monograph will be shipped automatically to the library on approval. Libraries may reject and return to the vendor titles they deem unworthy.
- The monograph will be announced to the library via a paper notification slip and/or electronically (usually by means of web access).
- The monograph will not be shipped or announced. It is excluded or "de-selected" based on the library's profile.

Acquiring books automatically on approval also provides the most cost-effective way of bringing material into the library. The expensive process of searching, identifying and ordering titles is left to the vendor instead of the library.[7]

Apart from these basic shared elements, vendor approval methodologies vary widely and may yield significant and disparate outcomes. The profiling principle described below are those of YBP Library Services.

- Identification of a "universe" of imprints subject to the profiling process. The vendor's mandate is to profile all monographs published by these eligible imprints. It is not feasible to cover every scholarly imprint, but it is possible to comprehensively cover more than 90% of titles of interest to academic libraries. Having a defined list also lends a reassuring predictability to approval coverage.
- A commitment to examine, catalog and describe each monograph with the "book-in-hand" by trained professionals in addition to computer support. In this way the precision and complexity demanded by library instructions can be satisfied.
- Face-to-face meetings and discussions with all selectors, including academic staff, in the crafting of the initial profile. Successful profiles are never finished. They must be flexible enough to ac-

commodate the evolving collection interests of each library. To that end, regular joint evaluation of the profile is necessary.

The profile as "de-selection" may be fairly described as a series of filters through which each monograph must pass. A title that successfully passes through all filters is sent to the library on approval. If at any point in the process, the library's instructions restrict that title to a notification announcement, that announcement will be sent to the library in lieu of the book. Similarly, if the library's instructions exclude the title, no book will be shipped and no announcement will be made. The filters are always applied in the same order.

In brief, the profiling filters are:

- *Series instructions:* The Library's instructions regarding specific series titles. For example, all titles on standing order may be excluded at this point. There is no point in profiling monographs in series that are already being acquired by other means.
- *Imprint/publisher instructions:* The library's instructions regarding each of the imprints in the approval universe. A library may wish to exclude a number of imprints, restrict others to notification slips and leave the remainder open to automatic book shipments at this stage. The choice belongs to the selectors.
- *Non-subject parameter instructions:* The library's instructions regarding a myriad of relevant characteristics including intended audience, format, language, size, price, binding, etc.
- *Narrative overrides and/or aspects:* Because no classification scheme (Library of Congress, Dewey Decimal, National Library of Medicine, etc.) is adequate to precisely accommodate demanding collection development requirements, it is sometimes necessary to include written narrative instructions into the profile. This is especially true for interdisciplinary subjects such as Gender Studies or Environmental Studies–which may be classified in any number of areas.
- *Subject instructions:* Library instructions based on classification.

Effective profiling is confronted with some unique challenges in the Australian context. primarily designed in the US, profiling methodologies must be adapted to or superimposed upon a different Australian reality. In the traditional model, it is the librarians that are the chief custodians of the profile. However, the US subject bibliographer or librarian-as-selector model is most often absent in Australia. Instead it is the faculty and academic staff that is largely responsible for selection. For may academics, profiling methodologies are literally foreign to them as they assume a level of common language and understanding that librarians and vendors share. Care must be taken to involve the academic staff. However, it is an undeniable fact that many, busy with other duties, have little time or patience for profile creation or maintenance. Consequently, an unintended result of profile implementation may be a subtle, but very real, shift of collection responsibility away from academic staff and toward librarians.

Already we have described the principles by which profiling has occurred in the traditional nuclear library. If we are to move beyond that model into the collaborative, a new range of issues readily emerges. These include, the essentials of the system, the targets for collecting, the role and extent of funding, the nature of service agreements, the need to create sustainability, and the nature of administration.

DEMOGRAPHICS OF LIBRARIES

In the case of Australia, the dominant characteristic of the modes of historical and current organisation is distributed. This is a lesson that should be acknowledged and built upon. No schemes of Access and delivery have focussed on centralised models as in the British Library at Boston Spa. Australia has relied upon the collected strengths of the whole rather than the one. To test this hypothesis it is proposed to limit the included collections to those in the Victorian academic libraries. These libraries are all members of a group called CAVAL. The hypothesis can be tested amongst this group of libraries and then extended, if successful, to the larger group consisting of academic, special, and state libraries. The role of the National Library of Australia is indeterminate in this. The NLA has described its collecting purpose as being in the area of Australiana. In addition, the NLA manages the national bibliographic database–KINETICA. This database acts as a bibliographic utility but also as a record of national collecting performance. All significant collections in the country are recorded on this database. The NLA also has legislative requirements to facilitate and encourage issues of national interest. The National has conducted some of the very interesting analyses already included in this paper. In the second phase of this proposal the NLA should have a strong coordinating role to play. In the first instance, the pilot proposal should operate in Victoria only, and only amongst the academic libraries.

TARGETS

It has already been highlighted that less than 50% of English language publishing is being collected in Australia on an annual basis. To totally reverse this situation would not be a sensible solution. Even 20 years ago, the collecting level was only 67%. To establish a quantum target is obviously desirable. The measurement of success (or failure) is much easier. It would also be the case that to return to 100% of English language published output would be quite expensive. On the assumption that there is a 50,000 volume gap in annual collecting the cost for materials alone could be in the order of 7.5 to 8 million dollars. To further assume that it would be highly desirable to increase the rate of collecting in the Pacific Rim and Asian materials then the cost would obviously rise.

This equation is still inadequate. It is predicted that the rate of publication will decline with the unavailability of paper pulp over the next twenty years or so. The range of research disciplines which the universities are concentrating upon and the disciplines of national research focus are considerably more manageable. It is the contention of this proposal that a range of disciplines would be chosen to test collecting practices against. The aggregation of the collecting capacity of the nine University Libraries in Victoria in an autocratic fashion would be considerable. The days of such autocratic behaviour are either long past or yet to emerge. The creation of a top-slice fiscal capability would be essential if the testing of the gap is to emerge. The critical point to remember is that the collecting would be across the range of libraries and not only in the major libraries.

In his book, *The Death of Competition*, James Moore sees a world where traditional industry boundaries arc irrelevant and businesses are coevolving, unpredictable organisms within a constantly shifting business ecosystem that no-one controls (Moore, 1997). This is a vastly different world where competition exists, not for the good of an individual business, but to assist in the evolution of the overall business ecosystem. Moore defines a business ecosystem as "an economic community supported by a foundation of interacting organizations and individuals" (Moore, 1997: Ch. 2, 6). This community includes suppliers, producers, competitors and other stakeholders and allows for the emergence of leadership roles which "enable members to move towards shared visions . . . and to find mutually supportive roles"[8] Moore talks about the key elements of organisational strategy in such an environment, using the "information space" as an example:

- Rediscover and reinforce your "strongholds"
- Use these competencies to create new interrelated sub-systems
- Invest in identifying and capturing "the undefended hill"
- Find a niche where there is no-one else
- Develop the required competencies
- Make the investment required to dominate
- Work with many partners to create a defendable position
- Consider occupying the leadership position in the system

Competition between the partners still exists, but it is defined more broadly as part of the coevolution and survival of the whole system.[9]

Even though libraries may not think of themselves as businesses, the "biological system" metaphor is a useful way to explore the changing relationships of both social and economic institutions in the emerging digital age. Organisational strategy and processes are important, often more important than the technology–"having the right organization matters as much as delivering the right tools" (Seadle, 1998: 11).[10]

The capturing of this capability by "many partners" to deliver high quality, and quantity of targeted information in. a collaborative fashion is very much the "undefended hill"; the "leadership position" will create marketing strength for the parent universities even though there is a inherent tension between those institutions.

To further partner with a vendor in order to make this happen can create excellence. It is as Moore described above–"co-evolution." This suggests the best of the worlds of collaboration and synergy–the parallel adaptation of organisational identities for mutual benefit.

This proposal envisages that the group of libraries would undertake to purchase a target percentage of all materials published in English and a range of other languages across a specified range of disciplines. Each would have target title purchases and dollar expenditures, which would be monitored and reported on a regular basis.

PRACTICAL SOLUTIONS

How can this goal be achieved? As libraries seek to collect an expanding universe of publication with limited resources, there are now tools available to support cooperative collection development. Within the context of library consortia, no single model exists to direct our work. However, there exist a number of approaches that can be adopted singly or in concert. The key is the identification of overlap or duplication among and between members of the group. Some overlap is, of course, desirable. Duplicate core collections in shared disciplines among individual institutions will not disappear.[11] However, the identification of particular individual strengths in target disciplines provides fertile ground for addressing unneeded group overlap and raising the total percentage of published monographs held by the group. These approaches include:

Comparative Reporting: Comparative and retrospective reporting is a simple matter of relating one library's vendor transaction data or profile instructions to similar data for one or several other libraries.

- Shipment History: Various retrospective comparisons help consortia to identify and analyze historical collection development patterns of member libraries. For example, the report templates can include:
  - Shipment History and Unique Titles, Sorted by Imprint
  - Shipment History and Unique Titles, Sorted by LC Sub-Class
  - Approval Press Coverage and Standing Order Comparisons: When two or more libraries think together about sharing responsibility for a broad-based collection in the context of approval services, simple comparisons of existing imprint and standing order instructions provide a useful starting point. Example comparisons can include:
    - Comparative Approval Plan Press Coverage
    - Comparative Standing Order Instructions
    - A "consortial view" within the vendor's database: This supports the daily acquisitions workflow of libraries by providing a consortia-wide view of sales transactions outside of profiles (i.e., firm orders) and immediate control at the item level. When accessing a title, libraries will see not only their own institution's transaction history, but that of their group members as well. Acquisitions decisions can then be

made based on the holdings of the group and not just the individual institution.

Shared Profiling-Cooperative Collection Development Through Coordinated Approval Plan Profiles: In addition to comparative reporting capabilities, tools are needed to draft and manage coordinated approval plan profiles. Models for shared profiling already exist within individual institutions (UC Berkeley, Stanford, etc.) and can be readily adapted by consortia.

- Relational Database: At the heart of this concept is a sophisticated relational database of library account specifications including approval plan profiles and shipment details. This database becomes a dynamic tool for monitoring, displaying, and evaluating the impact of approval plan profiles on collections within a single library, multiple libraries on campus, or across institutions.
- A Third Dimension: Using the relational database, and various data manipulation tools, it is possible to go beyond standard two dimensional reporting, to a three dimensional view that incorporates the collecting patterns of multiple institutions on a third axis. Add to this, the percentages of the available universe of new titles, and it is possible for a consortium to devise strategies for coordinating their approval profiles. Ultimately the consortium will have enough information to maximize collection breadth by jointly acquiring a larger percentage of the whole.
- Predictive Capability: In addition, shared profiling will allow vendor customer service representatives and bibliographers to perform "what if" analyses of approval profiles. Analyses of this type will allow users to evaluate the impact of potential profile changes on collection patterns. Bibliographers will be able to quantify, in both numbers of titles and dollars of expenditure, the result of adding or removing individual publishers to an approval plan, including or excluding particular publication formats, or the addition of subject coverage.

SHARED CONSORTIA PROFILING

To illustrate these approaches, it might be useful to use a hypothetical example of three Australian libraries that wish to raise their shared percentage of English language monograph holdings to 70%. Certain agreements and assumptions have been made among the group of three. The core (duplicate) collection consists of instances where at least two of the members believe they must have the title in their own collections. Above, or in addition to, the core, only one member needs to own the title.

For the five subjects represented in the first chart, Library One collects fewer than 50 percent of the titles available in all but subject 1 (Chart 1). As will be shown, however, by uniquely collecting titles in other subjects, Library one helps the consortium achieve its goal of collecting 70 percent of the English-language books for a subject.

Libraries Two and Three see the core for subjects 1 and 5 similarly; that is, in those subjects they are collecting many of the same books, while in subject 4, they are collecting the same percentage of available books (30 percent), but for this subject, they are collecting different titles. Yet, in the picture presented here, these differences are invisible (see Chart 2). Why? Because each library was, until now, locked into looking only at its own collection. We cannot tell from these graphs of the libraries' collections how much or how little overlap exists in any subject.

Showing the three libraries together fails to indicate, again, where the collections overlap and where they supplement one another (see Chart 3).

But the shared profile clearly shows the advantage of a consortial approach (see Chart 4). At the back of the cube, the bar represented indicates the percentage of total titles available in the five subjects from at least one of the three libraries. Further, the area visible above the bars for the individual libraries represents the titles housed in only one library but available to the consortium.

The shared profile permits considerable flexibility. In subjects 2, 3,

CHART 1. Library One

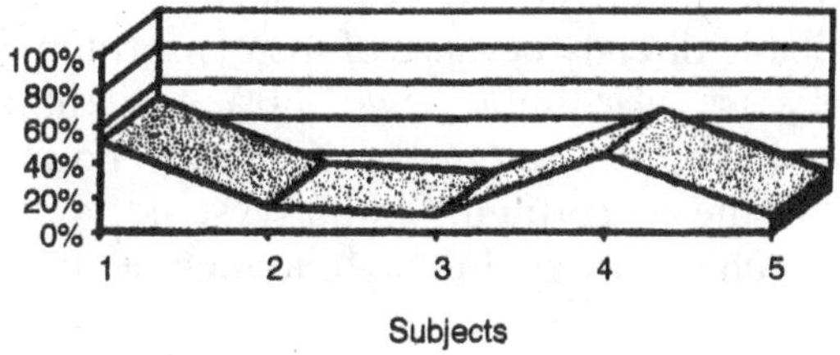

CHART 2. Libraries Two and Three

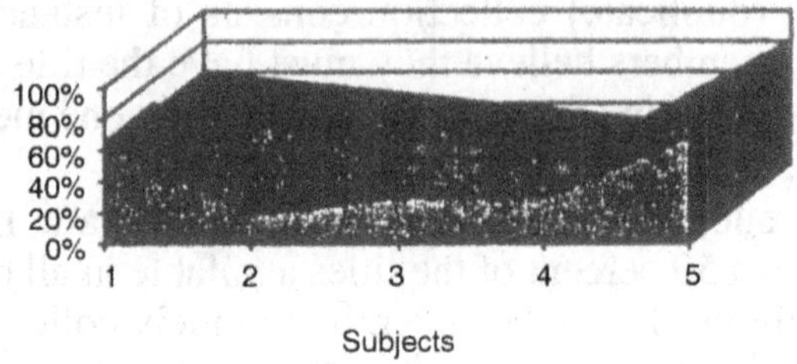

CHART 3. The Three Libraries

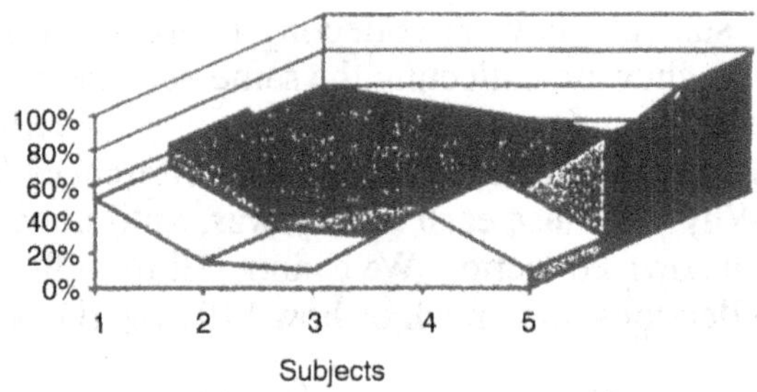

CHART 4. A Three-Library Shared Profile

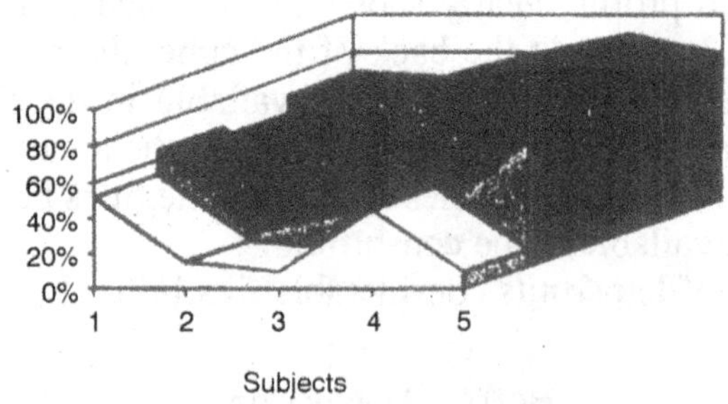

and 4 the consortium achieves its goal of collecting 70 percent or more of the books available directly because of the consortium. In subject 3, library three collects 40%; library two, 30%; and library one, 10 percent of the books in the discipline, and because no overlap exists, the total is 80% for the consortium. Similarly, subjects 2 and 4 enable the consortium to achieve its goal though no member can do so on its own.

By contrast, in subject 1, each library collects at least 50% of the titles available, but because of overlap, the total achieved is 67% of the titles in the subject, short of the consortium's goal. In subject 5, on the other hand, the consortium achieves its goal because library three alone specializes in the subject. (That is, all titles in the very small collection of library one in the subject and in the larger collection of library two are included in the titles collected by library three.)

But the important information in the shared profile is contained in the bar. You might imagine that the cube represented by the chart is with piled books, each title a discrete data point, making the cube a relational database. The range visible at the back represents titles bought only once, patrons satisfied, and books collected by only one.

SERVICE AGREEMENTS

This paper has highlighted that library systems in Australia have been strong on systemic Access and Delivery mechanisms. Having said this, it would be essential to formalise these arrangements in the form of service agreements. These agreements would detail the standards by which access would be achieved by the library users, the tools by which they would be able to achieve access and the times which would be guaranteed for delivery as well as the form of delivery. In this partnership each partner is equally responsible for acquisition, access and delivery. Each set of library users gain out of the arrangement, no one set is independent of the other; each set of library users has truly collaborated; the system has co-evolved to a new level of acquisition, access and delivery.

A related issue is the issue of long-term storage and the role of consortium repositories. Having purchased the material and achieved the designed targets, it would be important to sustain the system objectives. The lack of physical space with individual libraries and the lack of funding for physical expansion will require some form of action on repositories for the collective good.

SUSTAINABILITY

It has been argued above that 'top-sliced' funding was highly desirable in order to test the proposition of this paper. It is clear also that the first and most important issue to be dealt with in this exercise is the "end-game." To fail to detail the funding arrangement beyond the initial funding impetus is to court disaster. The "end-game" strategy ts to achieve sustainability or to at least move strongly down that path. One way of achieving this is to impose an impost of say $4.00 on each inter-loan amongst the members and to impose a similar impost of $2.00 on each in-person loan. The sum of these imposts would go into a central fund designed to sustain and expand on the initial strategy.

THE FUTURE

What is the future if it is not something that we have designed? As de Kerckhove said, "the future can and should be more a matter of choice than of destiny." This proposal builds on historic and current systemic modes of operating, it has incorporated proposals such as the Distributed National Collection, it has provided shape to initiatives such as JANUS, and it has dealt with the dual pillars of our generation: accountability and sustainability. Most importantly, it has taken as its goal, the provision of excellence in service and collection to the users who are the raison d'être of the libraries individually and collectively.

NOTES

1. Editorial in *The Australian Library Journal*, vol. 47, No. 4, November 1998.

2. De Kerckhove, Derek. *Connected intelligence: The arrival of the web society.* London: Kegan Paul, 1997.

3. Currency graphs 2 and 3 are used with permission. They are generated and retrieved from a plotting formula and software using our own parameters on Prof. Antweiler's website (*http://pacific.commerce.ubc.ca/xr/*). His home page states:

> This page and the FX database software are ©1998-99 by Prof. Werner Antweiler, University of British Columbia, Vancouver, Canada. Permission to download data through the retrieval interface and reproduce images generated by the plot interface is granted provided that the source and this copyright are acknowledged.

The time period shown in diagram is 1/Jan/1995-3/Sep/1999.

4. Overseas monograph collecting in Australia: Observations based on the National Bibliographic Database (NBD). National Library of Australia, July 1998: 12.

5. KINETICA is the National Bibliographic Database for Australia. It is the successor to the Australian Bibliographic Network (ABN). It is both a bibliographic utility and a record of national holdings.

6. LIDDAS is a software development in Australia supported by the Australia Vice-Chancellor's Committee and Fretwell Downing. It provides inter-loan management software, unmediated searching, and virtual catalogue searching across the consortium collective membership.

7. The cost effectiveness of approval plans has been noted many times in the literature. One very cogent example may be found in "The economics of monographs acquisitions: A time/cost study conducted at Iowa State University," by Dilys Morris and Pamela Z. Rebarcak. *Library Acquisitions: Practice and Theory.* Vol. 20, Issue 1, Cover date: Spring 1996. ISSN 03646408.

8. Moore, James F. *The death of competition: Leadership and strategy in the age of business ecosystems.* New York: Harper Business, 1996, Ch. 2, 7.

9. op cit.: 16-19.

10. Seadle, Michael. "The raw and cooked among librarians." *Library Hi Tech* 16(3-4) 1998: 7-11.

11. For a detailed study of overlap among academic libraries see "Approval Plan Overlap: A Study of Four Libraries." Nardini, Robert F., Charles M. Getchell, Jr., and Thomas E. Cheever. Co-published simultaneously in *Acquisitions Librarian* (The Haworth Press, Inc.) No. 16, 1996, pp. 75-97; and *Approval Plans: Issues and Innovations* (ed. John H. Sandy), The Haworth Press, Inc., 1996, pp. 75-97.

Back to the Future: Building the Florida Library Research Consortium

Martha Hruska
Kathy Arsenault

In 1996, library directors from the University of Florida, Florida State University, and the University of South Florida (Florida's largest state universities) proposed a cooperative collection development initiative. The libraries of the State University System had experienced successful cooperative projects for over a decade, all enabled by improved technology. These cooperative projects started most notably with the 1987 Florida Center for Library Automation's implementation of LUIS. This NOTIS based online catalog gave the state's widely dispersed universities instant access to one another's collection holdings for the first time. This capability gradually enabled a major change in how Florida libraries could build their research collections.

Improved telecommunications, including e-mail, conference calls, fax and Ariel networks, provided an infrastructure to greatly facilitate interlibrary cooperation. More recent examples of State University System initiatives facilitated by technology are the migration of LUIS to a web-based format and the coordinated selection of jointly pur-

---

Martha Hruska is Associate Director for Technical Services, University of Florida.
Kathy Arsenault is Collection Development Librarian, University of South Florida, St. Petersburg.

The authors are grateful to Rosann Bazirjian and Sam Gowan, former Program Team members, for their invaluable assistance with the FLRC project.

[Haworth co-indexing entry note]: "Back to the Future: Building the Florida Library Research Consortium." Hruska, Martha, Kathy Arsenault. Co-published simultaneously in *Collection Management* (The Haworth Information Press, an imprint of The Haworth Press, Inc.) Vol. 24, No. 1/2, 2000, pp. 79-85; and: *Creating New Strategies for Cooperative Collection Development* (ed: Milton T. Wolf and Marjorie E. Bloss) The Haworth Information Press, an imprint of The Haworth Press, Inc., 2000, pp. 79-85. Single or multiple copies of this article are available for a fee from The Haworth Document Delivery Service [1-800-342-9678, 9:00 a.m. - 5:00 p.m. (EST). E-mail address: getinfo@haworthpressinc. com].

© 2000 by The Haworth Press, Inc. All rights reserved.

chased electronic resources. The combination of these experiences provided a context that makes a more cooperative collection development of research materials seem feasible.

The library directors from Florida, Florida State, and South Florida appointed representatives to develop and implement a proposal for an even more expansive cooperative collection development among the three libraries. A literature search quickly identified a model and inspiration: the North Carolina Triangle Research Libraries Network (TRLN), which over its fifty year history has developed me of the richest collections of research material in the nation (Patricia Buck Dominguez and Luke Swindler, "Cooperative Collection Development at the Research Triangle University Libraries: A Model for the Nation," *College & Research Libraries* [Nov. 1993] 470-496). Unfortunately the "Florida triangle" faces problems that the TRLN does not: Tallahassee, Tampa, and Gainesville are separated by distances of from 129 to 246 miles, a large triangle indeed. In addition, the TRLN consortium builds on strong preexisting institutional commitments to collaboration.

The Florida planning team therefore had three major tasks: (1) to develop a structure and operating procedures for the organization, (2) to develop and implement significant improvements to the ILL system linking the universities, (3) to select and foster subject teams for a pilot cooperative collection development effort.

1. *Structure and operating procedures:* The planning team recommended to the library directors that team members become the advisory board of the newly named Florida Library Research Consortium (FLRC) that would link the general university libraries of Florida, Florida State and South Florida, while making provision for other state universities to participate when appropriate. The Advisory Board members agreed to work with cataloging and ILL departments in expanding cooperative functions, to establish and mentor subject teams, and to report regularly to the library directors. It agreed to restrict cooperative proposals to Conspectus levels 4 and 5 material. Materials would be purchased and housed by the individual libraries, but loans across campuses of any materials would be encouraged.

2. *Improvements to the ILL system linking the universities:* All State university libraries had participated, since the early 1980s, in the Florida Library Information Network (FLIN), an interlibrary loan network Although services were free to state university students, FLIN pre-

scribed the usual restrictions on interlibrary loans: no reference books, journal issues, media, microform, or other special format material would be lent, and loan periods would be brief (two or three weeks). Advisory Board members quickly recalled that these strictures would seriously limit cooperation. If research level materials were to be jointly selected, access should be provided to each university's graduate students and faculty whenever possible regardless of the material's format. In addition, borrowers were to be treated uniformly across universities, with the same borrowing privileges available to FLRC researchers as would be available to the home university's equivalents. The University of South Florida, a metropolitan university with three regional campuses, advertises itself as "one university, regionally dispersed." FLRC borrowed the concept and resolved to become, as much as possible, "one library, regionally dispersed."

3. *Subject teams:* The Advisory Board selected 4 subject teams in areas where each university offered advanced degrees with complementary specialties. Theater, marine science, anthropology, and French studies teams were designated. The Advisory Board requested that team members attend a workshop in Gainesville to meet one another and plan for their year's activities. Patricia Dominguez of the University of North Carolina, one of the authors of the article on the TLRN, agreed to attend and act as facilitator to the teams. Teams were given basic tasks: (1) to evaluate academic programs at each university to determine current and future research needs, (2) to evaluate current collections and evaluate strengths and weaknesses and to develop a working definition for research level materials, (3) to determine primary collecting and selection responsibilities, (4) to select and encumber approximately $15,000 of research materials, divided among all three libraries. Each university contributed a special allocation of $20,000 so that the 4 subject teams would have both an incentive to participate and a reasonable deadline for their tasks. In future years, it was expected that cooperation would become institutionalized so that special allocations would not be necessary.

In the three years since its inception, the Florida Library Research Cooperative has worked hard to establish a program that benefits each of the participating libraries. The FLRC has grown slowly but deliberately to the point where it now includes seven subject teams. Anthropology, theater, and marine science continue from the original four teams, joined by religious studies, British history, art, and music. Each of these has agreed on joint collection building policies, closely related to local research needs, that detail the areas in which each library will focus. The subject teams have been actively building collections based on these policies over the last two years. Over 1200 jointly selected items have been purchased, including microform, media, periodical subscriptions and back files, and monographs. For example, marine science librarians agreed to select various journal subscriptions and back files not currently available in Florida libraries. The theater team purchased play scripts and specialized performance videos in both English and foreign languages. Anthropology divided responsibility for dissertations, selected microform collections, and ethnographic videotapes. Subject specialists are encouraged to spend departmental funds as much as possible with an eye towards the other cooperating libraries' collections, so the 1200 specially purchased FLRC items greatly underestimates the impact of the program.

In 1998, "Guidelines for Shared Resources" were approved and implemented. These guidelines expand on traditional interlibrary lending practices and are based on the premise that the participating libraries are committed to sharing their research holdings as much as possible. The guiding principle in developing these policies was 'default to yes,' unless requested materials are too fragile, valuable, or heavily used to transport off site. Since media, microforms, and journal back files have been popular purchases for our subject teams, traditional state university system lending policies have been adapted to make these formats available to all FLRC faculty and graduate students. Special Collections and Reference departments are also encouraged to think creatively to provide needed research materials across campuses, taking advantage of fax or scanning to provide desired materials within fair use copyright limits. Materials may also be lent department to department for on site consultation. Happily, the ten Florida state university system libraries are also working together to provide a new and speedier courier service among all the libraries.

LESSONS LEARNED

Respect your elders: The North Carolina Research Triangle libraries' experience over the past fifty years provides valuable guidance. Patricia Dominguez's advice to the original FLRC organizational meeting participants stressed the importance of voluntary agreements that serve the institutional interests of each participant. She suggested division of collecting responsibilities by easily understood objective concepts such as geography or format whenever possible. To date, the advisory board has found that traditional humanities or social science subjects are most amenable to cooperative agreements. Marine science, in which the collection development team was able to allocate subject specialty by geography, has been the only science program undertaken. Ms. Dominguez also advised restricting agreements to research level materials and integrating cooperative collection development with regular collection building as much as possible, making it an integral part of collection development rather than an expendable 'frill.' Appropriate subjects, in Ms. Dominguez's experience, can be neither too central (since passions run highest) or too marginal (since continuing support may be vulnerable) to the libraries' missions. The Advisory Group has followed these guidelines as much as possible as it identifies and mentors new subject groups.

The more things change, the more they stay the same: In spite of the radical changes that technology has brought to our libraries, cooperative collection development has focused on fairly traditional materials. With the exception of theater and anthropology videotapes, faculty groups consulted by our subject teams were quite traditional in their requests for materials. Retrospective collection building of serials and monographs was the overwhelming faculty preference. In the few cases in which faculty were interested in electronic sources, licensing agreements and the small size of our purchasing pool made cooperative savings virtually impossible. Requests were referred to the State University System electronic collections committee instead. In addition to collection preferences, participants revealed a strong need for face to face communication in addition to entail and conference calls. Without exception, teams were unable to build trust and creatively brainstorm unless they got to know one another in person. Although long-distance communication was able to facilitate discrete decisions, the relationships essential to successful collaboration inevitably required getting together with the FLRC advisory board to kick start the teams' activities.

You can lead a horse to water but you can't make him drink: Even with the vision of the library directors and a solid program infrastructure, the FLRC participants are finding that the key to the program's success is the commitment of the subject staff involved. The collaboration required for cooperative collection building is ultimately dependent on the commitment of the staff and the quality of their relationships. The FLRC libraries, UF, USF and FSU, are all organized quite differently. Funding for library materials and the materials selection process are handled differently in each of these institutions. This has simply meant that each of the subject team representatives operates from a unique environment with different incentives and types of assignments. In spite of strong and consistent administrative support, subject teams experienced widely varying outcomes. In subject areas where the FLRC program has been most successful, the team members have defined their own common purpose and where their efforts can best complement one another. These teams have used the Advisory Group for support, not for management. The teams that have not coalesced have, for various reasons, been unable to see the mutual benefit of the program and sometimes negatively reacted to a sense that the overall program is managed too heavily from the top down. To enhance the program further and to add subject teams, the Program Committee must continue to provide very supportive direction and incentives. Additional subject staff will need to be assigned and they will need assurance of resource support for the program, in terms of their own time and the funding resources to build the research collections. Ideally, each library participant would be trained in bibliography and responsible for selection in his or her subject areas.

NEXT STEPS

Having built a structure and an infrastructure for FLRC, the participating libraries face additional hurdles. The extended research collections of the three libraries must be integrated with local collections so effectively that FLRC is transparent to library staff and users. Eventually, it is hoped, patrons will be able to search the three library catalogs simultaneously. Staff at all levels should be aware and committed to look beyond their local collections to exploit the expanded resources available to them. Both the opportunities available and the responsibilities required from FLRC must be part of staff members' daily routines. Second, the FLRC will work on coordinating digital resources. A web site and discussion list for staff and a public web site for researchers are currently in the planning states. Cooperative digital special collections and preservation initiatives are also anticipated. As more unique research resources appear in digital form and the means of sharing print materials through scanning becomes increasingly common and available, the librarians who make cooperative programs work will be the ones shaping the future of access to research materials. Third, subject teams should be nurtured and expanded. In the Florida Board of Regents' recent classification of the Florida state supported universities, Florida State University, University of Florida, and University of South Florida were designated as Research I universities. This distinction confirms a strategic priority for these universities to develop and further build their doctoral and research programs. The FLRC has established itself as a research library cooperative to support this renewed direction for the universities. The FLRC continuing to build a strong core group of successful programs is essential to develop the track record necessary for additional funding opportunities, a major possibility for enhancing Florida research collections.

The FLRC experience has proven that although technological innovations make cooperation a possibility, very traditional library values, realities and competencies, including interpersonal skills, subject knowledge, and bibliographical expertise, are essential to make cooperation a reality. Furthermore, scholarly commitment to traditional print collections has so far made retrospective monographs, microform collections, dissertations, and journal back files the typical selections of subject teams. Libraries undertaking cooperative collection development projects, just as in their planning for assimilation of electronic information, are challenged to think beyond the boundaries of their physical buildings and collections without abandoning the values and strengths of current practice. Cooperative collection development, it appears, leads back to the future.

Last Copy Depository: Cooperative Collection Management Centers in the Electronic Age

Vernon N. Kisling, Jr.
Stephanie C. Haas
Pamela S. Cenzer

INTRODUCTION

As we move from paper to pixels, we are witnessing an important transition in the creation, ownership, dissemination, and archiving of information. One aspect of this transition has been a changing role for library consortia. Traditionally, consortia have facilitated cooperative

---

Vernon N. Kisling, Jr., is Collection Management Coordinator, Stephanie C. Haas is Environmental Librarian, and Pamela S. Cenzer is Serials Librarian, Marston Science Library, University of Florida.

This paper was presented at the Creating New Strategies for Cooperative Collection Development Conference, Aberdeen Woods Conference Center, Atlanta, Georgia, November 12-14, 1999.

[Haworth co-indexing entry note]: "Last Copy Depository: Cooperative Collection Management Centers in the Electronic Age." Kisling, Vernon N., Jr., Stephanie C. Haas, and Pamela S. Cenzer. Co-published simultaneously in *Collection Management* (The Haworth Information Press, an imprint of The Haworth Press, Inc.) Vol. 24, No. 1/2, 2000, pp. 87-92; and: *Creating New Strategies for Cooperative Collection Development* (ed: Milton T. Wolf and Marjorie E. Bloss) The Haworth Information Press, an imprint of The Haworth Press, Inc., 2000, pp. 87-92. Single or multiple copies of this article are available for a fee from The Haworth Document Delivery Service [1-800-342-9678, 9:00 a.m. - 5:00 p.m. (EST). E-mail address: getinfo@haworthpressinc.com].

© 2000 by The Haworth Press, Inc. All rights reserved.

acquisition of print material, but the electronic library is having a significant impact on this role. With space problems, weeding, and a greater reliance on electronic resources, archiving strategies for print and electronic resources require an expanded role for consortia. The purpose of this paper is to explore this expanded role using last copy depositories.

CURRENT POLICIES

Based on information available from exploratory survey by the authors, ARL, RLG, SAA and recent articles, it appears that the impact of electronic resources has created certain trends which should be of concern to the profession:

- *A dependence on others to "archive" electronic publications.* According to a 1994 ARL survey on electronic journal policies and procedures (SPEC Flyer 201), 54% of their libraries depend on an outside source (the publisher or a consortium) for "archival" copies of electronic journals. Another 26% maintain an electronic "archive" copy, and the remaining 20% have no arrangement for "archival" copies. Results of the authors' informal survey among southeastern academic libraries tend to agree with the ARL findings. This situation will only escalate when licensing agreements provide for access to the material rather than ownership.
- *An acceptance of inappropriate standards for archiving electronic publications.* An electronic copy of an electronic publication is not an acceptable archival format and is an impractical method (because of the constant migrating that would be required).
- *A superficial checking of regional holdings before weeding research collections.* In addition, weeding print material is often justified because the material is available in microform or electronically. However, electronic material may not be maintained at the library, except perhaps as an electronic copy stored in a Systems Office computer, and even this may not be done as libraries move toward a policy of "access rather than ownership."
- *A lack of last copy policies.* Even if a title is available in microform or electronically, there should be improved safeguards against disposing of the last best copy of a title in order to pre-

serve the cultural artifact as well as its content. No one expects this to happen, but without appropriate care, even the most common titles will eventually dwindle down to a few copies.

DEFINING THE CONCEPT

A last copy depository is considered here to be a regional cooperative depository for the last copy of English language titles held at the region's academic/research libraries. Because these titles would be the last copies within the region, the depository would also serve an archival function. Journals would be an initial concern, but monographs and other publications would be included. Titles available in both print and electronically would continue to be held in their paper format and/or as microfilm copies. Titles available only electronically would be held in paper or as microfilm copies. Current titles available only in print would still be retained at the libraries unless the libraries choose to transfer the last copy of these titles to the depository. The depository facility would be a separate storage and archival facility in order to be more cost and space effective for the library system it supports.

Organizationally, each last copy depository would be part of a national system of regional centers. CRL began in a similar fashion for its region, but has since emphasized unique materials, particularly foreign titles. This has been an appropriate policy for its first fifty years, since there was a need for foreign materials and there was not a concern over the loss of English language materials in their original condition. When looking toward its next fifty years, it would benefit the library community if CRL, in cooperation with regional academic/research library consortia, would lead a coordination effort to establish regional centers to preserve and archive English language print materials, as well as to properly archive electronic materials. The reasons for such an effort are provided more fully in the following discussion of the issues.

ISSUES

Commercialization of electronic resources. Allowing publishers and vendors to maintain and "archive" journals (as well as other publications) presents a number of risk factors:

- Will they maintain their electronic "archives" over time, or will the profit motive adversely affect the commitment to maintain the "archive"?
- What will become of the "archives" when another publisher acquires their titles?
- How will libraries know titles exist electronically, find URLs, and access these titles (particularly for non-journal publications such as reports)?
- If libraries do not have copies of the titles, will there be cost controls on the prices charged by the publisher/vendor for document delivery?
- Is it in society's best interest to have libraries, the traditional repository for the preservation of scholarship, relinquish this function to commercial publishers and vendors? Will this role be abdicated in the electronic age because of a format change?

When negotiating contracts for full text electronic resources, libraries should require the publisher/vendor to provide a paper or microfilm copy of all titles as an archival copy. In order to avoid excessive duplication at the libraries (as is now the case with titles available in both formats), this archival copy could be sent to the depository that would serve the region's libraries. Not even sources such as JSTOR, which maintains paper copies of everything they have in electronic form, should be trusted as the sole repository of archival copies. Having one such facility is inadequate and at some future date it is quite possible that a commercial publisher or vendor will acquire JSTOR, as was (CARL) UnCover. Regional last copy depositories, on the other hand, would be library operated archival centers and would be a deterrent to any monopolistic control over the access to titles when these documents are only available electronically, and only from the publishers/vendors.

Access vs. ownership. An important aspect of this possible monopolistic control by the publishers/vendors is the issue of access vs. ownership. It appears that librarians consider access to documents, rather than owning the documents, a blessing. However, this increases the potential for monopolistic control over these documents. If libraries do not own the documents, which is counter to our traditional role, we cannot manage, organize, or archive the documents. Collection management will be compromised and librarians will have less control over information sources relevant for local patrons. If publishers/vendors have the sole copy of documents, they can escalate and manipulate prices for subscriptions and document delivery. However, if libraries insist on having a paper/microfilm copy of titles, these archival copies will deter uncontrolled price escalation. Considering recent experience with the costs of journals, electronic packages, and licensing agreements, it should be apparent that this issue is a matter for serious concern.

Archiving electronic resources. Another issue that needs serious review is the concept of electronically archiving electronic documents. One of the major problems with electronic copy is the perpetual need to migrate the copy to newer technologies. The effort and costs of doing so are enormous, and will depend on long-term commitments on the part of the libraries (or the owners of the original electronic document). Based on practical experience, long-term commitments cannot be relied upon. Libraries have too many budget difficulties and commercial operations base their decisions on the bottom line. Providing a one-time production of a paper or microfilm copy (a true archival copy) of these titles for the last copy depositories will ultimately be cost effective and far less labor intensive.

Loss of our literary cultural heritage. Space problems and subsequent weeding are causing a gradual, but increasing loss of print material. Having monographs or journal issues available on microfilm or electronically in a last copy depository ameliorates the angst of deselecting.

Eventually (and probably before anyone notices) this will result in the loss of titles in their original formats. This is a matter of saving not just the information content, but the items themselves as cultural artifacts. Preserving this body of publications cannot continue to be done at the libraries where space is needed for newer titles, special collections, computers (to access a growing number of electronic resources), study space for the students, and other space needs.

CONCLUSION

A regional system of last copy depositories is needed for the twenty-first century in order to:

- retain and archive our English language print publications,
- properly archive our English language electronic publications,

- utilize our academic library space in a more effective manner,
- permit libraries to concentrate on newer publications and special collections,
- to, perhaps, provide for cooperative acquisition,
- provide back-up access for commercial document delivery as a deterrent to monopolistic control by the publishers/vendors,
- to maintain the traditional role of libraries as repositories and organizers of our literary cultural heritage.

For the foreseeable future libraries will be responsible for the management of at least two collections: one print and one electronic. Last copy depositories would be effective adjuncts to libraries as they attempt to manage the still growing body of printed materials. The depositories would also provide a coordinated way of maintaining and archiving the tremendous growth in electronic resources. By preserving our print heritage and by owning and properly archiving the electronic heritage, libraries–with the support of last copy depositories–will continue to fulfill the role as repositories for our accumulated body of knowledge.

An Experiment in Cooperative Collection Development: South Asia Vernaculars Among the Research Triangle Universities

E. Christian Filstrup
Jordan M. Scepanski
Tony K. Stewart

In January 1999, the executive committee of *The Triangle South Asia Consortium* (TriSAC, an educational cooperative of the specialized South Asia faculties of Duke University, North Carolina Central University, North Carolina State University, and University of North Carolina at Chapel Hill) submitted a formal request to the *Triangle Research Libraries Network* (TRLN, a library collaborative of the same four campuses) to attempt an experiment in coordinated collection development in European and vernacular materials dedicated to South Asia. This proposal continues a long tradition of area studies cooperation among members of TRLN. It also charts new territory in two ways: it gives a shared bibliographer full responsibility for developing the South Asia collections on four campuses; and it creates a multi-campus faculty group that operates as a unified "super-depart-

---

E. Christian Filstrup is Associate Director for Collection Management, Organization, and Preservation, North Carolina State University Libraries.

Jordan M. Scepanski is Executive Director, Triangle Research Libraries Network.

Tony K. Stewart is Associate Professor of Religion, North Carolina State University.

[Haworth co-indexing entry note]: "An Experiment in Cooperative Collection Development: South Asia Vernaculars Among the Research Triangle Universities." Filstrup, E. Christian, Jordan M. Scepanski, and Tony K. Stewart. Co-published simultaneously in *Collection Management* (The Haworth Information Press, an imprint of The Haworth Press, Inc.) Vol. 24, No. 1/2, 2000, pp. 93-104; and: *Creating New Strategies for Cooperative Collection Development* (ed: Milton T. Wolf and Marjorie E. Bloss) The Haworth Information Press, an imprint of The Haworth Press, Inc., 2000, pp. 93-104. Single or multiple copies of this article are available for a fee from The Haworth Document Delivery Service [1-800-342-9678, 9:00 a.m. - 5:00 p.m. (EST). E-mail address: getinfo@haworthpressinc.com].

© 2000 by The Haworth Press, Inc. All rights reserved.

ment" in representing faculty interests to the bibliographer. The request, many years in the making, was possible because of the happy conjunction of three interlocking institutional developments, two historical and one current:

1. Duke University's long standing commitment to South Asia collections;
2. strong cooperation over the years among the members of TRLN in building coordinated collections; and
3. the remarkable degree of formal and informal interaction during the last twelve years among the faculty focusing on South Asia at the four universities, interaction that has revitalized and expanded the study of the region on the campuses.

DUKE AND SOUTH ASIA COLLECTIONS

Duke University joined the Library of Congress South Asian program in the early 1960s and has employed a South Asia specialist ever since.[1] Like many early participants in the Library of Congress P. L. 480 program[2] Duke acquired materials in most vernacular languages through the sixties and into the early seventies. This short-lived attempt at comprehensiveness was fed by a program that provided materials for only a small annual membership fee ($500). Publications were purchased with local currency which the U.S. government owned in abundance. But though the purchase price of these materials was negligible, processing costs ran high, especially for non-Roman script languages, and the sheer quantity of receipts stirred second thoughts among many participating libraries about the range of their acquisitions under the program. In the early 1970s, to more closely match collections with the research emphases of the university, Duke's South Asia bibliographer, Avinash Maheshwary, who still holds this position, pared down the vernacular language profile to Bengali, Hindi, Marathi, Sanskrit, and Urdu. In 1986, the program profile was reduced further to English only. Overall, Duke has research level collections of English-language South Asia material, with imprints from both South Asia and non-South Asia sources. It is particularly strong in government documents and has a large collection of pamphlets. Vernacular collections in the five languages mentioned above are strong through publication dates in the mid-1980s, but since that time only selected titles have been acquired. In a more recent development, NC State joined the Library of Congress South Asia program in 1998 and acquires small numbers of Hindi and Urdu publications to support undergraduate language instruction and obtains English-language materials in science and technology from the region.

TRLN COOPERATION

Cooperative collection development among North Carolina's research institutions predated the formal establishment of the Triangle Research Libraries Network by more than forty years. Duke and UNC-Chapel Hill, faced with depression-era budgets, began systematically collaborating in building their collections in the 1930s.[3] Although an initial effort foundered because it was too ambitious and detailed, in the 1940s the two campuses applied the lessons they learned to Latin American publications. This time they were successful and a long and rich history of cooperation in area studies began. The Latin American effort evinced four conditions critical to area studies cooperation:

1. it was a relatively new discipline on both campuses;
2. the effort was launched with external funding;
3. the assignment of collecting responsibilities was simple enough for bibliographers to facilitate and for users to comprehend; and
4. faculty on both campuses saw the two collections as their own.

The relative youth of Latin American studies in the 1940s meant that neither campus had strongly vested interests in particular collections. Starting more or less ab ovo meant the two libraries could specialize without overriding or overlaying existing collections that did not follow the new division of responsibility. Initial external funding allowed the two universities to establish collection budgets that did not compete with other needs. Often libraries are asked to establish cooperative arrangements in order to make existing funds go farther. This is very difficult because it usually is a direct threat to someone's prized collection. Most of TRLN's cooperative arrangements have involved additional funding, allowing bibliographers to concentrate on building new or expanded collections. Duke and UNC-CH divided Latin America by country, an arrangement simple for both the bibliographers and for the users. The more complex the lines of demarcation, the higher the administrative costs, the more savvy required of users, and the greater likelihood of the arrangement failing. Finally, faculty agreed at the outset that location of materials on another campus was a fair price to pay for collections much larger than either campus could build on its own.

Based on the success of cooperative Latin American collection development, over the years Duke and UNC-CH, later joined by North Carolina State University, established similar arrangements for Commonwealth countries, Western Europe, Slavic and East European nations, Africa, East Asia, and most recently South Asia.[4] On the simple-to-administer/simple-to-comprehend scale, these arrangements range from Africa which is divided by national language (anglophone, francophone, lusophone) to Europe where responsibilities are split along much finer lines, e.g., northern France to Duke, southern France to UNC-CH. Currently TRLN libraries participate in Title VI programs for Latin America, Western Europe, Slavic and Eastern Europe, and East Asia. The first three programs boast standing as National Resource Centers (NRC). Cooperation among the TRLN libraries benefits from close proximity, daily van delivery, and since the mid-1980s, easy access to each other's online catalogs.

FACULTY INITIATIVES IN SOUTH ASIA

The January 1999 request made by the Triangle South Asia Consortium proposed to TRLN that it undertake an experiment in dispersed collection development and management. It targeted the languages currently taught or planned to be taught by faculty within TriSAC: Bengali, Hindi, Persian, Tamil, and Urdu. The proposed effort was an integral piece of TriSAC's long-term development plan, which includes a current application to the US Department of Education to become a Title VI National Resource Center for South Asia.

Intellectual Center

The NRC application is the result of faculty-initiated cooperation among the South Asia specialists that started modestly as a monthly "works-in-progress" colloquium organized by North Carolina State

University faculty members. This colloquium began an exchange that benefited largely from its informality, enforced by meeting in the homes of faculty members rather than on campuses, in a direct effort to overcome the institutional divisions inevitably assumed in the university setting. Those conversations, joined instantly by faculty at Duke and UNC-CH, continue today with thirty-five regular *South Asia specialists* (and more than double that number of ancillary faculty, other professionals, and graduate students interested in South Asia). It has grown into the vital organization now called the Triangle South Asia Consortium. The colloquium served as the intellectual center and incubator of cooperative initiatives for the faculty, meeting for 118 consecutive months (including summers). More than 140 colloquia have been held to date.

Reorganization

In 1989, members of the colloquium elected an executive committee, composed of two representatives each from the original three campuses. It later expanded membership to include North Carolina Central University, while augmenting the number of representatives to three each. The committee makes policy decisions and recommends to the directors programs to be pursued. Tony Stewart of North Carolina State University was the sole director for the first nine years of the organization's operation, but when the group's activities became too dispersed and numerous, TriSAC reorganized and public functions were assumed by Afroz Taj of NCSU, who became executive director. Stewart took responsibility for the institutional side of the operations through the *North Carolina Center for South Asia Studies* (NCCSAS), which serves as the experimental teaching and research wing of the group, and which is in the process of receiving UNC system sanction as a research "center." Today, the *activities of TriSAC and the NCCSAS* span the full range of university and public functions, reflecting the diversity of faculty interests.

Cooperative Programs

"Cooperative Programs" of TriSAC include the monthly colloquium, occasional seminars, guest speakers, hosting of professional conferences, multi-disciplinary and single-discipline workshops, the running

of temporary research institutes and cooperative projects, museum exhibits (in association with the Ackland Museum at UNC-CH), team-teaching courses in the cultural and literary history of South Asia, and innovative tele-video instruction, including a successful language core in Hindi-Urdu. Directed by the executive committee, involvement in cooperative activities has been and remains self-selecting, with faculty participating to the degree that suits their research, teaching, and personal temperament.

Public Programs

"Public Programs" include literary gatherings (e.g., Urdu Majlis, the Bangla Samiti, etc.), music and dance performances (in liaison with the Classical Indian Music and Dance Society), multi-campus film series, study abroad programs, student associations on each campus, outreach to community colleges and K-12 teachers, a weekly radio program of Hindi music titled "Geet Bazaar," and the delivery of TriSAC's *web page* and occasional newsletter. Many of these programs bring together students and faculty with members of the local South Asia community.

Center Responsibilities

NCCSAS-sponsored activities include all intra- and inter-institutional programs. NCCSAS serves as the focal point for fund-raising and *grants* for research (e.g., Rockefeller Foundation, National Endowment for the Humanities, U.S. Department of Education, Council of American Overseas Research Centers). The center has won more than $1.2 million over the last two years for projects developing innovative language instruction in the classroom and through electronic media. It also has partnered with The University of Chicago and Columbia University on a digital dictionary project. Other functions include the administration of TriSAC's finances, the situating of visiting scholars, and all public relations. It is through the offices of NCCSAS that TriSAC is connected directly to TRLN, with Director Stewart serving as library liaison.

COOPERATIVE COLLECTION DEVELOPMENT PLAN

Initiation of Request

A series of *resolutions* passed by the TriSAC Executive Committee on 18 January 1999 were vetted through TRLN's *Committee on Information Resources* (CIR), which "plans, oversees, and coordinates all TRLN activity related to the identification, acquisition, organization, access, use, and preservation of all information-related materials, print and non-print, paper and electronic." CIR's most important current activities include facilitating joint licensing of electronic resources, expanding intra-TRLN document delivery based upon a model developed at North Carolina State University called *TripSaver*, and sponsoring overlap studies of the collections of the four campuses and of approval plans with the same vendor.

Institutional Responsibilities

Negotiations between TriSAC and the Committee on Information Resources were fairly easy for two very important reasons:

1. The TriSAC Executive Committee had in its usual fashion forged a basic consensus among faculty that the TRLN agreement to acquire in these languages should override considerations of location, on the condition that TRLN could deliver materials to locations on the four campuses within 48 hours; and
2. TriSAC agreed to support TRLN acquisitions through direct subsidies built into the proposed NRC grant budget and other grants currently in-hand and planned.

Desirability of Dispersed Collecting

The arrangement assumes that the most basic materials for teaching first and second year language will be available in duplicate across the campuses, but for research-depth collecting, responsibility would be divided. From the beginning TriSAC avoided the pitfalls of trying to assign languages according to local faculty interest and instead kept in the foreground the collective strength resulting from sharing the burden. It is only a slight overstatement to say that it will not matter which library/campus houses material in a particular language. Initially Duke has been assigned responsibility for Bengal and Persian, building on historical interests; UNC-CH will take Tamil, a completely new language on that campus; NCSU will house Hindi and Urdu, the two vernaculars that have been systematically acquired on a limited basis during the last five years; and NCCU will collect only in English, no vernacular. Duke has also agreed to resume acquiring materials in Marathi and Gujarati, while maintaining the two classical languages of Sanskrit and Pali.

Faculty Expertise vs. Vernacular Location

In this dispersed arrangement, faculty research interests are divorced from location. For example, a professor of Religious Studies at UNC-CH, who studies Persian and Sufi literature, will have to rely on holdings in these areas at Duke, while instructors of Hindi and Urdu, will turn to NCSU, and so forth. Such an approach requires, of course, that each library be responsive to requests from faculty on the other campuses. A formal mechanism to assure the system works will be required, but precedent for inter-institutional service among the TRLN institutions exists. Bibliographers in area studies programs routinely purchase materials requested by faculty at other institutions. With growth of collections, the allocation of languages could change as faculty come and go, but TRLN has agreed to make such changes only with the cooperation and consent of the TriSAC executive committee. Consequently, a new hire in Tamil at NCSU would know from the outset that her historical collection would reside at Duke and the current collection at UNC-CH. Should she lobby to change collecting responsibility, her request would be vetted through the TriSAC executive committee and only on its recommendation would the affected libraries respond. In this scenario, TriSAC would operate as a multicampus or "super department" that mediates faculty requests, and any change in allocation of languages would be made only with TriSAC consensus. As the process begins, there already is a growing recognition on the part of the TriSAC executive committee that the responsibility for Hindi may place too great a burden on any one campus (its annual volume count easily matching all the rest combined), so that this language may have to be subdivided.

Delivery of Materials

From the user perspective, ownership and delivery are closely linked. Local ownership generally means unmediated access to a text. Dispersing ownership of print materials among the campuses inevitably increases delivery time. Traditional inter-library loan service will not suffice. Negotiation between TRLN and TriSAC resulted in a commitment to delivery of materials within a 48 hour window. NC State's current *TripSaver* service meets this standard and is being planned for all four campuses.

Shared Bibliographer

The other major component of the effort, one integral to the TriSAC NRC proposal is a shared bibliographer dedicated exclusively to building South Asia collections and providing appropriate services. This person will shoulder two large tasks: combined collection development for the four campuses; and liaison work with students and faculty. The shared South Asia bibliographer will bring to TRLN an unprecedented degree of cooperative collection development. This bibliographer will translate the curricular and research needs of four campuses into a unified profile against which the Library of Congress office will acquire monographs. For all faculty on the four campuses, the bibliographer will coordinate selection of individual monographic titles published outside India and select journal subscriptions. This attention to the collections needs of the four campuses is central to the position; it is not in addition to other core responsibilities. The first task will be largely manageable from a single site, Duke University. While the collection development duties can more or less be accomplished from a central office, this position's liaison responsibilities will necessitate a certain amount of travelling among campuses and require a degree of cloning unprecedented in earlier cooperative efforts. The advantages of telephony and e-mail clearly will ease the task, but face-to-face contact remains a central requirement of the position. As video-conferencing becomes more locally manageable the travel may be diminished. The challenge is to create a presence on all four campuses without reducing the bibliographer to a nomad. The position as currently planned by Duke, TRLN, and TriSAC, calls for an initial three-year subsidy from TriSAC's NRC budget, with the remainder of the cost assumed by Duke. At the end of the three-year period of the grant, Duke will assume the bulk of the responsibility for funding the position, with support from the other universities through TRLN.

Making Four Collections Function as One

The establishment of a National Resource Center presents a number of other challenges to the TRLN libraries. One is development of a coherent collection development policy that guides acquisition at all of the libraries. This policy needs two foci. One is building appropriate undergraduate collections. The challenge here is to be highly selective by level of difficulty. Undergraduates need easy-to-read texts, popular magazines, and newspapers as well as dictionaries and other basic reference materials. The other focus is on building research collections specific to faculty and graduate student needs. Meeting this challenge entails being highly subject-specific, faculty by faculty. Again, the match is between the library responsible for collecting the language and the faculty member wherever resident. The elaborate collections profile developed by the Library of Congress office in New Delhi should help on both scores. It allows selection of both basic texts and research level materials by subject. Duke has long experience working with this profile.

Cataloging

To the degree that TRLN libraries acquire their materials through the LC office in New Delhi, the libraries should be able to catalog South Asia vernaculars with graduate students. All materials come with catalog cards and catalog copy is available on the bibliographic networks within a few months of receipt of the items. The main requirement for these graduate students would be familiarity with script. They can learn basic cataloging rules and procedures without much difficulty. NC State has employed a graduate student to catalog Hindi and Urdu for the last two years. In the initial phase at least, individual libraries will pay for cataloging from local budgets. In this scenario, the same cataloger(s) could work in more than one library. A more advanced form of shared cataloging could be a South Asia cataloging unit in one library, but the benefits of centralizing would have to be weighed against the costs of keeping track of ownership and moving materials from one campus to another.

CONCLUSION

The plan to pursue cooperative collection development in South Asia vernaculars among the Research Triangle Universities is unusual, even extraordinary. While the esoteric and specialized nature of the materials involved argues for such an approach and the proximity of the campuses to each other and the relative complementarity of their South Asia-related programs make eminently sensible an integrated effort at providing library support, it is nevertheless a significant undertaking. To be sure, Duke University's long-term investment in South Asia materials provides a rich resource base from which to pursue building of collections worthy of a National Resource Center. And the trust and confidence developed over decades among faculty members and librarians at TRLN institutions as they engaged in joint collections building clearly makes this endeavor easier. But it is the interest and initiative of faculty in suggesting the arrangement that is of major note. Their teaching, research, and service partnerships in other areas contribute to a willingness to experiment with a different means of realizing library support, as does their recognition of the inability of any one of their four institutions to develop comprehensive South Asia teaching and research resources on its own. It is, however, noteworthy that faculty from various disciplines and from four rather different institutions have been able to come together and suggest to their libraries that a collaborative effort is appropriate and that they not only are willing to support it, but to take leadership in seeing it become a reality. Challenges remain and success will be measured ultimately by how effectively the information needs of students and faculty in South Asia studies are being met. But faculty-librarian partnerships, inter-institutional approaches, and collaborative experimentation offer new opportunity for responding to those needs.

NOTES

1. For a history of Duke's South Asia collections, see Maheshwary, Avinash, "An overview of resources for South Asia studies at Duke." *Duke Libraries* (Fall 1988): 6-8.

2. See Patterson, Maureen, "The South Asian P.L. 480 Library of Congress, library program." *Journal of Asian Studies* (August 1969): 743-754.

3. For a history of cooperation among TRLN libraries, see Dominguez, Patricia B. and Luke Swindler, "Cooperative collection development at the Research Triangle university libraries: A model for the nation." *College & Research Libraries* (November 1993): 470-496.

4. For a full inventory of TRLN cooperative arrangements, see *http://www.lib.unc.edu/cdd/crs/index.html.*

The Whole Is Greater Than the Sum of Its Parts

Milton T. Wolf
Marjorie E. Bloss

There is more information available today than at anytime before in history. And by tomorrow there will be even more; by next year there will be twice as much as today! Even rabbit pullulation pales by comparison with information production. But with all the information that is out there, it seems more difficult than ever before to get what you want, when you want it.

It appears, unfortunately, that most libraries and not-for-profit information-providing institutions, like museums, archives and other cultural entities, are suffering from the same problem: too much information, too little money. And, while technology has made some of the information morass more manageable, it has also magnified the problem. For example, getting useful information from the ever-burgeoning Internet is like filtering a cesspool for nutrition.

What you see, more often than not, is that "as the infrastructure of the digital library [museum, archive, etc.] emerges, a range of trends is gradually leading to the disappearance of human help in patron interactions."[1] Like pumping your own gasoline, we'll all be soon pumping our own information, for "the logic [of digital resources], the pertinent concept is user self-sufficiency."[2] As the downsizing of our staffs and collections continues, we download more of our former services and substance to the end user.

Milton Wolf is Senior Vice President for Collection Programs and Marjorie Bloss is Vice President for Library Operations, The Center for Research Libraries.

[Haworth co-indexing entry note]: "The Whole Is Greater Than the Sum of Its Parts." Wolf, Milton T., and Marjorie E. Bloss. Co-published simultaneously in *Collection Management* (The Haworth Information Press, an imprint of The Haworth Press, Inc.) Vol. 24, No. 1/2, 2000, pp. 105-118; and: *Creating New Strategies for Cooperative Collection Development* (ed: Milton T. Wolf and Marjorie E. Bloss) The Haworth Information Press, an imprint of The Haworth Press, Inc., 2000, pp. 105-118. Single or multiple copies of this article are available for a fee from The Haworth Document Delivery Service [1-800-342-9678, 9:00 a.m. - 5:00 p.m. (EST). E-mail address: getinfo@haworthpressinc.com].

© 2000 by The Haworth Press, Inc. All rights reserved.

The grand purpose, it would seem, is to make the end user "more self-sufficient in searching, retrieving, and evaluating information in a multitude of formats, and thus prepare them for a world where information and knowledge currently doubles every year and is expected to double every 73 days by the year 2020."[3] Now don't get us wrong, we're not against utilizing technology to make life better. Nor do we want to throw out the technological baby with the bath water, for it certainly can help us filter through the mountains of data and facts that are threatening to push an information fire hose down our throats when all we want is a cool, informing drink. To paraphrase Emerson, we either ride technology, or it will ride us.

No, the real problem is that information and its technologies have become Big Business (some of it truly Silicon Snake Oil Business). And Big Business's agenda, naturally enough, has more to do with making money, the transfer of institutional information power, and the fear and loathing of diverse publications and information outside of its control. Content that hasn't been legitimized by the commercial process, often in conjunction with the imprimatur of the corporate/research community, is one of the least discussed problems of the scholarly communication crisis. Serving the public diverse information through non-profit institutions is not high on the for-profit sector's agenda because the information provided by non-profits often is contrary to the world view promoted by the for-profit sector. Information control is Big Business!

An article in this February's *Wall Street Journal* says, "Scientists are increasingly supported by for-profit companies, but a new study shows that critical fact is seldom revealed in published research."[4] The article goes on to say, "The important person is the reader, and if the financial conflict might alter their perception of the validity of results, then the reader should have those conflicts revealed."[5] But don't count on it happening soon. Powerful vested interests, in a Byzantine partnership with scientists, are packaging information mind-food for your thoughtless digestion.

Jim Davis, formerly the Western Regional Director for Computer Professionals for Social Responsibility, puts it this way:

> If information can't turn a profit, it won't be developed or stored, regardless of its social value. The president of commercial database vendor Dialog was quoted in 1986 as saying "We can't

> afford an investment in databases that are not going to earn their keep and pay back their development costs, he answered, "Humanities." [Davis goes on to say] . . . Pharmaceuticals (information products) comprise [even] a more dramatic example–for instance, a 1991 World Health Organization report lamented the fact that development of new tuberculosis-fighting drugs all but stopped 25 years ago (even though three million die every year from the disease) because the drugs are "not a big profit maker."[6]

And, in a recent article entitled "The Politics of Cultural Authority" Wayne Wiegand, professor at the University of Wisconsin/Madison School of Library and Information Studies, remarks upon this relationship between knowledge, as it is commercially packaged, and power. He says:

> In the past 20 years or so an army of critical theorists . . . have been questioning the whole concept of "objective" knowledge, and analyzing connections between power and the values assigned to knowledge in its different forms. What they have discovered is that knowledge in any form is never disinterested, never totally objective, and that a discernible link exists between power and the kinds of knowledge people consider most valuable. Because knowledge is never disinterested, powerful people with a vested interest in certain kinds of knowledge work hard to elevate that knowledge to a privileged position. There, they believe, it will have the best chance to influence everyone else.[7]

What is important to gather from the above two quotes is that in the present milieu of "cultural authority," librarians, curators, archivists are considered merely "handlers of information products," having very little to do with determining the value of those products. The corporate structure that dominates the publishing industry and calls the research tune for a significant portion of the academy, especially in the sciences, is making it very clear that it does not want information handlers to evaluate content (i.e., select). It just wants us to buy its prepackaged and validated information–and pay (for you won't have any money left for alternative materials once you have been provided with the profit-sector's information)! Much censorship is really just a lack of money to buy alternatives. While research libraries would like to buy most of what the mainstream commercial sci/tech publishers generate, especially the serial publications, they can't afford all of them, let alone alternative points of view!

But there are things that we can do, should do, to ameliorate this situation. While it is probably beyond our abilities to enter into the lists with the corporate power brokers to affect their continuous machinations to sell us bell-and-whistle baubles, submerging technologies, and ersatz Solyent Green wonder products, we can join together through cooperative ventures that cut across traditionally accepted barriers to pursue mutually beneficial partnerships. After all, we are really all here to serve the information user. If we combine our collections and services, in a rationalized way, we can provide more from less, but we will have to jettison some of our antediluvian attitudes.

And one of these outmoded concepts is that of the self-sufficient library, museum, archive or any other information-serving institution. The traditional research library goal, for example, of building and maintaining large, self-sufficient, collections is not only anachronistic, it is also economically unsound. The rapid emergence and evolution of electronic technologies finally make it feasible for information institutions to build on local strengths and yet to collaborate on information issues across geographical boundaries–and types of libraries! However, our preindustrial mindset about ownership often cancels out our technical prowess.

As long as cultural information institutions rank themselves by the criteria of ownership (volumes and manuscripts held, artifacts owned, photos digitized, staff employed, and budgets expended) and nothing else, they will continue to represent quantity not quality. "Build a large, monumental institution (preferably with lions and griffins guarding the front doors), fill it with materials, and they will come" has been the hallmark of much of the cultural information enterprise for generations. One of the reasons for this is mainly because it is simpler to amass quantities of things than it is to discriminate intelligently. Certainly it is less controversial and time consuming than essaying the worth of the content, not to mention substantially less expensive than thoughtful selection (and the concomitant cost of bibliographers)! It is "selected information," driven by a definite intellectual goal or vision that makes an information institution valuable–not the number of widgets housed within. We should not be ranking our institutions by the tonnage!

We are guilty of schooling several generations in the belief that their own library collections, if properly developed, could serve all the needs of their clientele locally–with an occasional foray into interlibrary loan. The unfortunate result of this hubris, coupled with a long period of double-digit purchasing inflation and the simultaneous downsizing of budgets, is that most library collections are becoming more homogeneous as libraries are forced to satisfy core, local needs of demand first. (In other words, a good portion of everyone's acquisitions budget is consumed in sustaining subscriptions to *Time* magazine, *TV GUIDE*, *U.S. News and World Report*, etc.)

In the research libraries, ARL expenditure figures for library materials show again in 1997-98 that while libraries are spending more, they continue to get less. For much of the last two decades, libraries shifted expenditures from monographs to meet some of the demands of increasing serial prices. Data show that while libraries more than doubled expenditures for serials from 1986 to 1997, libraries purchased 6% fewer serial titles–not to mention the decline in monographic acquisitions (the number of monographs purchased by research libraries fell by 25%!).

In short, librarians have, of necessity, put their clientele on a core collection starvation diet, depriving them of those nutritious sources that used to distinguish one library from another, those materials that enable thinking outside the box of commercially purveyed pabulum. This fast-mindfood-collecting syndrome, the MacLibrary Syndrome, that focuses on the core at the expense of the periphery, is threatening information users with a severe case of content-deprived informational deficiency and resulting in less diverse scholarly research.

As has been indicated, we didn't get to this pitiful situation all by ourselves. Over the past 15 years, our budgets have been squeezed not only by funding cutbacks at our parent institutions, but also by inflation. At the same time, there has been a dramatic increase in the number of worldwide publications; and concurrently the impact and cost of technology on how we do business and the changing configurations in how we acquire resources for our collections (e.g., licensing agreements, consortial purchases, etc.) have significantly altered our daily operations. These realities have helped produce the very reasons for the homogeneity in our collections, and the excuses we give for their lack of diversity.

We may have, however, finally arrived at that crossroads where our self-aggrandized collecting provincialism is resulting in less information, rather than more, for our clientele. Approximately two percent of today's publishers account for 75% of U.S. titles produced. And the pricing and copyright practices of many of these commercial publishers have so constricted the flow of diverse information that it is not an exaggeration to say that they, in effect, control the major research publishing venues.

In truth, there is a well-entrenched, global commercial monopoly on the distribution and approval of ideas, and we, as selectors, often contribute to its hegemony by our slothful collection habits. "Content," too often, has become what our commercial enterprises define and distribute, and what we often unwittingly purchase–largely because few institutions any longer can afford to devote the number of staff hours required, or the money necessary to the time-consuming, professional job of evaluative selection! Again, it is much easier to let the computer automatically renew our subscriptions, shuffle our artifacts–even if it is a lot of intellectual detritus, or let the patron slurp around the Internet where one can get lots of hits of unauthenticated bilge and dross. Somehow this is not consoling.

While we may make strong arguments that our shrinking budgets, the financial demands of supporting computer technology, and staff downsizing all have reduced the time and funds available for analyzing the worth of our current and retrospective acquisitions, it is equally true that we are not seeing the opportunities for positive change that lie before us–if we would only agree to communicate, cooperate, and collaborate!

While we ostensibly sing the song and talk the talk of hanging together, we, in fact, more often hang separately when it comes to resource sharing and cooperation.

As one wag recently observed, partnership is often another word for seeking funding from some outside agency. And once we get the money, we frequently go our own ways–until the next funding proposal or consortial agreement promises something for nothing.

A recent Mellon Foundation Report makes it clear that the "viability of the traditional model of the library" is unlikely to meet the information needs of the emerging global village. Ann Okerson, in that Report, sums it up

> In the face of this pricing crisis, libraries have responded essentially by redistributing their resources, a mode of response that

> cannot go on indefinitely. Instead there is a growing realization that no research institution can hope to sustain a self-sufficient collection into the indefinite future. Even before the "crisis," libraries were actively collaborating and sharing resources. Under the circumstances described in the study, and even absent new technologies, libraries would have been led to pursue "without walls" philosophies energetically.[8]

"Without walls," however, means more than electronic access to virtual libraries, museums, and archives, it also means pursuing partnerships that provide gateways to other collections, sharing our staff–even sharing our buildings! It means enlarging our conceptions of collection development and shaping collections in concert with each other–even across geographical and political boundaries.

But our traditional attitudes about ownership must be overcome if we are to re-orient ourselves to the challenges and rewards of constructing complementary information resources that provide the depth of knowledge necessary for thorough research and that contain all the diverse materials our clientele need. Otherwise, we are going to continue to build boring, vanilla, cultural information institutions that are content-deficient, and unlikely to lead to a healthy and multicultural society of respectful dissent–not to mention a more democratic forum for the critical examination of ideas

Working in cultural information institutions is no longer for the feint of heart, and if we don't learn to work more cooperatively, we will be hung separately by an economic-political machine that is as relentless as it is blind. If we are going to see more clearly, we will have to envision and enact our future roles differently than in the past. If the traditional concept of creating and maintaining large self-sufficient collections of books, manuscripts and artifacts is not yet dead, it is only waiting on the arrival of the taxidermist for the *coup de grace*.

Our future lies in giving away our information institutions to our communities, in combining our resources and in facilitating and interpreting the cultural information dialogue. Paraphrasing Dylan Thomas, let us not go gently into the commercial info night, let us rage, rage, against the dying light of content, substance, and value. Vow that you will not be just an information handler of pre-packaged commercial pablum, engineered to reduce your communities to thoughtless, unexamined lives. The silent majority all live in graveyards!

Robert Archibald, president of the Missouri Historical Society, exhorts cultural institutions "to abandon the pedestals of authority that wall us off from those we serve and enter into the fray of discourse about important things in our communities."[9] He argues that "history is not fact, that objects do not speak for themselves, that science is value-laden, that art is perspective, that technology is not neutral, that memory is not static, that there are no fixed canons, and hence . . . institutional claims of objectivity, authority, and truth [are] disingenuous."[10]

Counter the commercial information juggernaut with the principles of inclusion and collaboration. We can revitalize our non-profit cultural information centers if we understand that "successful collaboration requires shared vision, a shared plan, and shared resources. Unless this is agreed to at the outset, relationships will be difficult and the results one-sided "[For] successful collaborations build trust and relationships, magnify resources, and achieve results that exceed the separate capabilities of collaborating organizations."[11]

Archibald goes on to say that "We no longer ask isolated questions such as 'What should we collect, conserve, exhibit, publish, research or what programs should we offer?' These are strategies and resources. The questions we ask now are focused on what strategies and resources can best facilitate discussion of enduring community concerns."[12]

As for technology, it can certainly assist us, especially in communicating and enacting our collaborations. Nevertheless, with all our new technology, the most recent study of interlibrary loan done by the Association of Research Libraries came to the conclusion that there has been no significant change during the last decade in the two-week turnaround time for getting books and information between libraries, even though volume is up over 50%! And beware of those who assure you that there will be cost savings because of computerization. The research to date argues against such a sanguine, if not deceitful, view. Much to the chagrin of the computerholics, the overall productivity of U.S. industry during the past twenty years (except for a few high tech companies), a period of massive institutionalization of computer systems, has actually decreased slightly.

That the computer has changed how we work, however, cannot be denied. That it has encouraged constant reorganization, as we all hurry to fit in with the Machine's new bells and whistles (euphemistically called "re-tooling, or staff training"); that it now accounts for the most significant outlay of increasing expenditures in most organizations; that a burgeoning group of computer tenders and tweakers continues to grow; and that in some places information technology has become a substitute for individualized information service; this is all too true. Like the bank teller and the formerly ubiquitous gas station attendant, the knowledgeable, personal reference service provider (the information interpreter) has been replaced by a machine.

When the cost of technology decreases the money available for acquiring the astronomically increasing universe of publications; when copyright law becomes a barrier to the exchange of information and can be used as a monopolistic club to fend off competition; and when content is determined by "what the corporate/academic oligarchy sells";[13] the resulting vanilla research libraries and information institutions become a harbinger of the intellectual stagnation that will inevitably follow.

Neither information nor ideas are capable of (in)voluntary action. People, however, are, but without access to diverse information resources we will witness a less kind and less gentle society (not to mention, less democratic). Information does want to be free and like the brain drain prior to World War II, when thinkers flocked to the more liberal environment of the United States, ideas will seek new shelter if we do not treat them well.

Do not be surprised if the world wide web, that international information agora, does not spawn some entrepreneurial types who start selling information that is really useful and relevant to its clients "by the drink," so to speak. We are already seeing at the Center for Research Libraries the rise of the "independent reader/scholar," who, not affiliated with any institution, is hungrily searching the electronic fields of data in search of "content." This global phenomenon has some far-reaching consequences for information institutions, and for society in general. As information professionals, as interpreters and guides to the information gateways, we should encourage a more discriminating use of information; that is our forte, and we should do all that we can to promote this aspect of our professional expertise. Interpreting information is the mark of professionalism.

The worldwide explosion of information works in our favor: almost everyone is now burping up information junk. There is data, data everywhere, but not a lot to think. As Sue Myburgh, a senior lecturer at the University of South Australia, notes in her essay on "information retrieval vs. data retrieval":

> This dichotomy is situated in the encounter that takes place between the information retrievalists, on the one hand, and the data retrievalists, on the other; those who labor with qualitative research methods, as against those to whom quantitative research is all.

Put another way:

> The field of information retrieval can be divided along the lines of its system-based and user-based concerns. While the system-based view is concerned with efficient search techniques to match query and document representation, the user-based view must account for the cognitive state of the searcher and the problem solving context.[14]

Both methods require sophisticated knowledge of the information universe, but the user-based one is a tailored process, as unique as the individual; or as the community that the information institution serves–and it is in this arena that most of us excel. This is our turf, our metier, our future. Forget the personal trainer, the personal banker, it's the personal information provider whom everyone will want! It's "content" that people will pay for, go to museums and archives to view, touch and learn from. And we are superbly placed to interpret and present information, making it meaningful and accessible to those who need it.

We don't just dispense information; that's what bookstores do. We educate by providing possible interpretations, by adding value–even by advocating. Certainly we must be sensitive and aware of the latest buzz, largely manufactured by today's increasingly yellow journalism, but we must also be professionally tuned to the underlying issues. And we must constantly customize our limited resources through cooperative endeavors to the needs of our communities, realizing that "as the digital era explodes" our institutional walls, "the definition of community takes on worldwide dimensions."[15] We are really building one world library!

So let's not get caught up with the behemoth Publisher/Government/Research Complex or the computer engineers who, having lost sight of their objectives, redouble their efforts. They are already burying their heads in the information morass that they have unwittingly created. By the time they get it straightened out, we can be even further down the information road, doing what we do best: collecting, conserving, exhibiting, servicing and interpreting the complex information world.

This is not to say that we should not lobby for modifications to the present political/economic structure, to point out the fallacies of commercial information legerdemain, to educate our clientele about the intricacies and the vested interests of the Information Age, but we should be spending more time, the majority of our time, doing what we can do (evaluating, selecting and collaborating), should do, and, if done well, would ameliorate considerably the "crisis" we face–not to mention the goodwill we would accrue with our users. Collaboration is not just a front for getting grants or making consortial purchases; it is not a buzzword, it's a life style (in many ways it's like marriage: love, honor and negotiate).

Collaborators don't care who's on top. Collaboration means "sharing" control–sometimes even not being in control. And what is this craven need we seem to have for autonomy? And what has it actually gotten us? A series of vanilla cultural information institutions with more technology and less staff.

While we don't know all the ways we can learn to share, we do know that we could do a lot more than we are doing–and it's less expensive in the long run than the pernicious game we are playing now of "one-book upmanship." In a recent speech Tom Sanville urged libraries to cross-pollinate with other information institutions, to join together in groups like OhioLink (a state-sponsored collaboration of all types of information institutions) to realize the lowering of costs of the information unit.

It reminds me of that old parable about the various body parts arguing about which one is the most important one. They all are important and must work in harmony. And so should we! The sum of our parts is greater than any one of us. We are building one world cultural information resource and it's time we became conscious of this and moved with that purpose.

One of the greatest cultural resources, the Library of Congress (even though it is not a National Library), still makes major collecting decisions, like deciding no longer to collect comprehensively in certain areas, without alerting the rest of us in a timely manner. There are innumerable collections scattered across this country and the world that we have little or no knowledge of. There are magnificent collections rotting in basements, attics and closets that would enrich our national heritage and broaden the content that we could offer our clientele if we would only learn to work more closely together–and select, even locally, less of the detritus belched up by the commercial publishers. With a little more cohesion (similar to ARL's SPARC initiative), we could even influence these bottom-line commercial enterprises to provide what our clients really need, maybe even support some new publishers and information purveyors who were more in tune with content, society, and, heaven knows, civilization.

The ultimate objective of cooperative institutional information development and sharing is to maximize the materials to which our clientele, yours and mine, have access while minimizing local budget expenditures. Surely, this alone can serve as a blueprint for the journey we must embark upon if we are to hang together.

The best summation I can provide you is from an article in *Information Technology and Libraries* by Jordan M. Scepanski, Executive Director, Triangle Research Libraries Network:

> Among the first steps that can be taken in re-thinking how service to the public is rendered is for librarians [curators, archivists and other cultural information providers] to assert their professional expertise. The obvious problems with information today is its overabundance. There is more of it than can be handled. Peter Lyman, of the University of California at Berkeley, has pointed out that libraries originally were created to deal with the problem of information scarcity; that is, to bring together in one place, for the use of the many, items that were few in number so that they could be shared. Now there is too much rather than too little. There also is too much of too little. That is, so much of the information that is overwhelming everyone is of poor quality or of little value. There is a lot that is of little consequence. If the traditional library, then, was the answer to a paucity of information, the new [information specialist] is the solution to its plenitude. There has never been a more critical need for the talents of professionals who not only know how to find information, but how also to evaluate it. The role of the [information specialist]

> can no longer be one of pointing the way for the user, nor even of just teaching that user how to find what is needed. [We] must now teach both how to find what is needed and how to assess what is found. [We] are information experts, and that expertise extends beyond knowing where to look for things. [We] do know how to differentiate good data from bad, current information from that which is dated, reliable sources from those that are less so. And given the intense subject specializations of content experts–most especially faculty members at universities–and their subsequently narrowly drawn knowledge of their fields, coupled with the extraordinary expansion of scholarship in every field, good librarians frequently know the literature of a given discipline better than many of its practitioners and teaching and research experts. To change, public service [information specialists] have to be recognized as information experts and accept that they are so. No longer can they, or society, heed that old admonition, drilled into so many in [professional] schools, that [we] don't make judgments about the information [we] help people find. If [we] don't make such judgments no one will, and clients will be the worse for [our] timidity. [We] should return to the public librarian's approach of an earlier era, that of the "readers advisor," the librarian whose knowledge of the disciplines and of [the] literature and of the reader's interest and needs allowed functioning as a guide and a counselor. [We] once again need to guide and counsel. [We] need to advise and to teach.[16]

It is time for us to re-dedicate ourselves to the value-added things we bring to the information arena, to facilitate the information gateways for our users, to collaborate across institutional and geographical boundaries, to share our dwindling resources and magnify them through cooperative strategies, to create an international conspectus for preserving the recorded knowledge of civilization, and to put our always limited funds toward our overarching visions.

Over the years it has become almost a cliche to urge people to "think globally, act locally." Could we possibly add a parenthetical addendum to "act locally (with global intent)"? After all, whether you realize it or not, we are building one library. And all of you are its bibliographers!

NOTES

1. Heckart, Ronald J. "Machine Help and Human Help in the Emerging Digital Library," *College & Research Libraries*, V. 59, no. 3 (May 1998), 250.

2. *Ibid.*

3. Bosseau, Don L. "Where Are We Now? Some Thoughts About Expansionism," *Journal of Academic Librarianship*, V. 24, no. 5 (September 1998), 390.

4. King, Ralph T., Jr., "Medical Journals Rarely Disclose Researchers' Ties," *Wall Street Journal* (February 2, 1999), p. B1.

5. *Ibid.*, p. B4

6. Jim Davis. "The Incompatibility of Capitalism and Information," *Intertek.* V. 3.4 (1993), 19.

7. Wayne A. Wiegand. "The Politics of Cultural Authority," *American Libraries*. V. 29 (January 1998), 81.

8. Okerson, Ann, in Synopsis to *University Libraries and Scholarly Communication* by Anthony M. Cummings et al. (The Association of Research Libraries for the Andrew W. Mellon Foundation, November 1992), p. xxii.

9. Archibald, Robert, "Narratives for a New Century," *Museum News*, V. 77, no. 6 (November/December 1998), 37.

10. *Ibid.*

11. *Ibid.*, 42.

12. *Ibid.*, 40.

13. *Ibid.*

14. Sue Myburgh, "The Clash of the Titans: Information Retrieval vs. Data Retrieval," in *Information Imagineering: Meeting at the Interface*. Milton T. Wolf Pat Ensor, and Mary Augusta Thomas, Eds. (Chicago: American Library Association, 1998), pp. 53-54.

15. Hage, Christine Lind, "Books, Bytes, Buildings, and Bodies: Public Libraries in the 21st Century," *American Libraries*, V. 30, no. 1 (January 1999), 79.

16. Jordan M. Scepanski. "Public Services in a Telecommuting World," *Information Technology and Libraries,* V. 15 (March 1966): 44.

CONSORTIA, COOPERATIVES, AND CONSTERNATION

The Printed Book: Still in Need of CCD

Anna H. Perrault

Librarians in the U.S. have spent most of the 20th century developing cooperation for resource sharing. This has been accomplished mainly through networks and consortia providing both the apparatus and culture for resource sharing. Although we have probably not yet reached the limits of "interlibrary" cooperation, in the 21st century we will need to focus on and develop types of cooperation other than among ourselves. The technological advances of the last half of the 20th century have enabled and set the stage for new forms of cooperation. The Internet has created an international free exchange of ideas. This changed and charged atmosphere of an information commons has eased the way for international cooperation. How can we as collection development specialists and research library administrators take advantage of this new culture of an international information commons?

Anna H. Perrault is Associate Professor, School of Library and Information Science, University of South Florida.

[Haworth co-indexing entry note]: "The Printed Book: Still in Need of CCD." Perrault, Anna H. Co-published simultaneously in *Collection Management* (The Haworth Information Press, an imprint of The Haworth Press, Inc.) Vol. 24, No. 1/2, 2000, pp. 119-136; and: *Creating New Strategies for Cooperative Collection Development* (ed: Milton T. Wolf and Marjorie E. Bloss) The Haworth Information Press, an imprint of The Haworth Press, Inc., 2000, pp. 119-136. Single or multiple copies of this article are available for a fee from The Haworth Document Delivery Service [1-800-342-9678, 9:00 a.m. - 5:00 p.m. (EST). E-mail address: getinfo@haworthpressinc.com].

© 2000 by The Haworth Press, Inc. All rights reserved.

This paper will first briefly review the present situation of the virtual book. Then I will present some research findings on the monographic collections of academic libraries–the state of the book as a printed resource in the "national collection" or the "commons" of resources available to us. After which there will be some conclusions, interpretations and suggestions for CCD.

We have just about gotten to the point at which, solving copyright problems, resources sharing of journal articles is, and will largely be, through electronic transfer. The access vs. ownership paradigm is working for journals. Sure, there are licensing and copyright problems, but for reader acceptance, electronic access to articles and reports is proving to be preferable to printed volumes. This is in a research context. The popular magazine and newspaper in electronic format have not reached that kind of user acceptance level. That level of acceptance has also not been reached for longer texts or the "virtual book."

For the immediate foreseeable future the uses of the virtual book would seem to be:

- *Research reports.* In several varieties, research reports are finding wide acceptance. Theses, dissertations, pre-prints and other unpublished research reports, because of the low demand for these individual documents, can be stored on CD or sent via FTP. They can be promulgated by the author(s) and mounted on web servers. Inevitably, to be read or receive much use they are downloaded and printed out. But they are quasi, not really virtual books.

- *Scholarly texts.* While there has been acceptance of electronic text projects, especially in the humanities, these have thus far been very expensive projects and there is not much indication that the numbers of electronic scholarly texts will totally replace printed texts in the near future. These electronic texts are providing access points for analysis that are not afforded by printed texts. But they seem to be functioning as supplementary to print and the expense of mounting and maintaining the sites works against their proliferation. One characteristic is that many of them are international efforts.

- *Textbooks.* With distance education becoming a growing mode for delivery of education, the webpage is becoming more important than the textbook. While most faculty right now regard the materials placed on a course website as supplementary to the textbook, I think the printed textbook will gradually be replaced by electronic modules which make interactive learning possible. An alternative to the web-based delivery of instructional materials is an electronic book, in CD-ROM, DVD, or e-book format. This form of virtual book will initially find the widest acceptance, but in academe, rather than with the general public.

While much hard information and data, e.g., U.S. government websites of the Department of Commerce, U.S. Geological survey, databases like LEXIS-NEXIS, are now available through the web, these are still documents to be downloaded and used in a reference nature–not necessarily in their entirety. They are not texts which we would classify as a "virtual book" For the kind of reading and flipping around which occurs with longer texts, print or printout seems to be the preferred format.

The Internet is used and accepted by the general public only for brief information pieces. Interest erodes when a document is "pages" long and can't be printed or downloaded and printed out in easy format. The desired length of the document seems to correlate with the short attention span of many internet users.

While the internet has certainly gained widespread acceptance among the general public and acceptance, if not credibility, among information professionals as a source of information, publishers, by and large, do not see the internet or "virtual book" as replacing their printed book products. As Jane Cart of the British Library said at IFLA in 1998 in Amsterdam, "For general publishers, the internet is not a publishing medium. For the more adventurous of them, it is an increasingly effective promotional medium . . . "[1]

There are many ways in which we make use of the format of the printed book, most of which we do not consider amenable to the virtual formats now current. Research in book form is not just text on page. It is illustrated with photographs, reproductions of art works, graphics and diagrams. Not to say that these cannot also be included in electronic versions. I do think the web page format is having great influence upon the formatting of printed works. But the book as reading, visual package, we all know, is not regarded as the same thing in electronic form. Yes, we can incorporate hot links, which is one reason I think its acceptance in education is rapid, but we still can't carry it around, mark on it, or put a bookmark in it. If the printed book disappears, it will not be replaced by the virtual book in exactly the same way–that is, the content can be made virtual, but the format can never be made virtual. In short,

> The problem with virtual books is that they are not printed; and the problem with printed books is that they are not virtual.

In the new British Library at St. Pancras as part of an interactive exhibition on communication there is a computer which asks visitors their opinion on the future of the book. The results thus far are that the majority think the printed book will be around for another 50 years.[2] This means that most people now living do not see the printed book disappearing in their lifetime. So in a few short years, the printed work, which was formerly regarded as going the way of the dodo bird and fast falling out of favor, has made a remarkable recovery.

If the printed work will still be a staple of library collections, what will be the goals of CCD in collecting printed works? What do we hope to accomplish in a collective sense? Is it to insure that at least one copy of all publications can be found in a library somewhere? Is it to insure that all materials deemed of research value are collected by at least one academic library? Somewhere? What would be the collecting goals of an international information commons? Before we attempt to answer these questions, it might be useful to have some knowledge of the present state of collecting print monographs in U.S. academic libraries.

ACADEMIC LIBRARY MONOGRAPH COLLECTIONS

With this assessment of the current situation of the virtual book, that is, that print is going to be primary format of longer monographic works for many years to come, I would like to present some research findings with regard to the present state of academic library monograph collections. Over the past 15 years, I have studied monograph collections in academic libraries. The studies have been on numbers of titles and have de-emphasized the volume count mentality. These studies have tracked the changing nature of academic library collections by subject and language. One study examined collections by median age.[3]

Both research and library statistical series have established that the latter 1980s was a period of low collecting intensity for monographs in U.S. academic libraries, especially in foreign languages.[4] There are few comparative data to compare the 1980s with earlier time frames, but from the vantage point of the 1990s, the 1980s still appear to have been a low point for academic library monograph collections. There has been a gain in the number of titles added and in the number of unique titles in the 1990s. In the 1990s there is not much in the way of shifts between broad areas of knowledge, but the shifts had already taken place in the 1980s.

A few findings from recent data are presented here as a background for discussion of CCD. The data extracted are from the OCLC/AMIGOS Collection Analysis CD, 1997 edition. These are aggregated data which give us an idea of what the "national collection" is like. That is, the resources in a distributed collection of U.S. academic libraries which are ostensibly available to everyone through resources sharing. From these data, I have tracked collecting patterns in academic libraries for the period 1987-1995. The data are displayed for three peer groupings of academic libraries. The most interesting of these findings for our purposes are the data on unique titles by subject and language and proportions of collections by language.

Table 1 and Figure 1 display the number of unique titles within three peer groups of academic libraries compared with the number of unique titles in the aggregated database of the OCLC/AMIGOS CACD.[1] From this graph we can see that the number of unique titles in the ARL peer group corresponds closely to the number of unique titles in the CACD database (peer group 14). The ARL (peer group 1) owns

TABLE 1. Unique Titles by Year for All Peer Groups–All Languages

	1987	1988	1989	1990	1991	1992	1993	1994	1995	TOTAL
Peer Group 1	44,379	45,343	46,329	50,353	50,962	53,141	53,062	50,322	44,856	438,747
Peer Group 4	29,522	29,600	30,105	31,779	30,989	31,388	31,361	29,956	26,578	271,278
Peer Group 7	23,587	23,977	25,410	26,435	26,525	26,600	26,201	25,276	23,246	227,257
Peer Group 14	50,069	50,918	51,262	57,282	55,441	57,666	57,304	53,096	47,514	480,552

FIGURE 1. Unique Titles by Year for All Peer Groups–All Languages

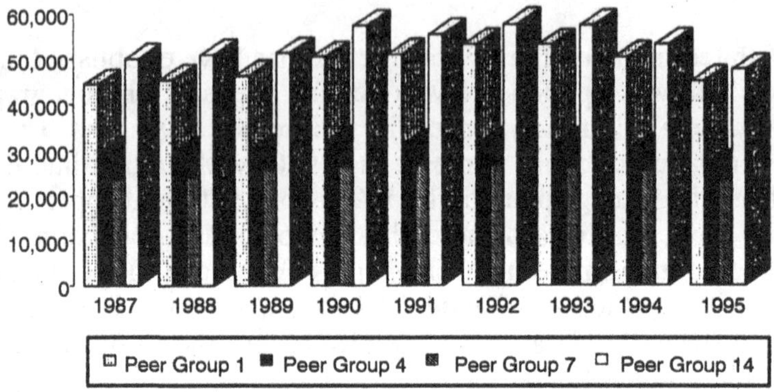

a large proportion of the total number of titles in the database. In fact, it can be said that the ARL library holdings "drive" the database. The ARL group titles are contained within the number for the whole group, so we can see that most of the unique titles can be accounted for by the ARL group. This is not surprising, since these are the largest research libraries in the database and they would be expected to have the largest number of unique titles that is more diverse collections than the smaller size academic, public and special libraries which make up the remainder of the library holdings in the CACD.

The other two peer groupings, 4 and 7, have a much lower level of numbers of titles. Peer group 4 (Large) is the next grouping in size of collections to the ARL group, 123 academic libraries, most of which are from institutions that would be considered research in that they grant doctoral degrees. The number of acquisitions are far below those of the ARL peer group. The third peer group (Medium) is composed of 227 more libraries from even smaller institutions, mainly four-year undergraduate or college libraries with a few graduate programs. There is a wide variety of mission, but these are predominantly not research institutions. The number of libraries in peer group 7 is larger than peer group 4, but the average number of unique titles is lower than for peer group 4.

We would like to think that the non-ARL institutions would make their own contributions to the information commons, but the data I have show that the contribution is mainly in increasing the number of holding libraries overall, not in contributing to the diversity of unique titles.

Since the purpose of this paper is to ultimately make suggestions for some changes in thinking and the data are provided for background, I am not going to show numerous graphs, but instead will summarize the findings with regard to unique titles by subject and by languages. In comparing the number of unique titles by three broad subject groupings of humanities, social sciences, and sciences, some interesting patterns emerge.

- Until 1991, the entire database contained a larger number of unique titles in the humanities than did the ARL group. In other words, other libraries were contributing unique titles. But, beginning in 1992 the ARL peer group goes slightly ahead of the aggregated database, indicating that there are not many unique titles in the database that are not owned by some ARL library. Or put another way, the majority of the unique titles in the humanities are owned by ARL libraries.
- For the humanities both peer groups 4 and 7 have much lower numbers and proportions of total in unique titles than the ARL and the CACD database. For peer group 7, the proportion of unique titles is even lower than in peer group 4.
- In the social sciences,[2] for the ARL group, in all years, there are fewer unique titles in the social sciences than in the entire database, which means that there are quite a few titles in the database for which no ARL library had a location symbol in the database. The pattern for the other peer groups of smaller size academic libraries is similar in that there are a larger number of unique titles in the social sciences than in the humanities but a smaller proportion than for the aggregated database.
- In the sciences, the ARL group has fewer unique titles than the database until 1994. For the last 2 years of data, the ARL group and the entire database are even.
- The pattern in the sciences for both peer groups 4 and 7 are very similar. The number of titles each year does not fluctuate a lot and the absolute numbers for both groups are very close.

My earlier research in the composition of ARL collections in the latter 1980s showed a decrease in unique titles in the humanities. This dataset presented here shows an increase in unique titles in the early

1990s. For the humanities in peer group 1, the ARL libraries, there is a low of 15,639 unique titles in 1987 to a high of 18,769 in 1993. In 1987 and 1988, the ARL libraries had fewer unique titles than the aggregated database, i.e., there were titles in the database that no ARL library owned. Beginning in 1991, the ARL libraries have more unique titles than the database. The small differences in the number of unique titles between the database and the ARL group mean that the majority of the unique titles are owned by ARL libraries. From the devastating years in the late 1980s, there seems to be some recovery in that the number of unique titles does rise in the early 1990s.

To summarize for unique titles, the ARL libraries hold the preponderance of unique titles in the humanities, with the large and medium-sized academic libraries tending to have more unique titles in the social sciences than in the humanities. For all peer groups the number of unique titles in the sciences declines moving forward in time.

We may be seeing a pattern of fewer unique titles in the sciences because of electronic information sources or publication patterns. These data can be interpreted as there being much more of an agreed upon core of materials in the sciences than the humanities and social sciences. This pattern also obtains in approval plan data which show the universe of titles in the sciences to be rather small. Thus, in be sciences, everyone buys the same titles. Since monographs in be sciences tend to summarize established research findings, a low number of unique titles in the sciences may be an appropriate collecting pattern.

For measurements closer to the present, the data become less reliable. The very materials which should be quickly entered into the bibliographic databases, i.e., unique titles and foreign language titles, are customarily the last to be cataloged. Thus we see a diminution in the number of unique titles as we move forward in time. It cannot be said that a decline is taking place. The data could be a function of cataloging lag. The easy copy cataloging with just adding holdings symbols is the body of materials which show up in the bibliographic databases. The unique materials take much longer–an opposite situation from what is desirable for CCD and resource sharing, not to mention research.

Now, a few findings with respect to foreign language titles. In the latter 1980s as the acquisitions situation for monographs continued to deteriorate, foreign language acquisitions were the hardest hit. No one would dispute this today. Without giving a great deal of detail, I will simply summarize the major points with respect to foreign language collecting that can be ascertained from the same dataset as the findings on unique titles presented above. Table 2 shows the percentage of foreign language titles which are unique by year and peer group.

- Proportionately, for the CACD database (peer group 14), non-English language unique titles make up 11% of all titles. All unique titles, that is all languages, comprise 23% of the CACD peer group 14 by publication year. Slightly less than half of all unique titles are foreign language titles.
- For the ARL group the percentage of total in foreign language unique titles was near 14% in 1987, but fluctuates in a downward trend to less than 11% in 1994, 1995. The ARL group overall unique titles increased from 1987 to 1995, but the non-English unique titles decreased in that time span.

More specific analysis not shown in Table 2 reveals that

- The numbers of unique titles in the foreign languages are small in all but French, German, and Spanish. The numbers for Arabic and Japanese are too low to comment upon.
- From 1987 to the early 1990s, the number of unique titles in non-English acquisitions in ARL libraries increased in the humanities and social sciences, but began to decrease in the sciences beginning in 1992.
- In peer group 4, the number of foreign language unique titles in the social sciences and sciences steadily decreases beginning in 1987. The humanities show slight variation in the number of unique titles with the exception of a much larger number in one year, 1992.

TABLE 2. Percent Total Titles that Are Unique–Non-English

	1987	1988	1989	1990	1991	1992	1993	1994	1995	TOTAL
Peer Group 1	13.89%	11.14%	10.86%	11.16%	10.97%	11.44%	11.49%	10.92%	10.48%	438,747
Peer Group 4	5.62%	5.45%	5.37%	5.09%	4.79%	5.44%	4.57%	4.64%	4.39%	271,278
Peer Group 7	3.19%	3.15%	3.17%	2.96%	2.91%	2.77%	2.67%	2.77%	2.32%	227,257
Peer Group 14	11.80%	11.77%	11.28%	11.67%	11.38%	11.84%	11.96%	11.35%	10.97%	480,552

- In peer group 7, the number of foreign language unique titles in the sciences is very low; the number in the humanities and social sciences remain relatively constant until 1993 in which the social sciences begin to decline.
- In the sciences and technology the ARL group and peer group 14 show the same pattern and the numbers are close together; peer group 14 does have slightly higher numbers than the ARL group, indicating that there are a few sci/tech unique titles in foreign languages not held by ARL libraries.
- In almost all non-English languages, the humanities have the largest number of unique titles in all peer groups and all languages. The exceptions are in German and Spanish, in peer groups 1 and 14 in which there are more unique titles in the social sciences than in the humanities.
- In Russian language materials, for both peer groups 1 and 14, in the early years, the majority of unique titles are in the social sciences, but this reverses in the 1990s to a majority in the humanities in most years. Chinese displays an almost opposite pattern to Russian.

An attempt can be made to ascertain the percentage of book production being acquired by geographic publishing area. Redd-Scott summarized a number of studies conducted under the auspices of the ARL of library collecting patterns according to area of publication.[5] This is a comprehensive summary of area studies collecting in U.S. and Canadian academic libraries. The ARL study, research by Perrault, and studies on literature loss conducted by Schwartz,[6] all confirm the decline in the acquisition of foreign language publications. A few examples of the percentage coverage of book publication output in the first half of the 1990s are provided below.

Using the same OCLC/AMIGOS dataset as above and book production or approval plan figures an approximation of the percentage of coverage can be arrived at.

- For German language imprints, the ARL libraries have approximately 14,000-15,000 titles per year. From approval plan figures for German academic books, the number of books judged suitable for academic libraries hovered around 22,000.[7] The ARL libraries collectively acquired approximately 68% of the German academic books.

- For French language imprints, in the years 1987-1994, the ARL libraries have approximately 10,000 titles per year. Total book production for France in those years averages 41,000 to 45,000 per year.[8] Thus the ARL libraries acquired approximately 22-25% of French book production. Another indication of coverage for French language imprints is from RLG. In adding current cataloging records from the bibliotheque nationale de France for monographs cataloged since 1997, 90% of the records described items that were unique to the RLG union catalog.[9] This is a further indication that the coverage of French language materials by U.S. libraries is low.
- From approval plan coverage for U.S. and British English language materials the coverage by ARL libraries ranges from 67%-70% from 1991-1994.[10] Indicators are that book production and sales in the U.S. leveled off or decreased in the early 1990s. In fact, 1987 was the high point in volume of book production in the U.S. since World War II, with 1990 being the lowest point. Beginning in 1995, there have been large increases in U.S. book production.[11]

Thus, it appears that U.S. academic libraries in the aggregate were acquiring 67-70% of approval plan offerings in 1991-1994. The average for German language books is in the same range with respect to academic approval plan offerings. The figures for French language are not comparable, because the total is overall French book production, not approval plan offerings, but there are indications that a much lower percentage of French book production is being acquired by U.S. libraries than English and German language publications. Coverage for other languages is lower than for the three predominant language groupings.

The percentage coverage is naturally higher when it is measured by approval plan statistics since these are for titles appropriate for academic libraries. The percentage coverage is naturally lower when measured against total book production by country.

There is one non-U.S. study which pursued the question of the coverage of books by language. The National Library of the Netherlands sponsored a study to assess the current state of collection development in the Netherlands. The research project aimed to assess the coverage of the aggregate collection of Dutch libraries. The collections of foreign publications of an academic nature published in the 1990s in some 20 subject areas were compared with the collections of several authoritative German libraries. For German language publications, on the average, the coverage was around 50% with some disciplines in the humanities lower yet. After subject specialists examined the lists of publications not held by any Dutch library, those eliminated as not necessary raised the coverage to 70%, which the researcher considers to be low. The same study found that the German libraries were adequately covering German language publications. The researcher makes the point that probably neither the Dutch nor German libraries are adequately covering major U.S publications.[12]

We don't know what the unique holdings of the major European, Latin American, Asian, etc., national libraries or universities look like. In fact, we don't know what percentage of national publication is acquired and preserved by foreign national and university libraries. The problem of achieving both national and foreign language coverage for academic libraries is recognized abroad as well as in the U.S. Elizabeth Chapman, in an IFLA paper in Copenhagen in 1997 says, "National self-sufficiency is a concern throughout Europe." She suggests that "the most likely area for cooperation is the purchase of Non-English language publications."[13]

INTERNATIONAL COOPERATIVE COLLECTION DEVELOPMENT

The libraries of individual countries are having a difficult time assuring the archiving and availability of publications published in their own countries, much less attempting international coverage, except in comprehensive special collections. It seems best to admit that U.S. research libraries and consortia cannot attempt comprehensive international coverage. I am not suggesting we abandon the cooperative projects we have nourished so carefully. CRL, AFL, PRLG, have accomplished a great deal working in conjunction with area studies associations and foreign national and university libraries. I am suggesting that this cooperative collection development needs to become an international agenda that matches the new spirit of the international information commons.

Earlier in this paper, I used the phrase "national collection." This phrase is used in Australia but has never really caught on in the U.S.

There is an implication in this phrase that there is some common ownership that these resources in the bibliographic utility databases are national resources–same with the "distributed collection." With the concept of an international information commons, there is the idea that whatever resources exist are available for the shared use of all. Is it possible that the Internet is engendering a mind set that makes the concept of an information commons more acceptable? The Internet exists and grows through the unfettered contributions of millions. With the exception of passwords on corporate or for fee sites, the commons is for use by everyone. In an international information commons, every person and every library will acquire and use those units of information in which they are most interested and share all resources, especially the unique resources. But the resources, e.g., printed books, are not electronic.

A more restricted concept of an electronic information commons as a membership organization, which mounts indexes, and archives electronic research documents, was proposed by Gregory and Perrault at NASIG in 1997.[14] The commons is a membership organization that retains copyright for all commons materials. The commons licenses and sells products, such as CD-ROM course books. The CIC consortia for the publication of electronic science journals is a similar concept.

The collecting goal in the research library community in North America for most of the latter half of the 20th century has been cooperative collection development. That is, the emphasis was on the acquisition of materials through the designation or acceptance of collecting responsibility by an institution according to subject or area of study. This collecting responsibility was comprehensive. And the logical corollary to cooperative collection development is that the unique materials be shared with the users of other institutions who participated in the CCD program. The mentality in this cooperative collection development/resource sharing philosophy is that the universe of research materials would be covered through this division of collecting responsibility. It has come to the point that we, the U.S. institutions, need to realize that world publication output cannot be comprehensively covered by U.S. libraries alone. In the last 25-30 years, academic librarians have first had to admit that no library can collect comprehensively and then to convince faculty of this impossibility. We now have to realize that the collective collecting ability of North American research libraries is limited in the same way. As Milton

Wolf said in a CRL online discussion, " . . . whether we know it or not all libraries are building a worldwide collection right now–only rather poorly."[15] We cannot collectively acquire even one copy of world publication output. The emphasis needs to shift to international resources sharing with acquisitions responsibility both at home and abroad. I don't think it is abdicating our mission to admit that we cannot financially cover all domestic and foreign book production. The answer has to be increased international cooperation both within and without the library community.

It is time to turn to libraries in other countries and ask the question, are you acquiring and maintaining collections of publications from your country? And furthermore, would you consider this a responsibility of yours as a contribution to the furtherance of knowledge and to the information commons of world publication output? CCD cannot be just the U.S. acquiring materials from all over the world. The "world" has to agree that it is everyone's responsibility. And furthermore, the "world" involves more players than just libraries. Publishers need to be part of the solution.

PUBLISHERS AS PARTNERS

Although SPARC and JSTOR have begun publisher partnerships with respect to journals, much more remains to be accomplished in this avenue of cooperation. U.S. libraries cannot be sure that everything published in the U.S. finds a home in at least one library. Yes, that's what the copyright copies to LC program is supposed to accomplish. But there are trade titles that LC doesn't seem to own. Publishers (all kinds, types, sizes) should be encouraged to select a depository library, a partner, whatever term becomes fashionable, to receive copies of all of that publisher's output. Most University presses have such arrangements with their university libraries. Since this is for archival purposes, the material need not be transferred until disposal of inventory, or some designated time period, say 5 years, in which the peak sales period has passed. This would include all material licensed or sold by unit or subscription. The publisher would agree to hold one copy of each title published until the title is no longer offered for sale by the publisher. At that point, the titles would be transferred to the partner library which would agree to archive the material and to make available any material requested for research. If in digital form and copies are sold from archival copies, the depository library could both make a little money and pay a royalty to the publisher/copyright holder. The fees to buy the archival copies would be much lower than the fees for licensing current material. JSTOR is an example of a centralized preservation clearinghouse for electronic journal backfiles. Libraries can belong to the consortia and not purchase and provide server space indefinitely for journal backfiles. In other words, it is not just the publisher giving assurances that the materials will be permanently archived, but also the consortia or library partner.

There could even be a symbol which the publisher could place on all works which indicates that the publisher is a participant in the publisher/library archiving project. This proposal posits an international system of library/publisher partnerships and an international spirit of cooperation to supply research materials worldwide.

I would especially like to see this implemented in Europe because the U.S. libraries are not able to acquire foreign language publications at the rate they could 10, 20, 30 years ago. There are many foreign publications which no U.S. library will own, and many U.S. publications which no foreign library will own. The number of scholars globally will probably remain small, which is all the more reason to rely on libraries in the country of origin to collect and lend those printed materials from their country. Such a global view is needed in the library community to encourage true internationalism.

My point in proposing this is to point out that we have always talked about CCD in terms of libraries cooperating with libraries. While there could still be more cooperation among libraries, we need to look outside of our own circle for assistance and cooperation in preserving recorded human knowledge. The dialogues that began as a result of the pricing crisis in the 1980s served to make the research arms of the publishing industry more aware of the difficulties libraries and universities face in acquiring publication output in order to provide access and preserve the materials. More consciousness raising remains in terms of the corporate conscience. If publishers are going to generate books, they need to be concerned about that final step–what happens after the sales have stopped. What happens if someone wants to read a book that was published 20 years ago? It is somewhat akin to having to restore the landscape after you have mined out the pit. With profits come some responsibility to contribute to the world good. And libraries can say "We'll assure that your publications become immortal. Just give us a copy to keep forever." And 20 years from now we wouldn't have to ask why a copy of a certain title can't be found anywhere in the world. There would be a least one copy in a library publisher archive somewhere in the world.

Marianne Scott, in a paper given at the 64th IFLA conference in Amsterdam in 1998, reviewed the many types of cooperation between libraries and publishers, many of them international in scope. These include collaboration in the development and establishment of standards, the ISBN, ISSN, ISMN, etc.; the adoption of CIP; and the, although not universal, widespread use of alkaline paper. Scott outlines six challenges that lie ahead for libraries and publishers in the future that need to be resolved in collaboration for the welfare of both groups. These include copyright and licensing issues, the development of standards for electronic data access and management and the preservation of digital media and archiving of digital documents.[16] I would add to this list the challenge of assuring the archiving and preservation of at least one copy of printed works. The assurance of this by direct deposit from the publisher to the depository source with a minimum of selection decision, middle-men, etc., would go a long way toward solving this dilemma.

We have worked very hard at CCD for specific areas of the globe, specific subject areas within consortia, but this has almost all been within the library arena and within the U.S. OCLC and RLG have accomplished a great deal in which bibliographic and collecting programs initiated in the U.S. have been extended to major universities and some national/public libraries abroad. Although more remains to be accomplished with these and similar programs, the mentality of cooperation for the preservation of knowledge through acquisition and preservation of both print and electronic resources needs to become a global effort. Not just that libraries in a few advanced countries acquire and preserve certain subjects, but that the publishing industry must realize that they can no longer assume that libraries are able to comprehensively in the aggregate without cooperation and assistance on their part. As information professionals we have been concerned with acquiring materials by individual unit selection or the entire run of journals title by title for quality and local needs. What I am advocating here is the acquisition of material by publisher origin, much as area studies acquire by region, regardless of individual unit worth or expense.

What is different about what I am proposing is:

- This cooperation is not limited to the library circle.
- It is international, not limited by country or region.

This calls for an international effort on the part of librarians and other information professionals, including the originating publishers. It also calls for cooperation by governments that have responsibility for the archiving and the preservation of their output of government information. This is truly a Herculean task of consciousness raising, planning, and cooperation worthy of the new millennium!

NOTES

1. A title is unique within a peer group if only one library within the group owns that title. A title may be unique in more than one peer group–that is, one library in each peer group could own the same title, but it would be unique in each peer group because only one library in each group owned the title. Thus, the number of unique titles in the CACD database means that only one library of all of the libraries in the database owns a title.

2. History is included in the social sciences.

REFERENCES

1. Jane Carr. "Library-publisher relations in the next millennium: A cross-bench perspective." *IFLA Journal* 24 (1998): 312-315.

2. Ibid., 314.

3. Anna H. Perrault. "The Shrinking national collection: A study of the effects of the diversion of funds from monographs to serials on the monograph collections of research libraries," *Library Acquisitions Practice & Theory*, 18, no. 1 (1994): 3-22; "The changing print resource base of academic research libraries in the United States," *JELIS (Journal of Education for Library and Information Science)* 36, no. 4 (Fall 1995): 1-16; "National collecting trends: Methods and findings," *Library and Information Science Research* 21, no. 1(1999): 47-67; "The Effects of high median age on currency of resources in community college library collections," *College & Research Libraries* 60, no. 4 (July 1999): 316-339 (co-authored with Richard Madaus, Ann Armbrister, Jeannie Dixon, and Rhonda Smith).

4. Ibid. Also *ARL Statistics* 1988-.

5. Jutta Reed-Scott, principal author. *Scholarship, Research Libraries, and Global Publishing* (Washington: DC, Association of Research Libraries, 1996).

6. Charles A. Schwartz, "Literature loss in anthropology," *Current Anthropology* 33 (June 1992): 315-317; "Empirical analysis of literature loss," *Library Re-*

sources and Technical Services, 38, no. 2 (April 1994): 133-138; "Literature loss in international relations," *PS: Political Science & Policy* 25 (December 1992): 720-723; "Gap analysis of book publication output and aggregate research collections in psychology," *American Psychologist* 48 (1993): 1151-52.

7. *Bowker annual*, 1998/1999: 514.

8. *Bowker annual*, 1998/1999: 538.

9. *Research Libraries Group News*, issue 48 (Winter 1999): 10.

10. Perrault, *LISR*: 57.

11. *Bowker annual*, 1998/1999: 521.

12. Henk Voorbij. "Are Dutch academic libraries keeping up with research material? The coverage of foreign academic publications in Dutch libraries," *Alexandria* 8 (1996): 189-204.

13. Elizabeth Chapman. "Buying shares in libraries: The economics of cooperative collection development," *IFLA Journal* 24 (1998): 102-106.

14. Vicki Gregory, Anna H. Perrault and David Whitemarsh. "The Web: A Means of Delivering and Publishing Serials with an Examination of Copyright Issues," in *Experimentation and Collaboration: Creating Serials for a New Millennium*. Proceedings of the North American Serials Group, 12th annual conference, Ann Arbor, MI, May 29-June 1, 1997, Charlene N. Simser and Michael A. Somers, Eds. The Haworth Press, Inc., 1998. Also as *Serials Librarian* 34 (1/2 and 3/4) 1998: 345-351.

15. Milton T. Wolf. "Cooperative collection management: Online discussion." *Collection Management* 23, no. 4 (1998): 65.

16. Marianne Scott. "Library-publisher relations in the next millennium: The library perspective" *IFLA Journal* 24 (1998): 316-319.

Grey Literature Poses New Challenges for Research Libraries

Julia M. Gelfand

Discussions today about information, publishing and the role libraries play in these dynamic times can be characterized as always about plenty, needing to be cutting edge, full of references to links between all sectors of the communication industry, role of e-commerce, convergence and constant innovation to keep consumers content, always feeling transformed with newness on the brink. This preoccupation with everything having to be "consumer-driven" suggests how libraries, and other service providers identify their priorities, respond to new opportunities to utilize the latest technologies, and anticipate what our future will be like.

Grey literature has had a struggling past, with recent emergence in popular culture and references to it in academic and conventional business circles. Because of its mixed welcome in formal settings such as libraries, its perceived value as uneven and its difficult challenges in being identified, collected, acquired, processed and oftentimes used, it has been part of the "underground," only recently surfacing due to other successes in electronic publishing and access. With the advent of the web in the last six years, grey literature has emerged to new prominence as creators of it have championed its cause and value by

---

Julia M. Gelfand is affiliated with the University of California, Irvine (e-mail: jgelfand@uci.edu).

This paper was presented at the CRL Conference on Cooperative Collection Development, November 12-14, 1999.

[Haworth co-indexing entry note]: "Grey Literature Poses New Challenges for Research Libraries." Gelfand, Julia M. Co-published simultaneously in *Collection Management* (The Haworth Information Press, an imprint of The Haworth Press, Inc.) Vol. 24, No. 1/2, 2000, pp. 137-147; and: *Creating New Strategies for Cooperative Collection Development* (ed: Milton T. Wolf and Marjorie E. Bloss) The Haworth Information Press, an imprint of The Haworth Press, Inc., 2000, pp. 137-147. Single or multiple copies of this article are available for a fee from The Haworth Document Delivery Service [1-800-342-9678, 9:00 a.m. - 5:00 p.m. (EST). E-mail address: getinfo@haworthpressinc.com].

© 2000 by The Haworth Press, Inc. All rights reserved.

making it increasingly available via the web. The ubiquitous nature of the web and such information sources are taking on long overdue and advanced roles in the administering of reference or public services in libraries.

One may think that they know what grey literature is, but defining it is not so pure and simple. It is neither black nor white, is how some people begin, meaning that it describes information that is neither proprietary and restricted, nor that which is totally in the public domain. Thus, grey symbolizes the blended or abstract hues that describe information which is produced at all levels by government, academic, business and industry enterprises, both in print and electronic formats, but which is not controlled by commercial publishing interests, and where publishing is not the primary business activity of the organization or authorship. Whether this is a vague or sufficient definition suggests that flexibility and an open mind are helpful in this interpretation.

This new tolerance for a rather great diversity of information product replaces previous decades of bashing grey literature when it was not feasible to direct the necessary resources to alleviate the previously mentioned challenges that once defined it. Those of us who defended the value of grey literature, promoted and studied it, were often on the defensive as research library management inquired why, when there were so many other compelling and competing demands, did it not have a greater role in our institutions and be more heavily requested by users. If the content of it was so valuable, why did it not become part of the standard practices of the publishing marketplace, going through traditional peer review and ending up as a commercial product that libraries pay for and could handle without special concerns? Why, when it was added to library collections, did it require such special processing, usually original cataloging?

Having been the target of these discussions countless times, I want to underscore the fact that I am about to commend library leaders today. I mean the administrators, managers, scholars, who finally see that with the investment of technology, and by engaging in more cooperative experiences and investments, they too can promote a greater tolerance for nontraditional resources and information. By latching onto pluralism, libraries have begun to realize that users need information packaged many ways, and they can no longer expect that only one method will be sufficient. Not everything fits perfectly on a shelf, in a drawer, or case, or has a clean URL to identify it. Anything complex, alternative or fugitive suffers from an analogous experience in libraries. There are innumerable obstacles–the economic, practical, and the process of converting to new ways, while maintaining the necessity and traditions to support print, which is not disappearing.

Libraries are commonly acquiring materials in multiple formats, subscribing to different packages of information that contain the same information. Not only are overlap, duplication, multiple access all too common, expensive and oftentimes unnecessary to support, that sometimes we are not even fully aware of the consequences there are with the litany of unknowns about electronic publishing and resources. Licensing and the dilemma of access versus ownership through leasing, struggling with authentication issues, concerns for archiving of materials, compatibility of technologies, the interface with the public catalog, all lead us to understand that there still is a bias or prejudice towards the simplicity of retaining print. Unlike other professions or theories, librarians and libraries can pick and choose which practice they choose to follow, keep or discard, based on economics, willingness to serve users creatively and in the way that many increasingly want to be served, and with the technological resources they think can be supported.

Scores of colleagues have more articulately than I addressed how the rules are changing. We are commonly directing library users to materials not part of our collection by offering better access to document supply options, more dependable and service oriented interlibrary loan procedures, and introducing hosts of other new services based on electronic communication and technical competencies.[1] Many libraries are accelerating their online environments, connectivity, and growing their digital resources because they have learned that by shunning, ignoring, denying users access, they are not letting in the content. The message is the critical thing; not the messenger.

Research libraries have faced this challenge in the past and have gone ahead and taken the plunge. Different issues and outcomes contributing to these advances include, acceptance of the MARC record, expanding the classification series to welcome new subject areas and multidisciplinary and cross-disciplinary matter, seeing more acceptance of mixed and multimedia product, and seeing vast new research areas open up with new collaboration and partnerships defining them. Examples of this may be how library collections treat women studies and feminist interpretations of a range of subjects, area studies, special resources such as dissertations, working papers, technical reports, standards, designs, preprints, datasets and quantification, and other merging and abstract disciplines and their supporting materials. These examples would not survive if users did not need, want, use and depend upon them for scholarly purposes. They all seem to threaten commercial publishing and traditional library collections, because users can increasingly gain access to these materials without going through the library as a gateway. Grey literature is often considered an end-user product, not meeting the criteria of library collection policies. The value-added elements commercial publishers, information providers and libraries have made are not always viewed as essential to improving the product, justifying far greater expense, or worth causing delays in letting users manipulate and access it, or contributing to the noticeable improvement in the allowance for instantaneous remote access.

Regardless of how change threatens hierarchical structures, resistance can be summarized as fear:

- The fear of eroding the foundation of libraries being warehouses for materials serving generations;
- The fear of a concept of authority, having to redefine documents, like the collection development policies that have been true for decades;
- The fear to organize information in new ways;
- The fear that such information will require greater reference and curatorial support;
- The fear to introduce how information with no price tag on it can have incredibly high value placed upon it;
- The fear of losing a competitive edge to a peer institution;
- And, the fear of losing control and seeing new relationships emerge between library staffs and their methods of obtaining and using their collections, and the different relationships now required by users with technical support staff and other new by-products of institutional reorganization and creative staffing models.

We need to continue to applaud library leadership who is open to diversity, and use grey literature to furthering greater inclusiveness instead of a cudgel to bar use. What we do know well from our library experiences, is that access has become key and some direction is needed to better organize the motley resources.

The difficult issues about nontraditional resources in our library collections can only be resolved when we realize that our "imperfect" world of bibliographic control needs to be refined. This has begun to take place in the last couple of years as electronic publishing has pushed the envelope demanding that our efforts to experiment will in time perfect the method. What we see is a plea for greater creativity in the library community, to do things differently, to open up new applications and make things less rigid. Promoting access with modified and abbreviated records is better than no access. Recognizing that "free" material from noncommercial sources may deserve an equal place in the public catalog, especially if it serves local user populations and is considered worthy content.

What research libraries need to do to handle the proliferation of information, including grey literature, is to realize that teaching and learning are no longer restricted to school and university alone but become a lifelong challenge and libraries must administratively become better knowledge managers, as must librarians. This can only be achieved if libraries improve at knowledge acquisitions. Like in museums or retail establishments, when you deal with a product line, there is a "certain life expectancy" that determines how much visibility it gets. It is important that you keep it moving and changing, responding to and reflective of trends. Librarians and users alike should keep themselves off balance anticipating necessary changes. That is what defines a research environment. Schoop writes, "The fast growing amount of globally available, immediately accessible but only in some cases really needed information calls for systematic information filtering, evaluation and application, thus providing reusable knowledge," and "when talking about knowledge we should make the following distinctions":

1. Data are stored facts and rules, which are not linked to individual tasks or decisions problems and thus not (yet) contain semantic
2. Information consists of 'rich data' applied to a specific context, thus possessing a certain semantic
3. knowledge is specific information linked to processes, which is understood by the user and in active use and change

before concluding that "knowledge as a whole has to be isolated into specific objects as knowledge components."[2]

With a +/− 3% error rate, and the fact that there are more than 4,882,000 public domain active web sites with more than 3,649,000 unique web sites and seeing an increase of more than 211% between 1997 to 1999, web volatility is enormous, with 44% of web sites in 1998 no longer live in 1999.[3] Terry Kuny, in his analysis of "The OCLC June 1999 Web Statistics," offers the following observations from the presented numbers:

> First, the web volatility is a very interesting number. It suggests that if you were to have one hundred randomly selected links listed in a document, that one year later 44% would be invalid within 12 months. This seems to have some pretty interesting implications for developers of subject (link) gateway services, anyone interested in digital preservation, and for indexing/cataloging of network resources.[4]

Implications for this in the library context are enormous. Beginning nearly three years ago, library selectors and bibliographers began the task of noting valuable resources for their library users, by creating subject homepages. The deficiencies in the search engines causing users confusion about the authority control of information, the credibility of the author or compiler (and thus they could not adequately evaluate the information), encouraged librarians to select and highlight resources of value and bring them to the attention of their users. This increasingly common responsibility has several ramifications in the research library environment. Users must become aware of such resources in an efficient, natural and effective way.

Librarians must maintain these pages and create them so that they serve users well with accurate and live links. New technical standards and competencies have been defined by libraries, with significant human and systems resources going into programs for technology training to support html, web design and other needed skill sets. With the proliferation of information, the increased volatility of the web, the urgency to develop better access, all of this indeed becomes a major organizational challenge. Subject homepages do have value, especially if they reduce the frustration level of users having to use large and slow search engines that do not clearly indicate how their output is generated and why searches can not be accurately repeated. Even with more sophisticated users, there is the confusion about whether retrieval is by reversed chronology, by relevancy ranking, frequency, domain, or any other method of indexing.

Additional workloads and different strategies make subject web sites a complicated deal to administer and sort out. Having subject expertise contributes to a better understanding about the information, layout of the site, comparison to other library resources, and how the information can be used. In the design of subject homepages, achieving compatibility and having standard formatting contributes to ease of use; the size, focus, direction and navigation of the site and its organizational nexus make it useful for some users and less so for others.

For some librarians, this is an extension of their collection development and management assignments, for others it is a completely new and different activity, which does not come naturally. With most librarians assigned to collect in a given subject area with responsibilities for all formats that can be supported, this activity has greater implications. Attention to print resources may be shortchanged, as the demands for additional handling may not be so critical today. However, for those library staff who prefer to teach their user communities how to retrieve relevant material, or who are not familiar enough with the subject, it becomes an extensive consumer of time and of again replicating resources. Not only are these new methods of pathfinders increasingly common and popular, and standard fare in most libraries today, but they reveal a lot about the library culture of that institution. If librarians are working in an understaffed environment, where their subject expertise does not lend itself to this activity well, there is not much assistance with which to back up the staff. The information cited in many homepages is not often cataloged; thus it is not part of the public holdings or online catalog. Hamaker calls for rethinking the role of library catalogs per Internet resources in a recent article.[5]

Currently in the world of print acquisitions, when one needs to collect books in a specific subject area. one can subscribe to an approval plan, that screens materials based on a profile of reading level, publisher, and other secondary sources of reviews and readers' advisory services exist. For journals in both the print and electronic milieu, there are indexing and citation analysis tools to validate material, serials agents and now aggregators that package information access for collections. In the web environment, it is much harder, although use statistics inform the web author or webmaster, how often the site has been accessed. In the spirit of collaboration, one good site or finding aid circulates and is linked to many other pages, thus homepage development is not always one of great creativity. In other technical services and cataloging functions, workloads of those engaged in processing are overwhelming, with backlogs mounting of electronic resources needing attention. Outsourcing experiences are more common and perhaps grey literature lends itself to that consideration, although managing the metadata should be done to local specifications. What appears to make greater sense is for libraries to subscribe to the indexing and cataloging of web products compiled by the national bibliographic utilities. For electronic journals, this is becoming de rigeur. For those materials that are not noted in the MARC record with a URL, the requirements of inputting that and then running a software program to detect dead or failed links is required. Cooperative cataloging on a more widespread basis would be a potential solution and may alleviate the need for users to consult all of the following, the online public catalog, the appropriate subject page and several search engines to find the appropriate material.

Often libraries are not receptive to adding materials that require supplemental technical support or software to utilize the material. Loading Adobe Acrobat readers was relegated to computer laboratories and office workstations rather than on terminals in public reading rooms until recently, when PDF became common. Still, libraries hear arguments about what role e-mail has in library reading rooms, even though users depend upon it for capturing their library research.

Many libraries are moving in the direction of licensing bibliographic software packages that offer users the ability to retain the reference for future review without having to conduct the search again. Examples of such software include EndNote, Reference Manager and ProCite. Around for nearly a decade, these products allow users to organize information in a highly customizable and personal way that is meaningful to the user. Having various search strategies by which to recall a reference or document, allows one to place it in one or more locations with notes about it. Considered "must have software" by many scientists and scholars and now students and general library users, these resources allow "the massive influx of information to turn into knowledge, which ensues innovative thinking."[6] Libraries are increasingly licensing this software and using it to enhance a variety of technical operations that are compatible with local OPAC management.

Grey literature lends well to the flexible structure of bibliographic software. This may be the only way that you would organize such information from such a wide range of sources that span all formats. Let's remember what the potential of a networked information environment is and what it is becoming. Increasingly, with more Z39.50 compatibility around, having EndNote allows for additional client support of collected references and information. Thus, bibliographic software becomes a more valuable resource to library users. They can organize their references from a variety of sources, adapt to a needed style manual when submitting a paper requiring a specified format, or follow "Instructions to Authors" without tracking down the journal. They can also download fulltext material in Z39.50 and incorporate this into the pedagogy of some classes. It is another example of knowledge management, commercially available to customize individually and institutionally. When our goal as librarians is to sharpen critical thinking skills and facilitate more knowledge management, why not take advantage of help that is there.

The "Axioms of Cooperative Collection Management"[7] build on the premise that cooperative collection development does not happen without significant commitments at the institutional levels and a willingness to utilize electronic technologies with a spirit of adaptability. The special attributes of grey literature include how flexible it can be to share and transfer across networks with accompanying user guides and other needed information, having the potential to communicate and work directly with the creator of the information.

Applications such as distance education, and course integrated instruction offer endless opportunities for faculty and librarians to collaborate on introducing resources to students. Classroom or laboratory use of information makes for more interactive learning experiences. Finding aids and instructional support are definitely critical to successful use of some grey literature. A windows-based environment offers users the ability to access and learn at the same time. Grey literature tends to be a collection resource developed over time, almost serial in nature; thus identifying and referencing key parts of the resource is important.

The new grey literature, which respects and emerges from our traditions, are in fact breaking the silence, bridging the gap between past and present, speaking out and grateful for their new home in a welcoming atmosphere of increasing value and importance. As grey literature advances to another stage of visibility, it can be noted that the academic library community has played a major role by including more electronic information in its holdings and supporting it with better bibliographic access and servicing. In October 1999, the fourth international conference of grey literature will be held. Many sponsors contribute to that conference, including national libraries, government agencies from around the globe, the intelligence community, academic libraries and research organizations. In addition, the Amsterdam based GreyNet tracks all activities related to scholarship about grey literature and hosts a web site devoted exclusively to grey literature interests.[8] A new journal, the *International Journal of Grey Literature* (MCB University Press (v. 1, #1 2000) debuts this year to promote the creative, academic, and service functions of grey literature.

Six years ago, I shared that academic research libraries showed only reluctance in accepting or promoting grey literature because there were many more competing demands for attention as we launched web access.[9] Since that time, libraries have begun to examine what they could do together and we see how networked telecommunications has changed our vision and work lives. Libraries continue to explore what they can do together, knowing full well that there are far too many obstacles in doing things alone. Consortia are a way of survival, and there are new interpretations and practices for each experience in cooperative ventures. Grey literature has not only sustained itself, but it has prospered enormously, however at a more modest pace than could be expected in research library collections. As interest in grey literature from the commercial sectors expands and better control and access is in place, the potential is obvious.

Still, the grey literature "movement" continues to define its products and themselves a tad differently depending on the position in the organizational structure. Many people sympathetic to grey literature concur that the impact of many changes in their institutions, be that in government, academe, industry, libraries or as independents, dictates how grey literature will be treated. What is clear, is that the value of grey literature is significantly greater due to electronic access and it is perceived to have more historical value, as its citation patterns indicate more credibility in scholarly activities.

Recent threads on active discussion listservs suggest the more widespread consensus that David Goodman expresses in an exchange about electronic availability to scholarly journals,

> Given (libraries') limited resources, we (librarians) are forced to make choices about what to provide by purchase and what to provide more indirectly. For a research library, I think it is valid to purchase emphasizing the material most valuable for the current and future research (and teaching) needs of our institutions.[10]

The challenge remains how we in libraries can improve upon that and share the responsibilities to accurately describe and share information as widely as possible. Technology will continue to transform how we conduct research and business and manage our resources. Grey literature is being created in digital formats at alarming speed, in all subject areas, around the globe, and it is often defied by adequate bibliographic description. As we celebrate half a century of organized cooperative collection development, perhaps we can expect this new century to usher in even more interest in expanding the notion of library collections. Until then, grey literature still presents a difficult conundrum for research libraries.

NOTES

1. Chuck Hamaker, "The Rules Have Changed: Library Catalogs and Internet Resources," *Charleston Advisor* (1/1), July 1999, 37.
2. E. Schoop, "Structured Documentation: An Approach to Identify and Model Knowledge Components for Learning Purposes," in Gaul, W. and Locarek-Junge, H., Eds. *Classification in the Information Age, Proceedings of the 22 Annual GfK1 Conference*, March 4-6, 1998. Berlin: Springer, 1998, 410.
3. Terry Kuny, contribution to *DIGLIB@INFOSERV.NLC-BNC.CA*, September 16, 1999.
4. Ibid.
5. Hamaker, 37-38.
6. EndNote User Stories, see *http://www.endnote.coni/ENApplication_Note.htm*
7. Richard J. Wood, "The Axioms, Barriers and Components of Cooperative Collection Development" in Gorman, G.E. and Miller, Ruth, Eds, *Collection Management in the 21st Century: A Handbook for Librarians*. Westport, CT: Greenwood Press, 1997, 242-244.
8. GreyNet *http://www.konbib.nl/infolev/greynet*
9. Julia Gelfand, "Academic Libraries and Collection Development Implications for Grey Literature," *Proceedings of the First International Conference on Grey Literature*, Amsterdam, December 13, 1993, 123-140.
10. David Goodman *(dgoodman@princeton.edu)* on *liblicense-1@lists.yale.edu*, September 25, 1999.

Challenges and Constraints for History Selectors

James P. Niessen
Susanne F. Roberts

Collection development librarians for history in research libraries enjoy many opportunities for cooperative action due to the breadth of their collections and responsibilities. However, they also face special challenges for historical materials that may be not be fully appreciated by advocates of cooperative collection development. Library support for history must encompass a broader range of specified, foreign-language, and retrospective material than many disciplines; this is what makes cooperative collection development for history unique. These requirements may place extraordinary demands on local funds that are then unavailable for cooperative projects, but the needs of historians may in the end be met only by resorting to a distributed collection. History is more wedded to the monograph in codex format than many other disciplines, both because of the importance of synthesis and narrative in the discipline and because most earlier specialized monographs will never be digitized. By virtue of mission and money, history selectors in research institutions are perhaps the most motivated and

---

James P. Niessen is Librarian for History and Foreign Languages, Texas Tech University Libraries.

Susanne F. Roberts is Librarian for European History and Coordinator of Humanities Collections, Sterling Memorial Library, Yale University.

The authors would like to thank the following individuals for their comments on drafts of this paper: Suzan McGinnis, Ann Okerson, and Louis Pitschmann.

[Haworth co-indexing entry note]: "Challenges and Constraints for History Selectors." Niessen, James P., and Susanne F. Roberts. Co-published simultaneously in *Collection Management* (The Haworth Information Press, an imprint of The Haworth Press, Inc.) Vol. 24, No. 1/2, 2000, pp. 149-173; and: *Creating New Strategies for Cooperative Collection Development* (ed: Milton T. Wolf and Marjorie E. Bloss) The Haworth Information Press, an imprint of The Haworth Press, Inc., 2000, pp. 149-173. Single or multiple copies of this article are available for a fee from The Haworth Document Delivery Service [1-800-342-9678, 9:00 a.m. - 5:00 p.m. (EST). E-mail address: getinfo@haworthpressinc.com].

© 2000 by The Haworth Press, Inc. All rights reserved.

best situated to share in cooperative efforts. Yet job responsibilities, budgetary pressures, organizational structures, and the expectations of their constituents may constrain them as much as their colleagues in smaller libraries.

The authors of this paper have selection responsibility for all or part of history at libraries ranked in the first and the third quartile of the Association of Research Libraries. Our thoughts about this topic received stimulus from the offline discussions with colleagues on *H-HistBibl*, a mailing list within *H-Net: Humanities & Social Sciences OnLine* dedicated, as its official mission states, to "the practice and study of bibliographic and library services in support of historical study and teaching."[1] Our presentation draws partly on our own experiences and partly on those of colleagues as described in their messages to H-Hist Bibl and elsewhere.

We have identified six topical areas that we will address in turn; James Niessen speaks from the perspective of an academic research library in the third quartile of the ARL, and Susanne Roberts from that of one in the first quartile.

WHAT ARE THE RESPONSIBILITIES AND DEMANDS ON THE TIME OF THE HISTORY SELECTOR?

The bibliographer or curator working exclusively in collection development is becoming less common in research libraries. The subject librarian exercises reference, outreach, and instruction as well as selection functions, perhaps having less time and energy than traditional bibliographers for outside activities as a result.

Niessen

In my five-year library career I cannot report fundamental changes in my formal responsibilities. Throughout this period the official title of the selector has been subject librarian, and the emphasis has been on the complementarity of our activity on the service desks, in user instruction, in the selection of resources, and in interaction with students and faculty in one's academic departments. The library's Information Services Department includes units for Reference, Government Documents, Liaison and Collection Development, and User

Instruction whose boundaries are extremely permeable. Many years ago, I am told, the library employed some people without library degrees who bore the title of bibliographer and worked in acquisitions, not reference. As recently as last year, some academic faculty members were designated by their departments to coordinate book orders for sending to the library. As I will describe in a later section, members of the faculty rather than library staff formerly did most of the actual selection of material bought with the history allocation. Our current system sought to rectify the inadequacies of that model.

The job description of the subject librarian at Texas Tech presumes autonomy and unpredictability in the demands on the selector's time. Not only are the disciplines and their information needs distinctive, but also the departments' traditions and expectations in relation to the library. In effect, the subject or liaison librarian model is an ongoing experiment, with no consistent standards in the balancing of functions (such as desk duty and reference selection against the form ordering for the circulating collection) traditionally carried out by Tech librarians. In some academic departments, the library committee, its chair, or individual professors are unusually active in collection development and the librarian makes no claim to subject expertise. In such cases, collection development is less time consuming because it consists primarily of processing faculty recommendations. Three areas are making increasing demands on selectors' time: website development, library instruction, and the consideration of electronic products. These also develop unevenly across the program due to culture (some departments are more likely to request instruction than others) and discipline (electronic products, especially indexes and e-journals, are demanded more in the hard sciences, less in the humanities). It is difficult to address all these responsibilities adequately, but they provide the selector with a unique fund of knowledge about the information needs and local collection of his primary clientele.

Comparing my funds to those of colleagues at larger libraries, I must ask whether the budget of a selector at this size of library can even permit collecting for non-local needs. I would argue that, presuming an adequate focus, it is possible. It has been fairly easy to arrange with some colleagues in the Big Twelve Plus consortium about some narrow areas of local emphasis. However, the many claims on one's time make it difficult to conduct the collection analysis and consultation of reviews that would be necessary for cooperative selection in broad targeted areas (Mosher & Pankake, 418, 427-8).

Roberts

As one of those formerly full-time collection development librarians or bibliographers whose basic responsibilities have recently multiplied, I bear witness to this trend and its possibly negative effects on cooperative collection development. In the spring of 1996, Yale's small Bibliography Department merged with the Reference Department, creating the Research Services and Collections department staffed by ten librarians. All the librarians now have subject and departmental liaison responsibilities, perform advanced subject reference and general reference, and offer general as well as subject specific instruction. Except for general reference, all of these (departmental liaison, advanced reference, and some instruction) had been the bibliographers' responsibilities on a smaller scale. Now, while my collecting areas have diminished slightly, these other responsibilities have dramatically increased, in part due to a new institutional emphasis on instruction and liaison functions. General reference has not become an institutional priority and yet requires a heavy staffing commitment from the librarians who develop the collections and provide liaison and instructional services; it draws hours of my time away from my primary collection development concerns. In addition, the structure of our department is now more complex; the collection development activities of a larger group of selectors, many of whom lack knowledge, skills, and experience in this field, require more coordinating effort–another of my responsibilities.

This multi-faceted model has become increasingly common in research libraries. Collection development responsibilities have, according to history selectors' reports, been treated by administrators as a kind of staff development opportunity rather than as functions requiring training, skill, and experience. Though it has some benefits, the model is remarkably inefficient and not particularly conducive to cooperative collection development. It carries, as colleagues experience it, very high overhead. Many more people must spend their time developing and maintaining awareness of the same array of reference tools rather than on building particular collections, and the same number must toil over budget requests instead of information requests. Spread thin, librarians' expertise in a subject or function becomes diluted, as does their attention; it is not possible to focus long or deeply on anything. Some history selectors report spending only about 25% of their time on collection development. Not only are collection development functions fragmented and split among numerous librarians with competing demands on their time, but also many of those librarians do not report directly–if at all–to administrators in charge of collection development and management.

Can effective cooperative programs thrive in such a milieu? When collection development librarians have multiple functions, and particularly when some of these are strongly oriented towards serving local users, the prospects for cooperative collection development may be less than optimal. Not only do fragmentation of time and multiplication of responsibilities take a toll on selectors' ability to initiate or participate in labor-intensive cooperative ventures–however much they might favor them–but service activities also subtly affect their point of view. General reference service, intense instruction, and liaison work tend to focus attention on local needs and local collections rather than cooperative collections or the national collection.[2] These public services functions heighten a selector's awareness of local research, teaching, and programmatic needs and enhance her ability to build collections to meet them and to anticipate future needs. This is true especially in larger research libraries with comprehensive collections and adequate budgets. What public service activities teach selectors about how historians work will be discussed below.

HOW ARE BUDGETARY ALLOCATIONS FOR COLLECTION DEVELOPMENT ADMINISTERED?

Separate budgetary lines may exist for individual formats and means of acquisition or for groups of disciplines; alternatively, selectors may control funds for all formats in a discipline. Sharing responsibility for a discipline with other library units may reduce the selector's capacity for outside collaboration.

Niessen

In his article on "Budgetary Methods for Collection Management," Eugene Wiemers, Jr. notes that the way budgets are organized has a major impact on selectors' autonomy and accountability (Wiemers, 108). At Texas Tech, the history selector has direct control over one part of history acquisitions, the formula-based firm order allocation for that subject. There is shared responsibility for the funds for approval plans, continuations, reference, and electronic publications, and selectors exercise only mediated influence over the portions of these budgets corresponding to their subjects. We are encouraged to return unwanted approval plan books, cancel subscriptions that have outlived their usefulness, and terminate reference titles that are now duplicated in electronic format. The selector's economic incentive to do so would be far stronger with selector-based budgeting where we can use the money saved thereby for the ordering of other titles. Approval plan books do not come in on our personal fund, although the dollar value of shipments accepted on each selector's portion of the approval plan does influence the next year's firm order money through the allocation formula. Standing orders instituted in wealthier days or under the influence of a long-departed faculty member are likely to go unexamined. These funding arrangements lead to variation in the rigorousness of the selection criteria: firm orders must be actively selected, approval plan titles may be returned if outrageously out of scope but we tend to keep them if they have any redeeming features, whereas the standing order titles are often very specialized works at steep prices. All of which is not to deny the efficacy of well-managed, well-monitored approval plans and standing orders. The spread of history acquisitions across several funds also makes it difficult for the selector to place a dollar value on acquisitions in his subject or to account for the future disposition of shared funds. This makes it harder to understand what you are currently doing and could do in cooperative projects with selectors in other libraries.

Outside the Texas Tech University Library (the main building of "the libraries"), we strive for a comprehensive collection on the history of the American Southwest and outstanding retrospective holdings on the history of the Vietnam War in our Southwest Collection/Special Collections Library. Once again budgetary separateness makes it difficult for me to get an overview of current collecting. Because the Southwest and Vietnam are also major curricular foci in our history department, the acquisition of archival, non-circulating copies of new monographs may not be sufficient on our commuting campus. To some extent I can factor in these special collections as I decide how to apportion my funds among historical fields, but knowing the demand for circulating copies I must see that the approval plan still covers titles in southwestern history and the Vietnam War fairly well. Thus the influence of our special collections on my own ordering is a complex one.

Roberts

The administration of budgetary allocations for collection development librarians at Yale is not per se an impediment to cooperative collection development. Allocations are made on a subject or regional basis and thus selectors control funds for all formats in a discipline. Some of our numerous approval plans are funded from central collection development funds, while some are paid from subject funds. In all cases, the shaping and monitoring of approval plan profiles and receipts rests in the hands of the subject librarians.

Several libraries in our system have overlapping responsibilities; for example, collections in religion (an important field for historians) are held in both the Sterling Memorial and Divinity libraries, and the history of science is collected in Sterling Memorial Library, the Kline Science Library, and the Medical Historical Library. Librarians at Yale increasingly try to cooperate internally to avoid duplication, develop important strengths, and take advantage of expertise in processing and cataloguing staff. This high level of internal cooperation, brought about at Yale in the past two decades by growing budgetary concerns, is not a necessary feature of large academic research libraries. Where it operates, however, it inculcates in selectors' attitudes or orientations and experience with potential for cooperative efforts outside the library.

The substantial budgets of large research libraries like Yale do not, however, necessarily foster cooperative collection development, but this has more to do with relative abundance than the structure of allocations. Selectors in such institutions are not necessarily complacent, but they may be under less pressure to look for collection resources elsewhere. With a large and prominent history department, collecting mandates at Yale are traditionally and necessarily broad, and budgetary allocations have supported comprehensive collecting in many areas as well as new departures. Purchase of large expensive items may be deferred for another fiscal year, or the cost may be spread out over several years, but for the most part we are still able to acquire material that supports local research and programs and builds on the library's considerable long-term strengths.

Selectors at Yale instantly adapt their budgets to changing programs and expectations. With adequate pressures, even long-standing reliance on other collections' strengths can break down in the face of changing research interests in a prestigious department and increasing demands, often from undergraduates. For decades, for example, Yale determinedly maintained a conspectus level three collection on South Asia, deferring to stronger collections at Columbia and Cornell. In recent years, the expanding horizons of historians and students have encouraged somewhat more active collecting of research materials in this field.

GROWING EXPENDITURES FOR ELECTRONIC DATA ARE LIKELY TO REDUCE THE SIGNIFICANCE OF LOCAL COLLECTION BUILDING

At many institutions, the selector's budget may decline in relative terms and be dedicated to general-use, high demand items. The CRL and certain regional centers may take on a greater role in specialized collection development. Participating libraries must then decide whether subject librarians should be involved in representing their institutions' needs to these consortia.

Niessen

In good times, the library budget can be a rising tide that lifts even the history selector's boat. This has been the case at Texas Tech, although the book budget has declined as a relative portion of the materials budget. Electronic publications rightly enjoy administrative favor at this time. For example, *JSTOR* and science e-journals facilitate immediate access to resources more cost-effectively than would be possible through traditional methods, while public access bibliographic utilities and online indexes do the same through interlibrary loan.

There are some troubling implications for history collecting because of the current budgetary preference for electronic publications, however. The importance of monographs and other retrospective materials and the doubtfulness that most of them will be digitized have already been mentioned. Even among indexes and journals, the benefits for historians are undermined by the eclecticism of the discipline. Moving historical indexes online involves investments for implementation by the vendors and technical support by libraries that may be prohibitive. Even *Historical Abstracts*, a recognized standby in paper, has come online only in the past year and has been difficult to sell to colleagues in my library. Part of the problem (this is my observation and reported by colleagues in other libraries) is that historians use *Historical Abstracts* in paper very little. The benefits of electronic databases should not be minimized, though. Through our membership in the LEIAN consortium (Llano Estacado Information Access Network, for West Texas and Eastern New Mexico) we have gamed access to a very large package of FirstSearch databases, including some of special interest to historians, such as *WorldCat*, *Arts & Humanities Search* (the *FirstSearch* version of the *Arts and Humanities Citation Index*) and *Humanities Abstracts*.

Electronic formats, and libraries' increasing expenditure for them, have even greater potential for mischief in the economics of journal publishing. As part of a survey of historians' use of information sources in 1997, I asked our sampling which historical journals they consulted at least once every three months. Only two titles, *American Historical Review* and *Journal of American History*, were designated by more than ten percent of respondents (*Use of Historical Information Study*, Table 62). Apart from a very few journals of record, historians prefer specialized journals whose conversion into e-journals will come late, if at all. Many electronic journals require plugins on users' computers. In January 1998 the Council of the American Historical Association endorsed a statement of concern about electronic journal publishing that had grown out of a conference at Indiana University on the future of historical journals. The *Statement on Intellectual Diversity* by the Coalition of History Editors for Publishing in the Future deplored the tendency of publishers and journal aggregators to select for electronic publication only those titles for electronic publication with a sufficiently broad readership base. The editors warned that if the content of all existing history journals were not brought into the electronic medium "the current orphaning process of journals in area studies and in specialized themes will soon diminish the historical profession at large" ("Statement," 36).

Texas Tech's ventures into cooperative collection development have been almost exclusively in the electronic arena. Our recent membership in the Center for Research Libraries (CRL) is the principal exception. The study evaluating the benefits of CRL membership by Rutledge and Swindler argues that promotion and staff participation contribute significantly to making membership worthwhile for dues-paying libraries. In its one year as a member, Texas Tech has yet to participate in acquisitions balloting. Not that this is unusual: Donald Simpson, President of the CRL, reported in 1987 that only slightly more than half of members had participated in balloting the previous year (Rutledge & Swindler, 415-16).

Roberts

In Robert J. Wood's "paradigm shift" individual selectors are increasingly constrained by consortial arrangements concerning the choices and offerings of electronic products (Wood, 233-4); this shift has not occurred at Yale. In the selection, for example, of large general undergraduate article-index and full-text databases, initially, at least, selectors were steered in the direction of *ProQuest* as one of the choices of the NorthEast Research Libraries (NERL) consortium. However, for a variety of reasons, we elected to add Wilson Web databases, and eventually because of the dissatisfaction of local users, we recently switched to EBSCOHost's *Academic Search*. In this case, the decisions were made with broad input from selectors and other librarians, and reference and general funds, not subject funds, assumed the costs.

The real danger is, of course, that expensive general reference tools as well as increasing numbers of online journals and subject specific databases will drain funds from the budgets formerly devoted to the print and microform sources of a field like history. Historical materials are finally beginning to appear in electronic formats in appreciable quantities; meanwhile the number and importance of "traditional" materials show no signs of diminishing. So far, large academic libraries can still afford both traditional and electronic resources. In fact, electronic offerings in history–while growing in number–consumed only 1% to 3% of history budgets at Yale in recent years. But somehow budgetary resources for electronic resources must be created, and these will come either "off the top" or from individual selectors' budgets. To create such budget lines as well as to simplify the payment process, selectors at Yale give over into central coffers subject funds for subscriptions to general electronic resources that they support; these then become centrally funded. Depending on how a library creates budgets for electronic resources, even selectors in large research libraries may in the end see a relative diminution of their purchasing power and be forced to cut back on exactly those marginal materials that no one else is collecting. The process may be so slow and unconscious that the results will be invisible for years. The challenge for history selectors in large research libraries is to be aware of decisions to diminish the scope of collecting and to collaborate usefully to mitigate the consequences for the national collection.

Many electronic resources are purchased or leased through inter-institutional cooperation, but these represent a special kind of cooperative collection development. Libraries don't share electronic resources in the same way that print or microform resources are shared: a single copy or subscription meeting the needs of several institutions. Instead, libraries pool staff and budgetary resources to negotiate favorable pricing and license terms. This pooling does happen at the administrative level, but it is possible–at least in large research libraries–to involve selectors in decisions about what products to acquire and how much of their funds to contribute. Selectors must always weigh alternatives. In some cases, these electronic resources (for example, *Periodical Contents Index* or *Arts and Humanities Citation Index*) enhance the value and utility of existing collections, and the spending of funds on this sort of collection enhancement is acceptable and indeed desirable.

If the CRL and other regional centers assume a larger role in specialized collecting, it is still possible and indeed advisable to involve subject librarians in the process of recommending purchases to CRL and voting their preferences on the ballots. I have had some success using this way of getting CRL to purchase microform collections necessary for the research of Yale graduate students. The democratic balloting process can, however, be at odds with individual member libraries' interests; the first two parts of a desired collection passed the balloting process and were purchased, but subsequent parts did not win enough votes to be purchased with available funds and were deferred for consideration the following year.

HOW MUCH INFLUENCE DOES THE SELECTOR HAVE IN THE ORGANIZATION OVER PROCESSING AND ACCESS PRIORITIES?

Successful cooperative collecting requires not only shared acquisition of materials but also shared information via catalog records and ILL policies that make works usable.

Niessen

Alongside economies of collecting, the selector must wrestle with economies in the processing of material. Calculations about the dollar cost of cataloging, catalog records, and even title tracings can lead to decisions of great interest to the selector and to potential borrowers. Does the set or series have a parent record in the catalog so that the selector can identify gaps in the holdings in order to address them? Can the local or remote user determine whether we own a particular item by author or title, or only by volume number? The Bibliographic Services Department rightly has decisive say in such decisions, since these departments dispose of their staff time and can judge the monetary cost of various options, but selectors need to be aware of their implications. collections also raise a quandary: even in the case of rare and nationally significant titles, does the expense of cataloging or providing them with the necessary preservation treatment stand in a satisfactory relation to the item's expected use value? Three years ago we acquired a six hundred volume collection of Russian books. I'm still struggling with these questions as the borderline remnants of the collection await disposition.

The Achilles' heel of reliance on a special non-circulating collection for part of collection development is the fact that it may not provide satisfactory access for local students and faculty. Even more evidently, non-circulating volumes are of limited value for the distributed national collection we are discussing. Granting physical access by a mobile researcher to a stationary collection is admittedly one form of resource sharing. Our library recognizes this through its support of modest research grants to our faculty for the support of travel to out-of-town collections. However, cooperative collection development presumes that resources themselves should be mobile or at least nearby. The more geographically remote a library is, as in the case of

Texas Tech in West Texas, the more important the role of interlibrary loan for cooperative collection development.

Interlibrary loan is another area of library operations where the selector's preference for resource sharing may encounter countervailing arguments aimed at maximizing efficiency. OCLC is the hands-down favorite of ILL staff in seeking resources outside the local collection, because of the convenience of patron-initiated requests through *WorldCat*, ease in locating holding libraries, messaging, and a streamlined fee management system (Jackson). If staff concede any fall-back option at all, it may be the expensive but almost equally convenient British Document Supply Centre. Staff may be reluctant to add RLIN, CRL, or even more specialized sources to the search routine of the paraprofessionals and student assistants who do most of the searching.

Selectors can play a role in interlibrary cooperation even where their budget, status within their library, or the overall size of a library collection and its budget would not seem to justify it. I am referring to the AAU/ARL German Resources Project *http/lcweb.loc.gov/loc/german/*, in which I have participated as a Texas Tech representative and working group member although "only" as a selector, and one from a library with relatively modest means, at that. Though my library is the smallest of those represented in the Project's Collection Development Working Group, my situation is not unique because the head of the Document Delivery Working Group is a selector and the head of the Bibliographic Control Working Group comes from an arts and letters college. As we have worked to put in place various initiatives over the past year, it has been interesting to note the low profile or lack of official participation of some major libraries whose collections and information needs would make them logical partners. As the results of our work have become better known, it is good to see that many additional libraries have joined us in recent months. The professional leave and travel money that facilitated my participation should be seen above all as an institutional contribution to this cooperative project. The participation of selectors in functional working groups outside their job descriptions highlights the interest of selectors in the collaboration of all functional units of their libraries in cooperation. Finally, when smaller libraries make their staff available for such projects it shows that these libraries can participate in this way, as well as through formal operational commitments.

Roberts

Individual selectors in large research libraries have varying levels of influence over institutional priorities for processing and access. Area studies specialists at Yale, who often control their own cataloguing units, are better placed to enter into and bring to fruition cooperative collecting programs than are selectors whose acquisitions flow through large general processing units that serve many units and whose priorities are set by others. The need to devote cataloguing resources to internal projects such as retrospective conversion can mitigate–at least temporarily–the success of cooperative ventures.

Selectors sometimes advocate, strenuously though not always successfully, access strategies that would exploit existing cooperative arrangements or foster awareness and use of new ones. Making library users and staff aware of the CRL's resources is an excellent case in point. As the selector for history, a discipline whose practitioners stand to benefit from CRL's holdings, I spent some years and more dollars trying to get tapes of the CRL catalog loaded into our OPAC so that users could see immediately the full range of available resources. The tape load was immanent for several years, but in the end it ran afoul of the more urgent priorities of our systems office and a host of probably excellent database-maintenance reasons for not loading them. Our current solution, as we wait for the capability of broadcast searching of Z39.50 databases, is to put a prominent link to the CRL catalog in the Web pages where we list the catalogs considered integral to Yale's bibliographic resources.

Selectors, as most of the literature emphasizes, cannot single-handedly achieve inter-institutional collaboration. Whether they initiate cooperative collecting projects or join in existing ones, broad local administrative commitment is vital. Between their clear traditional responsibilities and demanding new duties in reference and outreach, selectors need support to accommodate additional external activities that have local consequences and whose payoff is distant and unpredictable. Much energy in research libraries these days is directed towards developing digital libraries and cooperative purchasing of electronic resources; much less is devoted to cooperative collection development for more traditional materials.[3] Gaining support for engaging in cooperative collection development is one of the challenges.

WHAT IS THE CONSTITUENCY FOR WHOM THE COLLECTION IS BEING BUILT?

Due to budgetary scarcity or local tradition, faculty may control expenditures and prioritize material according to pedagogical relevance or their research, leading to the neglect of broader needs. The library can better build collections serving a wider community if selection decisions reside with the librarian.

Niessen

I referred in an earlier section to the evolution of the procedures for history selection at Texas Tech. The library at one time turned over the task of selection, and the disposition of the history fund, to the history department. This had the political benefit for the library that the history department could know that the fund was at its disposal and its decisions were final. In theory, nobody is a better judge of what is needed than the professors who know the literature, conduct research, and are frustrated in their teaching if their students can't get what they need. But academic departments are very political entities, with a strict hierarchy of various ranks of students and faculty. An ostensibly equitable system at Texas Tech provided that the history fund be divided up into equal allocations for each of the Americanists and larger amounts for each of the non-Americanists, the rationale being that the fields of the latter were less well served by the library's approval plan. A departmental committee determined the size of the individual allocations, and a grad student paid by the department collected the faculty's orders and forwarded them to the library.

One problem with our system of faculty entitlements was that the distribution was not truly equitable because the publishing universe and the approval plan profile were stronger in some fields than in others. A bigger problem was the inequality of faculty information needs and demands, because some were more active researchers than others and some designed their courses in such a way that their students made greater demands on the library. This led in turn to the greatest problem, namely that some professors never used their entitlements, which were returned to the departmental pot for the purchase of big-ticket items. In some years, a significant portion of the fund would go for specialized monographic sets or microform collections that would be used only occasionally or by only one professor, while the librarian lacked resources to address shortages of circulating materials that were encountered at the reference desk.

In place of the old system, I have maintained control of the allocation within the library and seen the percentage of orders based on faculty recommendations decline in these five years from nearly 100% to 60%. There was some opposition to the new system, but it is generally accepted today, for several reasons. I determine my spending priorities in consultation with the departmental library committee, invite faculty recommendations and distribute vendor slips to facilitate them, and deliver a spreadsheet with my history orders (identifying requesters for each title that had one) at the end of each year.

I have neglected two additional arguments for a predominant role of the faculty in selection: with small budgets the local ordering must be very selective, and small libraries are less likely to have librarians with the requisite skills and expertise. Where book budgets have stagnated, even very large libraries feel the need to address the most strongly expressed local needs rather than attempt to build a balanced collection or one that fills a function in a national collection. The librarian is more likely than the faculty to select with a national collection in mind. The stronger the degree of faculty control, the weaker a library's commitment will be to cooperative collection development.

Roberts

Collection development librarians in large academic institutions build collections for a broad constituency, one that they themselves help to define. The local constituents are, of course, among the most important. In the Yale Library system, faculty members neither directly select library materials, control expenditures, nor prioritize purchases according to their criteria of relevance. Departments as well as individual professors have a variety of ways of approaching library acquisitions: participating in library committees; making several requests/suggestions per week; sending shopping bags of review copies, or simply taking rich holdings for granted. Subject librarians assume the responsibility of maintaining awareness of research, teaching, and programmatic needs as well as breadth of coverage in general. They consult history department and other faculty members routinely about programmatic directions (new hires, new courses, new majors) as well as on the appropriateness of serials subscriptions/cancellations and the purchase of expensive microform as well as–increasingly–electronic resources.

Collection development for a large academic research library has a kind of built-in corrective to narrowly local preoccupations. Selectors for a major research collection are expected to consider other constituencies; traditional missions and adequate budgets afford the possibility of thinking broadly and comprehensively about collection development and acting on the dictum that "there is no access without ownership." The collections themselves resemble constituents. I continue, for example, strong collecting in British history, one of Yale's traditional strengths, despite the fluctuations of the program and teaching strengths and despite worries of some that British history is declining as an academic field. The notion of being a library of record carries an almost automatic concern for the national collection. This kind of broad thinking goes beyond mere pride in some worn-out notion of a comprehensive collection.

The national collection thus holds a place in the collection development and management strategies of selectors at large research libraries. My colleagues and I are still dutifully and comprehensively collecting in certain fields, like Rhaeto-Romanic literature, sigillography, and etiquette, that are remnants of older RLG assignments of "primary collecting responsibilities." With adequate funds, one can afford to subscribe to an obscure local European history journal for its relevance to the collection and because no other library reports holdings in the bibliographic utilities. An instance of major research libraries' responsibility for the national collection is evident in the large cooperative and federally funded preservation microfilming projects of the late 1980s and early 1990s. In an NEH-funded, RLG-sponsored filing project, Yale and Berkeley divided the field of American history at the Mississippi for the purpose of filming brittle books. These programs may not fully qualify as cooperative collection development, but they surely embodied cooperating at the national level. At Yale, subject selectors/bibliographers were closely involved in the genesis of and item-level decision-making for these programs. The experience of making reformatting decisions about brittle books in HEN-funded European, French, and British microfilming projects at Yale early in the 1990s altered permanently my preservation strategies. The national interest now figures in deciding whether to film a brittle book or simply photocopy it for the stacks.

Geography can be an important factor in cooperative collecting. Where consortia flourish in states or large urban areas, other research libraries are important regional constituents. Compared to some major academic libraries, Yale is somewhat isolated geographically from the cooperative arrangements in cities like Boston and New York. While there are certain specialties I rely on Harvard or New York Public to support, there are few actual agreements that figure prominently in collection development for history.

DOES THE MODEL OF DISTRIBUTED AND DIGITAL COLLECTIONS SUIT THE WAY HISTORIANS WORK?

Today's historians are trained in a traditional research library to browse in a physical collection of books and journals. Can they adjust to new working conditions, waiting for interlibrary loan or working with digital files? Cooperative collection development increases the need for user instruction.

Roberts

From the point of view of historians accustomed to working in major libraries, relying on other collections can limit the horizons of research at various stages in various ways. Historians work in many different ways, depending often on the kind of documentation they use for their research. Intellectual historians who focus on close reading of small numbers of individual texts might be content with the analytical power of digital resources; social and economic historians often need to go directly to the sources, spending months in foreign archives or at least poring over microfilms of archival documents. Their primary concern is with primary and secondary sources. For nearly all historians, retrospective materials are vital. Recent studies indicate–and my observations in recent years bear it out–that historians will change only slowly 'their ways of working and their relationship to libraries (Delgado & Lynch, 245-59).

In addition, different phases of historians' work require different levels of access to documents. Exploring topics for research often requires ready access to a broad range of materials and a mastery or at least survey of a large number of documents. Historians, for example, shaping a topic on attitudes towards imperial possessions or towards health and disease in the nineteenth century, may need to range over many volumes of numerous nineteenth century periodicals. For this reason, faculty at large research libraries are loathe even to have such materials transferred to off-site shelving facilities, much less get them on ILL or use them elsewhere. Scholars at smaller institutions must travel to major collections to do such work.

Some phases of actual research are best done with unimpeded access to research materials fundamental to the topic, whether these be printed sources, archival documents, or microforms of the latter. Interlibrary loan (except from CRL) is often inadequate for this purpose because of restrictions on quantity and time. Most libraries will only lend five microfiche or reels of film for a limited time and require that those borrowed be returned before more can be sent. When a collection contains hundreds of fiche or reels, such rules produce inefficiency and frustration for historians. Historians do, of course, find ILL useful in the advanced stages of their research; ILL brings them highly specialized monographs, articles, small numbers of microforms. General reference work, however, makes one acutely aware of how many faculty and students do not plan or simply do not have time for the two-to-three week ILL turn-around time. It is often not really a question of planning: the final stages of editing and proofreading a manuscript, despite the best planning, frequently end in an anxious last-minute scramble.

At the undergraduate level, ILL as currently administered is not an acceptable means of access even for infrequently used primary research materials like texts and documents sets in print or on microform. Instructional activities make abundantly clear that, especially for undergraduates, the rhythms of the academic calendar and assignments and restrictive due dates render ILL useless for providing primary materials for may research projects (Dannelly, 253). At Yale, undergraduates are encouraged to do real research in primary sources. The materials need to be on hand to be explored for potential topics and then to be used at the rhythm of undergraduate life, that is, sandwiched in with other course assignments. Senior essay or thesis writers rarely have the option of focussing their entire time for two weeks on the films that have just arrived on ILL. The culture of history research at Yale is such that undergraduates are encouraged to follow their own interests, often whether or not there are sources to work with. Faculty do not always try to steer them to materials we own. Thus we sometimes acquire microform collections in core fields even if they are held at CRL or elsewhere.

Library collections support not only research and teaching but also the work of history departments. One of my functions as subject liaison is to help sell the institution to candidates for faculty positions. Closer liaison ties with history departments reveal how heavily departments rely on the strength of library collections as a recruiting tool; in a certain sense these ties render selectors complicit in the larger system–noted in the literature–of recruitment and measurement, excellence and prestige, that drives research universities today. It is not only a question of competition and library pride in self-sufficiency (Wood, 235), but also of institutional success and all that hangs on it. Successful faculty hires maintain successful programs; both draw good students and graduate students and sustain institutional prestige. The quality of library collections and allocations are tightly entwined with this cyclical process.

Niessen

Historians place large amounts of data into a large context of related data. Concepts and subject terms are often themselves the object of interpretation, so that historians are frustrated with controlled vocabulary headings. While document surrogates presume to capture the "aboutness" of remote resources, historians value serendipity and may think spatially rather than conceptually about their information resources (Gilmore & Case, Tibbo). For all these reasons, the traditional historian's ideal "laboratory" environment is an eclectic and, above all, large collection in which one can physically browse the publications. Relying to a large extent on metadata in local catalogs, bibliographic utilities, and indexes to identify much of the material for request from a remote location is considered unsatisfactory. It is likely that many senior historians are accustomed to work this way and encourage their graduate students to do the same. Many of you have experienced the political sensitivity of talk about remote storage! Young faculty likely join the department at smaller schools directly from large Ph.D.-granting institutions that afford the luxury of magnificent collections, and they may be in for a shock.

The younger faculty have the advantage of greater familiarity with computers, the Internet, and databases. Accustomed to using these tools in other aspects of their lives, they are ready to experiment with their efficacy for their professional work. Institutional incentives for distance education and web teaching, Ethernet connections to faculty offices, and the conversion of many tools to online access with a site license for all local users regardless of location, reinforce the faculty's electronic skills. A big question, as Susanne Roberts also notes, is whether the tempo of student and faculty research can be reconciled to periodic waits for material that must be ordered from offsite. I would argue that historians who must learn to accommodate this reality will do so and will appreciate library instruction that helps their students do it, too. Library instruction for history alerts professors as well as students to the superiority of database searching over browsing for many research needs and demonstrates the use of bibliographic utilities and archival databases to locate remote resources. Through newsletters and classes we can also highlight digital treasure troves such as *American Memory* and *JSTOR* whose use is transforming historical teaching and research. We tell our faculty recruits not only about our traditional resources, but also about our strong commitment to service and our electronic offerings.

Historians are not collaborative in their work in precisely the way that natural scientists are; historical research and synthesis are more typically solitary and individual activities. However, the invisible college of historians has never been more important for professional life. I sit on the Executive Committee of *H-Net: Humanities & Social Sciences OnLine*. H-Net is a virtual organization of more than one hundred moderated Internet mailing lists, mostly in fields of history, with 100,000 subscribers worldwide. Roughly one third of historians in American higher education subscribe to one or more of our lists, and somewhat less than one third of all subscribers reside outside the United States. These historians come from a higher percentage of modestly endowed institutions than the leadership of the profession would lead one to suspect. Recently the Executive Committee held a retreat at Michigan State University, which provides much financial support for H-Net and houses its primary computer hosts. At our meeting with the Dean who is responsible for much of our financial support, it was striking to realize that Michigan State was the largest institution represented on our Executive Committee, and Texas Tech is the third largest. Their constrained financial circumstances may make

H-Netters more open to networking and new models of research and teaching.

The face of the historical profession presented by H-Net is different from that of the American Historical Association: less tied to large institutions and traditional measures of excellence, and above all more reliant upon networking and resource sharing. This face is supportive of the role of second tier institutions in cooperative collection development.

CONCLUSION

Subject librarians contribute to the quality of cooperative collection development through their knowledge of the literature, their methodology, understanding of working historians, and their concern for balance and quality in the local and distributed collection. Cooperative collecting ventures, while not yet appropriate for all subject areas, should not fail to integrate subject specialists and their valuable expertise. Selectors in small and medium sized research libraries can contribute to cooperative ventures in well defined areas where local interests mandate strong collections, and they can contribute staff time to organizational efforts such as the German Resources Project that do not have implications for local expenditures.

Libraries can maximize the contributions of subject librarians to cooperative collection development in several ways. Administrators must create environments that allow subject specialists time to analyze collections, to develop expertise and breadth of vision about collections and constituencies, and to focus on collaboration with other libraries. Administrators should foster structures and consultative practices that encourage and support collaboration. They can align institutional access and processing priorities with cooperative enterprises. Budgeting strategies can further enable subject librarians to collaborate in collection building if budgets are subject or selector-based and if approval plan profiling is under their control. Selectors with adequate control over budgetary resources are able to maintain collection breadth and develop depth as appropriate. And administrators can support cooperative endeavors such as the CRL and the German Resources Project in support of interlibrary goals that transcend cost-benefit analysis.

Growing expenditures for electronic resources should be monitored with sensitivity to the impact on subject-related budgets and to the continuing need in some disciplines for strong support of traditional resources.

History selectors themselves need not only to be vigilant about the consequences of choosing electronic resources over others lest the marginal materials that serve a far-ranging and eclectic discipline disappear from the national collection, but also to monitor their print collections to avoid needless redundancy of specialized material. While remaining attuned to the work habits of their constituents, history librarians need to seize every opportunity to educate their readers about the long-term benefits to the discipline of cooperative collection development.

Both libraries and historians pursue their goals in a variety of institutions. Most libraries rely to a greater or lesser extent on cooperative arrangements to meet their needs. The prestige of size, wealth, and tradition at the largest research universities offer great benefits, both for faculty and for the national collection. At the same time, library writers have warned of the implications of these positive traits for the readiness of the library to respond flexibly to change. Libraries with smaller, less comprehensive collections may need to collaborate more energetically to make research materials available. Models of cooperative collection development must be developed for different disciplines and types of libraries.

The success of cooperative collection development for electronic publications has primarily benefited the sciences, because they are journal-based disciplines. As we noted at the beginning, historians are unusually reliant on monographs. Even if improvements in ergonomics, video display, and desktop publishing make electronic monographs more feasible in the future, historians' need for diverse retrospective and foreign-language materials will preserve their predominant demand for physical books. From 1986 to 1997, ARL libraries' monographic expenditures rose only half as fast as monographic unit costs, 30% to 62%. Consequently, monographic purchases declined 14% (*Monograph and Serial Costs in ARL Libraries, 1986-1997*). United Nations statistics for the corresponding period indicate an increase in the annual number of new titles published worldwide (*Statistical Yearbook*). Historians are therefore increasingly reliant on resource sharing. Library budgets have, to date, permitted a spontaneous, undirected sort of cooperative collection development that has helped this system work. The continuation of current trends will increase the pressure on libraries, especially smaller ones, to overcome the obstacles we have described in this paper to active cooperation in the building of history collections.

NOTES

1. The discussion logs of the list may be reached from its Internet site at *http://www.h-net.msu.edu/~histbibl/*.

2. By the "national collection" we mean the aggregate of circulating–and thus available to practicing historians–holdings for history in North American libraries as measured by the North American title count. The "distributed national collection" has roughly the same meaning, but has a slightly more active, cooperative connotation.

3. One interesting exception to this statement is the user-initiated borrowing arrangement currently being developed by the Yale, Columbia and University of Pennsylvania libraries, which enjoys library and university support at the highest levels. Although it is a resource-sharing reader service rather than cooperative collection development enterprise, if it manages to reduce the interlibrary borrowing time it could have implications for the latter.

REFERENCES

Association of Research Libraries, Table: *Monograph and Serial Costs in ARL Libraries, 1986-1997*. Internet: *http://www.arl.org/stats/arlstat/1997_t2.html*

Collection management for the 21st century: A handbook for librarians. Edited by G. E. Gorman and Ruth H. Miller. The Greenwood library management collection, 0894-2986. Westport, Conn.: Greenwood Press, 1997.

Dannelly, Gay N. "Cooperation Is the Future of Collection Management and Development: OhioLINK and CIC." In *Collection management for the 21st century: A handbook for librarians*. Edited by G. E. Gorman and Ruth H. Miller. The Greenwood library management collection, 0894-2986. Westport, Conn.: Greenwood Press, 1997.

Delgado, Roberto and Lynch, Beverly P. "Future Historians: Their Quest for Information." *College & Research Libraries* 60, no. 3 (1999): 245-259.

Gilmore, Matthew B., and Donald O. Case. "Historians, Books, Computers, and the Library." *Library Trends* 40, no. 4 (Spring 1992), 667-96.

Hazen, Dan C. "Cooperative Collection Development: Compelling Theory, Inconsequential Results?" In *Collection management for the 21st century: A handbook for librarians*. Edited by G. E. Gorman and Ruth H. Miller. The Greenwood library management collection, 0894-2986. Westport, Conn.: Greenwood Press, 1997.

Jackson, Mary E. "Loan Stars: ILL Comes of Age." *Library Journal* 123 (February 1, 1998): 44-7.

Rutledge, John and Luke Swindler. "Evaluating Membership in a Resource-Sharing Program: The Center for Research Libraries." *College & Research Libraries* 49, no. 9 (1988): 409-24.

"Statement on Intellectual Diversity by the Coalition of History Editors for Publishing in the Future." *Perspectives*. February 1998: 36.

Tibbo, Helen R. *Abstracting Information Retrieval, and the Humanities: Providing*

Access to Historical Literature. ACRL Publications in Librarianship, no. 48. Chicago: American Library Association, 1993.

United Nations. *Statistical Yearbook.* New York: United Nations, 1992-.

Use of Historical Information Study. [Dublin, OH: OCLC, 1997]. An unpublished report tabulating the responses of a survey conducted by James P. Niessen of Texas Tech University and Richard Van Gorden of OCLC in the spring of 1997.

Wiemers, Eugene L., Jr. "Budgeting Methods for Collection Management." In *Collection Management for the 1990s*. Edited by Joseph J. Branin. Chicago and London: American Library Association, 1993.

Wolff, Milton T., ed. "Cooperative Collection Management: Online Discussion." In *Cooperative Collection Development: Significant Trends and Issues.* Edited by Donald B. Simpson. *Collection Management*, vol. 23, no. 4 (1988): 59-93.

Wood, Richard J., "The Axioms, Barriers, and Components of Cooperative Collection Development." In *Collection Management for the 21st Century: A Handbook for Librarians*. Edited by G. E. Gorman and Ruth H. Miller. The Greenwood library management collection, 0894-2986. Westport, Conn.: Greenwood Press, 1997.

Collecting Material on Natural Disasters: A Case Study in Co-Operative Collections Development

Linwood DeLong

Natural disasters are an inevitable aspect of human existence and when they occur near a populated center they result in a complex set of changes and disruptions to normal living patterns.[1] One researcher has noted that "in the last two decades, three million people were killed and an additional one billion people were affected by natural disasters. . . . Scientists predict that the social and economic costs associated with natural disasters will continue to rise."[2]

After the initial waves of disaster response teams and relief assistance organizations have sprung into action, collections development librarians should begin to take notice, because almost every natural disaster also generates a large number of studies, reports, investigations, and a lot of media coverage. It sometimes spawns citizen initiatives and it not infrequently initiates a complicated game of political maneuvering among politicians at different levels of government. The task of collecting material on a natural disaster poses some interesting challenges and, to be successful, requires many levels of cooperation. This paper will focus on the question of political cooperation, which can mean cooperation with government organizations, with indepen-

---

Linwood DeLong is affiliated with the University of Winnipeg Library, 515 Portage Avenue, Winnipeg, Manitoba, Canada, R3B 2E9 (e-mail: linwood.delong@uwinnipeg.ca).

[Haworth co-indexing entry note]: "Collecting Material on Natural Disasters: A Case Study in Co-Operative Collections Development." DeLong, Linwood. Co-published simultaneously in *Collection Management* (The Haworth Information Press, an imprint of The Haworth Press, Inc.) Vol. 24, No. 1/2, 2000, pp. 175-183; and: *Creating New Strategies for Cooperative Collection Development* (ed: Milton T. Wolf and Marjorie E. Bloss) The Haworth Information Press, an imprint of The Haworth Press, Inc., 2000, pp. 175-183. Single or multiple copies of this article are available for a fee from The Haworth Document Delivery Service [1-800-342-9678, 9:00 a.m. - 5:00 p.m. (EST). E-mail address: getinfo@haworthpressinc.com].

© 2000 by The Haworth Press, Inc. All rights reserved.

dent bodies established by the government, and with the informal political sector with its rich mixture of lobby groups and protesters.

Obtaining key government reports is usually not difficult. My library, The University of Winnipeg Library, is not an official depository library for the publications of any level of government, but letters or phone calls to the mayor's' office, to provincial and federal government offices and to the International Joint Commission resulted in our library being placed on the mailing lists for many of the significant reports from these bodies concerning our most recent natural disaster, the Red River Flood of 1997.

Typically, however these are summary reports, sometimes even political compromises that gloss over contentious issues, and they rarely reflect the full dimension of a government's response to a major disaster. A clearer picture emerges as one begins to search for detailed responses. The report from the State Emergency Management Agency of Missouri regarding the Mississippi Flood of 1993[3] lists fourteen major state departments as well as numerous sub-departments or agencies that were affected: the Department of Corrections, because a prison had to be evacuated; the Department of Mental Health, because of the necessity of "ensuring safety and shelter of clients housed in DMH facilities" (p. 56), and the Department of Higher Education, because the University of Missouri was felt to be "an unbiased source of information for Missouri citizens" (p. 51), just to name a few less obvious government departments. Frequently each state or provincial department will be required to issue at least an internal report on its disaster-related activities, and these reports may contain more detailed data and more detailed financial reporting than is found in the summary documents.

Furthermore, decisions by one government department or agency may have an impact on the manner in which other agencies deal with a disaster. As Stanley Changnon has noted, in the case of the 1993 Mississippi Flood some of the early problems were the inaccurate predictions of flood levels by the National Weather Service and the flood pronouncements by the U.S. Army Corps of Engineers.[4] Thus to understand the full magnitude of what happened in this flood it is not enough to know how much rain fell when and where, or how high the water levels became, it is also important to understand that key decisions about the re-routing of motor vehicle and railway traffic as well as the temporary stationing of river barges were delayed, because agencies assigned to these tasks were working with incorrect data. Federal officials at St. Louis and Des Moines issued several flood forecasts that contradicted each other, resulting not only in confused responses (Changnon p. 309) but also in an undermining of confidence in government departments at a time when it was very important that the general public pay close attention to what it was being told by government officials.

A good research collection pertaining to an event such as the 1993 flood would include as many disaster forecasts or new releases as possible, as well as the documentation on how government departments or agencies responded to or worked with this information. Obtaining information at this level may require working out formal or informal exchange agreements with librarians within these organizations, perhaps even initiating requests for information under access to information legislation.

Many natural disasters are also political disasters, or at least complicated political chess matches, as different levels of government either try to score political points by offering levels of compensation which the other level of government must match, or else seek justifiable reasons to hold compensation at low levels, knowing that the amount and form of compensation in any disaster immediately becomes a precedent for the next disaster. The Red River Flood of 1997 in Manitoba was no exception, and a key component in our collection relating to the 1997 Flood is the bundle of press releases issued by the federal and provincial governments relating to flood compensation formulae and payments, as well as press releases from opposition parties who chose to criticize the provincial government over what appeared to be an inadequate compensation strategy. Press releases from opposition parties are not normally part of a government documents depository program, and it was necessary to find a contact within the public relations office of the opposition parties who would look out for and send copies of press releases on this topic.

With advances in Internet technology it would be possible to establish a link in one's online catalogue between these documents and the records of the debates in both the federal and state or provincial legislatures regarding a disaster and its aftermath. However one chooses to arrange one's collection, it is important to collect material about all levels and forms of the political debate concerning a natural disaster and to seek the assistance of all participants in this discourse:

politicians of all stripes as well as organizations or individuals who make submissions to government hearings.

The political fallout from the 1997 flood in Manitoba resulted in much more than the infighting between different levels of government. One of the unusual features of Winnipeg's flood protection strategy is its Floodway, a water diversion canal almost the size of the Suez Canal that extends around one side of the city. It can be opened to accept excess water, whenever the Red River threatens to flood the city. To protect the Floodway against possible ice damage, the engineers had to design an unusual flood gate which, when opened, temporarily creates a backflow from the river to the surrounding areas, before the water starts to flow into the canal. The communities that surround Winnipeg thus find themselves in a tug-of-war situation with the city because the opening up of the Floodway, which saves the city from millions of dollars of damage, can result in an inundation of some of the surrounding communities. The Emergency Measures Organization flood forecasting authority did its best to calculate the expected water levels in all areas that might be affected by the flood, but for reasons that are still not understood, though hotly debated, the water level in one community rose several feet in one hour, just at the time that the Floodway was opened, resulting in a flooding of most of that community.[5]

Although the provincial government agreed to establish an independent commission to determine whether or not the Floodway was operated properly and whether the flood prediction authorities had done their work properly, citizens groups in these communities quickly became very distrustful of the composition of this review commission, accusing the government of filling it with political appointees. The citizens groups decided to hire their own consultants to prepare their own reports. Obtaining copies of these reports is a bit of a challenge, because citizen initiatives have no deposit mechanism for their reports, and frequently do not see university libraries as a logical place in which to conduct their attacks on the integrity of the government. It was necessary, therefore, to follow the local news media coverage of the flood very closely and to try to obtain contact information about any group or association that was planning to issue its own report on the flood. For our collection on the 1997 flood it is important to have items that document public perception of an event as well as scientific reports that may refute these perceptions.

Overall, the news media are a very important source of information about reports on a natural disaster, because affected groups or individuals often turn there to air their grievances, just as government departments or independent organizations use the news media to reply to criticisms or allegations. News media coverage also has the potential to strongly influence both the public's perception of a disaster and the manner in which politicians and government departments respond to this perception. Headlines that describe a flood as "a heroic struggle against the forces of nature" reinforce attitudes that the next flood must be fought with even greater vigour. It was only after the 1993 flood waters subsided and presidential review commissions were established that government policy began to shift from fighting floods, a policy that had also been strongly urged by the U.S. Corps of Army Engineers after the 1927 flood (Changnon, p. 247), to living beside the flood: encouraging farmers not to farm in marginal, flood-prone lands; restoring some land as wetlands; engaging in buyout programs to encourage people not to live in these lands; and ultimately recognizing that the Mississippi will flood again. Stanley Changnon's major study on the 1993 Mississippi flood notes that "news outlets, whether national or local, gave scant attention to the policy issues raised by the flood" (p. 229) and that coverage of other environmental disasters follows a similar pattern. Given these weaknesses in much of the media coverage, but also its potential to influence public perceptions about a disaster, librarians should preserve this political raw material. Libraries should try to assemble as many clippings files as possible (especially from local newspapers that are not indexed by commercial indexes) and encourage local televisions to preserve as much of their news footage as possible. Collection development librarians should bear in mind that documenting perceptions and interpretations of major catastrophic events is just as important as assembling collections of scientific data and reports.

The tremendous social and economic costs that are associated with natural disasters have led governments in different countries to establish disaster-related think tanks and major databases. Canada has organizations such as the Institute for Catastrophic Loss Reduction and the Canadian National Committee for the International Decade for Natural Disaster Reduction, Australia has its Emergency Management Australia, and the United States has organizations such as the Federal Emergency Management Agency, the National Hazards Research Center in

Boulder, Colorado, and the Scientific Assessment and Strategy Team (SAST). These organizations typically consist of representatives from major government departments, the academic community, private industry and non-government or not-for-profit organizations and are active not only in organizing conferences and workshops, assisting governments in formulating strategies to deal with and mitigate disasters, but also in issuing research papers, or at the least, newsletters that describe their activities. The SAST, which has assembled a 250 gigabyte, multi-disciplinary database pertaining to the upper Mississippi River Basin, distributes its information through the Internet (http://edcwww2.cr.usgs.gov/sast-home.html).

The lengthy report by the SAST on their efforts to assemble their database reads like a case study in co-operative collection development between scientists and agencies such as FEMA, the U.S. Army Corps of Engineers or the U.S. Geological Survey. It is sobering to read that there is "no clearing house or defined point of contact" for many of their data sets, that some data was obtained by chance, and that there is still a significant body of unpublished reports, proposals and plans that "should be catalogued and listed in a data directory that can be assessed through a readily available clearinghouse" (see "Database Development" at http://edcwww2.cr.usgs.gov/www/c2.htm). The Institute for Catastrophic Loss Reduction follows a similar co-operative approach. It contacted more than one thousand individuals in research and disaster management communities and it works closely with Emergency Preparedness Canada and the National Research Council.[6]

Clearly no university library can or should replicate the work that was undertaken by the SAST or any similar data collection organization, but libraries can ensure that they have detailed documentation on the scope and content of these databases. Research libraries or library consortia should actively cooperate with these organizations and ensure that research libraries form part of the information grid to which data collection organizations turn in their collection activities. At a time when government libraries are being downsized or eliminated, research libraries can co-operate with specialized libraries to ensure that important collections of historical data or information are preserved, organized and made accessible to a wider public.

Several specialized libraries devoted to natural disaster issues already exist. There is the group of approximately 40 libraries maintained by the U.S. Corps of Army Engineers (searchable at *http://lepac1.brodart.com/search/um/)* and the library maintained by the Natural Hazards Center (*http://www.Colorado.EDU/hazards/litbase/hazlib.htm*). According to its web site, the latter contains a database of about "17,000 reports, articles, brochures, and books, as well as a diverse assortment of . . . [other] publications." A search on the database of the USCAE on topics such as the Mississippi Flood of 1993 or the Exxon Valdez disaster yields about twenty-five documents. A similar number of hits results when one searches the Hazlit database of the Natural Hazards Center, though there is curiously virtually no overlap between the search results from these two databases. This may in part be explained by the limitations of the current retrieval software of the Hazlit database (each search retrieves only a portion of the total relevant holdings), but one should bear in mind that while university library catalogues in states that border the Mississippi typically list between 30 and 50 items pertaining to the 1993 Mississippi Flood, the University of Alaska catalogue lists over 700 items pertaining to the Exxon Valdez disaster. Both the USCAE and Hazlit databases contain some documents pertaining to the Red River Flood of 1997, but only a few documents pertaining to the Quebec ice storm of 1998 and, generally speaking, little in the way of grey literature or media reports.

The scope of issues raised by natural disasters and the breadth of information that researchers require is immense, because of the far-reaching impact of these events. The body of fresh water that flowed down the Mississippi River and into the Gulf of Mexico during the Flood of 1993 could be traced halfway up the eastern coast of the United States (Changnon, p. 279). One major study on the 1993 Flood includes not only detailed meteorological and hydrological reports but also investigations of crop insurance and flood insurance policies, land use policies, regional and national transportation systems, and agricultural production and housing policies. Even though the Winnipeg newspapers dubbed the 1997 Manitoba Flood the "Flood of the Century," scientists are studying the real possibility that the next flood could be much greater and are seeking to develop models to predict how great it could be, what precautions would be needed to respond to such an occurrence, and what hydrological or economic models can be used to calculate the effectiveness of different mitigation strategies. These scientists will also be visiting research libraries to see what material has been assembled to assist them with their investigations.

In conclusion, developing a meaningful collection of material pertaining to a natural disaster is an interesting challenge, because of the complexity of the environmental, economic, social and political issues created by a natural disaster and because of the large number of organizations that are drawn into the effort to deal with the short-term and long-term problems relating to the disaster. Obtaining this information is often not very expensive, but it does require a significant amount of cooperation among librarians in different organizations, who often have access to significant or unique materials, or between librarians and those who are directly dealing with the disaster. This can also mean attending scientific conferences and promoting the role of libraries in collecting material for disaster research, a role that conference organizers can easily overlook.

Academic libraries can play a unique role in this information gathering process because of their natural cooperative links with government and private research institutes, their established patterns for obtaining government reports and academic studies, and their political neutrality, which enables them to gather politically charged material that government libraries might be reluctant to collect. Apart from the obvious benefit of strengthening libraries' collections, assembling this material can also result in highly useful contacts between a library and the members of the public which it seeks to serve. It might even lead to increased funds for libraries to assemble such collections.

NOTES

1. An international Disasters Database has been created by the Centre for Research on the Epidemiology of Disaster at the Catholic University of Louvain, Belgium. A database of Canadian disasters has been produced by Emergency Preparedness Canada and is available at *http://www.epc-pcc.gc.ca/epc/epc_electronic_disaster_databa.html.* It is described in Carol Tudor, *EPC Electronic Disaster Database and Its Characteristics* (Project Report 97-1). Ottawa: Emergency Preparedness Canada, 1997.

2. Valerie Warmington, "Prevention Pays: The Socio-Economic Benefits of Preventing Disaster." International Decade for National Disaster Reduction: Canadian National Committee. Available: *http://www.rsc.ca/idndr/reports/prevent/toc.htm.*

3. State Emergency Management Agency, *The Response, Recovery and Lessons Learned from the Missouri Floods of 1993 and 1994.* Jefferson City, MO: The Agency, 1995.

4. Stanley Changnon, *The Great Flood of 1993: Causes, Impacts, and Responses* (Boulder: Westview Press, 1996): 27.

5. William Rannie, "The River Flood in Manitoba, Canada, *Prairie Perspectives: Geographical Essays,* vol. 1 (Winnipeg: University of Winnipeg, Dept. of Geography, 1998): 18.

6. Institute for Catastrophic Loss Reduction, "Building Resilient Communities," (Toronto: The Institute, 1999). See also the Placentia Bay Database, "a comprehensive inventory containing biological, physical, social and economic information for Placentia Bay [Newfoundland]" prepared by a private company, Chart, in co-operation with Environment Canada. Available: *http://www.chart.nf.net/database.htm.*

Dancing with Elephants: International Cooperation in an Interdependent (But Unequal) World

Dan Hazen

INTRODUCTION: COOPERATION AS PARADIGM, PANACEA, AND PROBLEM

Cooperation among North American libraries has a checkered past. Every clear-cut success, for example the National Union Catalog or the Name Authority Cooperative Program (NACO), seems to be offset by an effort of at best ambiguous results, say the Farmington Plan or the Conspectus.[1] The rhetoric proclaiming a new library paradigm of cooperative collection development, of "access rather than ownership," remains in the ascendant. Nonetheless, many of today's most promising initiatives are still built more around bibliographic technol-

Dan Hazen is affiliated with Harvard University.

[Haworth co-indexing entry note]: "Dancing with Elephants: International Cooperation in an Interdependent (But Unequal) World." Hazen, Dan. Co-published simultaneously in *Collection Management* (The Haworth Information Press, an imprint of The Haworth Press, Inc.) Vol. 24, No. 3/4, 2000, pp. 185-213; and: *Creating New Strategies for Cooperative Collection Development* (ed: Milton T. Wolf and Marjorie E. Bloss) The Haworth Information Press, an imprint of The Haworth Press, Inc., 2000, pp. 185-213. Single or multiple copies of this article are available for a fee from The Haworth Document Delivery Service [1-800-342-9678, 9:00 a.m. - 5:00 p.m. (EST). E-mail address: getinfo@haworthpressinc.com].

© 2000 by The Haworth Press, Inc. All rights reserved.

ogy than library collections, and around newly-created joint ventures rather than the institutions already in place. It's comforting to think that our latest effort has finally cracked the problem of collections cooperation, perhaps through improved bibliographic control and arrangements for interlibrary loan, or more carefully planned acquisitions programs, or even widespread digitization. But the historical record reveals a stutter-step process that deserves a more cautious approach.

The cooperative wheel of fortune has most recently brought forth the concept of "distributed collections." The associated programs tend to be narrow in topical focus and modest in their commitments and goals, and to emphasize peripheral materials that are unlikely to generate heavy demand. The "distributed collections" component within the AAU/ARL Latin Americanist Research Resources Project, for instance, invites participants to redirect seven percent of their Latin American monographs budget toward target areas that they choose themselves.[2] Priority cataloging is urged but not required, interlibrary loan commitments are limited to normal procedures within each institution, and even statistical expectations are tailored to local capabilities. The early results have been encouraging, not least for the project's energizing effect upon some bibliographers and institutions. Nonetheless, we're still a very long way from ensuring that all current Latin American publications of potential scholarly interest are readily available within the United States.

The ultimate success of the "distributed collections" model will depend upon participants from outside as well as within this country, since even the most comprehensive domestic program will leave many foreign imprints and other resources physically available only in their places of origin. Archival holdings are an obvious example, but a great many newspapers, pamphlets, and journals are likewise out of reach. Expanded cooperative programs might make these kinds of resources more accessible while benefiting overseas partners as well.

The calculus of cooperation seems so clear and compelling that implementation can appear only a matter of detail. International cooperation does suggest many fruitful combinations, but it is also substantially more complicated than we might wish to believe. Open recognition of the pitfalls and complexities should help us to construct realistic programs, and perhaps to avoid yet another cycle of hope (and hype) followed by disappointment.

This paper examines international cooperation using Latin America as an example. The region's cultural assumptions, institutional styles, and operational underpinnings are all quite different from our own, as are the resources available to its libraries and archives.[3] A number of past efforts illustrate how these contrasts can play out in practice. Latin America is also in the awkward position of being a subordinate within what is proclaimed as the "new world order." On the other hand, many argue that historical and even current examples of how the North/South divide has affected libraries and library cooperation will lose their force in the face of electronic technologies. A careful look at all the ingredients of successful programs can broaden the perspective. The essay concludes with some more modest suggestions on how we might proceed.

CROSS-REGIONAL PERSPECTIVES ON LIBRARIES AND ARCHIVES

It's tempting to assume that institutions are essentially the same regardless of location. Libraries, archives, and universities, for instance, may vary because some are rich and others poor, or due to specific circumstances of structure or administration. But they all share the same purposes, interests, and goals, and these are what count. Our discussion begins with a closer look at Latin American institutions, in an exercise that may cast a different light on these comfortable assumptions.

The Iberian Documentary Heritage: Bureaucrats, Writers, and Words

Spain built its colonial empire around bureaucrats and scribes. The mountains of documents generated during some three centuries of imperial rule have since been overlaid by even more paper from the republican period. The *expediente*, the administrative file constructed to chronicle a particular case, process, or problem, remains the basic building block of Latin American administration. The records are ubiquitous.

Latin America's written traditions are literary as well as bureaucratic. Printing presses were active well before 1600. In Mexico alone, more than ten thousand titles had been published by 1800.[4] Publishing exploded following independence, early in the nineteenth century. Output rose still further when, later in the century, immigrants flooded into many countries. However, print communication, though comparatively prolific, was through much of this history confined to a tiny literate elite. Press runs were therefore small. Only late in the nineteenth century did the full range of institutions associated with a literate culture begin to take shape, albeit with notable variations from country to country.

The region's strong heritage of documents and printed works contrasts with enduringly inadequate mechanisms to collect, control, or preserve these materials. Libraries have remained weak or non-existent. Archival documents as well as printed resources tend to be scattered among many institutions, none with both the mandate and the means to ensure that all appropriate materials are collected and preserved. The environment within which we would work offers the paradox of a massive written heritage that is in many instances unorganized, inaccessible, or uncollected.

The Cultural Roots of Libraries and Archives

Libraries and archives are created on the premise that there is a documentary stock worth gathering and organizing. Part of the underlying impulse may simply reflect the Western world's penchant for collecting and categorizing. Another element involves the means through which political entities define and assert themselves. Nations are validated, among other ways, when they maintain national archives and libraries, preferably in massive buildings that symbolize the strength, solidity, and stability of the state. These institutions affirm that there is a national culture–peoples, traditions, and history–sufficiently vital and coherent to warrant bringing its manifestations together within a monumental setting. Cults of culture, usually in its most erudite manifestations, may be part of the mix as well.

Many North Americans, while acknowledging these attributes of libraries and archives, would consider them no more than secondary features of institutions whose ends are really utilitarian–albeit in an exalted sort of way. Libraries exist to promote the informed citizenry which lies at the foundation of a functional democracy. Archives do the same, while also enabling efficient government and ensuring transparency in official transactions. Citizens are the customers and consumers, not such reified abstractions as "the nation" or "culture."[5]

Latin American societies have been less insistent in regarding information as a public good, rather tending to treat it as a private commodity connoting prestige or power. Neither libraries nor archives are widely perceived as protagonists in campaigns to strengthen democracy or to consolidate good government. Nor has an activist constituency demanding this role yet emerged. To the contrary, some of Latin America's social theorists have been at the forefront of those questioning the utility of mass literacy and traditional schooling.[6] Cross-cultural efforts involving libraries and archives may, from the first, be affected by very different perspectives on their meaning and value.

These contrasting views of cultural and social underpinnings may help explain why Latin American libraries and archives are so often few, small, and poor. The region's national and academic libraries would still seem like plausible partners for new cooperative programs. But when we look more closely, we even here find substantial differences from what our own models might lead us to expect.

Potential Partners and Their Cooperative Prospects

Most of Latin America's national libraries occupy impressive structures in their country's capital city. The appearances can be misleading, since most are also hamstrung by small budgets that allow for little more than basic operations. Acquisitions, for instance, are normally quite limited. Local publications are, in theory, received through legal deposit, but the laws are weak and uncertainly enforced. Nonetheless, the strongest holdings for each country are generally found in its national library.

In the absence of adequate alternatives, many national libraries serve as reading rooms for secondary and university students.[7] Latin America's national libraries are also enmeshed in politics. The top administrators are typically political appointees whose maximum tenure is fixed by the electoral cycle. Technical and support staff positions, while usually more secure, may also reflect patronage as well as competence. Programs and budgets are vulnerable to outside decisions. And only a few of these libraries enjoy both the authority and the ability to function as leaders in matters of library standards, national-level bibliographic control, training, or cooperation.

As a group, Latin America's national libraries seem problematic as long-term partners. What, then, of university and academic libraries, whose mandates are presumably similar to those of our own institutions? Here again the picture is mixed.

Public universities continue to dominate Latin American higher education in terms of student enrollments and library size. Only a few private universities have been around for more than a decade or two, though new institutions have more recently proliferated almost everywhere.[8] Some of these younger universities are very good but, in the absence of either standards or mechanisms for accreditation, many have the look and feel of diploma mills. All too frequently, their "libraries" amount to a few shelves of books in a back room or closet.

Latin America's older public universities, with their longer histories and generally better-established libraries, are those with which collections cooperation would seem most promising. These universities, in accord with longstanding regional tradition, are generally "autonomous": each one establishes its own method of governance, follows its own policies and priorities, and enforces its own procedures.[9] University authorities are chosen through elections in which students, employees, and faculty members normally have equal weight. Within the universities, those holding key administrative positions usually shift as the elected leaders change. Many public universities have virtually no funds for anything beyond faculty and staff salaries, plus an escalating burden of pensions. Admissions are open and fees are minimal, with even modest increases generating massive resistance. Mexico's flagship Universidad Nacional Autónoma de México (UNAM), for instance, recently attempted to raise tuition from about two cents to $60 per term, triggering strikes and demonstrations that have finally led university officials to proclaim the payments entirely voluntary.[10] Most faculty members work only part-time, combining their university positions with better-paying jobs. The sense of a scholarly community, as well as opportunities for contacts among all the members of that community, are correspondingly reduced.

Public universities are typically organized around "faculties" or schools, and perhaps special programs or institutes, each with its own library. In some cases the largest campus repository also functions as the central library for a university system. A scatter of completely autonomous units is equally common. Library budgets tend to be tiny, and acquisitions extremely limited. Recent holdings usually center on textbooks and similar materials that are likely to evoke only limited interest among researchers from other locations. On the other hand, some of these libraries may have strong historic collections, including newspapers and pamphlets. When the older public universities were still new, in the nineteenth century, they often were ceded libraries like those of the Jesuits, that had been confiscated by the state. Donations and extensive purchases were likewise noteworthy in the late-nineteenth and early twentieth centuries, when these then-elite institutions sought to lay the intellectual foundations for rapidly modernizing nations. While recent acquisitions have often slowed, the older holdings can be strong.

Bibliographic access is typically based on unit-specific card catalogs.[11] Most library automation relies on Micro-ISIS, a non-intuitive, non-MARC database management program, distributed gratis by UNESCO, that supports only a few library functions. This software, which encourages free-standing library catalogs in non-standard formats, has helped to foster an extremely fragmented bibliographic universe. Argentina's thirty-seven public universities, for instance, employ at least three mutually incompatible record formats in their Micro-ISIS catalogs, with additional local variations within each of these formats.

Most academic librarians only hold undergraduate degrees in library science. Staffs tend to be small, and libraries are often dumping grounds for employees who didn't work out somewhere else. Pay is low, and training opportunities are generally sparse. Public services have until recently centered on retrieving books from closed-stack collections, and a great deal of professional staff energy is typically directed toward original local cataloging.

With adjustments to reflect their different institutional structures, and always with a few happy exceptions, municipal and museum libraries, archives, and corporate and church collections share many of these same characteristics.[12] Latin America's bureaucratic legacy includes numerous notarial and judicial archives, frequently maintained apart from repositories for the executive branch, and in the case of some notarial archives actually owned by the functionary or his heirs. Religious orders constructed many of the region's earliest libraries, and parish and cathedral holdings can be likewise substantial. Finally, the region boasts a number of first-rate private collections. All these repositories are likely to hold documents, local newspapers, and other scarce materials. All tend to be understaffed and underfunded. All add to the depth of the region's untapped research resources. Unfortunately, their very limited possibilities make most of them unlikely partners for cooperative endeavors.

An increasing number of independent research institutes and documentation centers, some attached to non-governmental organizations, may carry greater promise. Their collections tend to be strong but narrow, and the nature of the parent institution often encourages dynamic approaches in acquiring and organizing information. Unfortunately, these generally young agencies are still only peripheral players in the overall information environment.

Summing Up: The Institutional Prospects for Cooperation

These characteristics of Latin America's archives and libraries carry a number of implications for international cooperation:

1. Many libraries and archives are subject both to the vagaries of electoral politics and to quick shifts in economic fortune. Continuity and long-term commitments may be problematic.
2. A preoccupation with identifying and then satisfying users' information needs is only gradually emerging. It remains quite common for answers to patrons' requests to begin and end in the local card catalog. Improved user services may not yet be perceived as the primary purpose even of internal adjustments, much less cooperative programs.
3. The region's librarians and archivists are committed to their professions, despite poor pay and sparse training opportunities. But the theoretical and technical knowledge required to implement successful new programs is often in short supply.
4. With scattered exceptions, bibliographic control is based on locally-created, non-standard records within systems using Micro-ISIS. Only a few bibliographic networks allow for shared records or resources. In most institutions, only a fraction of the total holdings are represented by automated records. Cooperation and resource sharing are more difficult as a result.
5. The Latin American holdings of greatest potential interest to overseas partners are likely to center on local imprints and historic materials, especially newspapers and pamphlets. Yet rarity, in conjunction with spotty bibliographic control, preservation

concerns, and local service priorities, may limit the accessibility of these resources even if cooperative agreements are in place.

LIBRARY COOPERATION IN GLOBAL AND HISTORICAL CONTEXTS: LOOKING FORWARD AND LOOKING BACK

The preceding section has considered Latin American libraries and archives as they in (too) many cases are, or have been until recently. Two additional factors need to be addressed in order to understand all of the barriers to change. The first centers on the models and rhetoric of our "global" present; the second looks to the checkered past of international library efforts.

The New World Order as Attraction and as Threat

The presumed common ground between research libraries in the North and the South may be both smaller and less solid than expected. We should be able to overcome most of the logistical or technical obstacles. Other barriers, however, may prove more difficult to address.

North American academic libraries, despite our convictions of often uncertain and forever inadequate support, enjoy lavishly privileged positions relative to most of our developing-world counterparts. Acquisitions are strong, staffs are competent, our educational models favor active libraries, and our parent institutions are by and large both solvent and focused. Perhaps even more significant, North American librarians enjoy fairly easy access both to decision-makers and to one another: The environment is rich in contacts and connections. Our Latin American colleagues can easily feel envy or resentment.

Northern Hemisphere descriptions of Latin American ("Southern") libraries and archives–the one offered just above is no exception–routinely focus on challenges, deficiencies, and limitations. The olympian detachment that so easily pervades these remarks will always be grating. An awareness of rank carries into the cooperative arena as well: permanently junior partners may be less enthusiastic about their status than their more privileged peers. The relative positioning of each player may also provide deeper grounds for doubt, since the benefits promised by cooperative programs are often most readily reaped by the stronger institutions. It should come as no surprise when potential partners balk at the prospect of unequal cooperative relationships.[13] When dancing with an elephant, the elephant usually leads. Some will forego the pleasure.

The broader world context suggests patterns of domination and dependence that can also impinge upon conversations concerning cooperation. Triumphalist assertions of "the end of history" proclaim a new global era in which a common experience of (Northern- and Western-led) economic integration and transformation will usher in universal democracy and prosperity.[14] Despite a few dissenting voices, neoliberal economics and a globalized marketplace are the order of the day. Even the grassroots empowerment sometimes associated with the Internet and other new technologies has thus far been conceived along lines native to the North.

This vision may seem unduly pessimistic, and the associated rhetoric overwrought as well as ungrateful. But many observers fear for fading national and local identities as, say, rock music and Hollywood movies crowd out local products, or as shopping malls and chain stores become ever more ubiquitous.[15] At the other extreme, religious and ethnic essentialism, or the rampant crime and extreme insecurity typical of many parts of the world, can suggest an emerging schism between "orderly" world regions characterized by liberalism and growth, and less favored zones doomed to Hobbesian anarchy. Either way, even self-determining institutions in peripheral regions are left with only limited freedom of action.

Several international agencies are exploring these issues within the context of their own development theories and programs.[16] Such analysis, in and of itself, helps to validate the concerns. The concept of "sustainable development" may provide the most promising focus for measures in support of cultural identities and historical patrimonies.

The rhetoric of administrative transparency, government efficiency, and "civil society" likewise encourages attention to all manner of official records. Skeptics, of course, may argue that the whole debate demonstrates yet again the desire to distill diversity into a single array of models, programs, and procedures that can be managed from without.

The increasingly insistent availability of international training, support, and products reflects genuine concern for Latin America's libraries and archives. Here again, it's easy to also deduce more interested motives. Functional bibliographic networks; for instance, require common formats and standards. Yet a library that decides to adopt the MARC format for bibliographic control, or that embraces microfilming procedures requiring multiple generations of high-quality film, will in the next instant confront the need for very expensive equipment and supplies. Automated library systems, computers, planetary cameras, silver halide film, conservation materials, and so on, are products that by and large come from the North. The "technical" elements required for full-fledged cooperation can be cumbersome and costly.

History and Its Weight

Today's terms of international interchange are often uneasy. The lessons of history can reinforce our would-be partners' cooperative misgivings. A quick review of but three examples of international activity, all within the broad area of preservation reformatting and each reflecting a different model for connecting with local institutions, may help illustrate the problems.

Around 1940, the Rockefeller Foundation funded a microfilming project whereby the John Carter Brown Library sent a cameraman to South America in order to strengthen U.S. holdings of colonial publications. The effort, which continued over several years, settled on the National Library of Chile's extraordinary José Toribio Medina Collection. The microfilm masters and copies alike, however, remained in the United States, with nothing to show for the project within Chile itself. The original effort was entirely extractive.[17]

About fifteen years later, in the 1950s, UNESCO began a short-lived project to microfilm and thereby rescue endangered archival holdings in Central America and the Caribbean. A mobile camera was dispatched to the region, and this time copies of the film were deposited onsite. In the absence of continuing support, however, almost all of the films eventually became lost or unusable. The effort brought few lasting results, even though host country needs were in this case paramount.

The Latin American Microform Project, LAMP, is a consortium, formed in the 1970s, that now includes about forty Latin Americanist collections from North America. LAMP deploys its pooled annual dues and occasional external funds for microfilming projects that focus on scarce or endangered research materials. Some LAMP projects are based within the United States, but most are sited in Latin America. Standard practice calls for LAMP to cover most or all of the filming costs, and to deposit both negative and positive copies of the film with the host institution. Whenever possible, filming is carried out using local laboratories and firms, in a deliberate effort to strengthen the region's technical capacity as well as minimize costs.

LAMP's copies of the film are managed and maintained through The Center for Research Libraries. The reels destined for Latin American hosts, however, face less certain fates. Climate-controlled storage vaults are almost unknown, and procedures for microfilm storage and use tend to be ad hoc. A good bit of the film has deteriorated, disappeared, or been damaged. Microfilm otherwise donated to or purchased by Latin American libraries and archives has frequently been (mis)treated the same.[18]

These internationally sponsored reformatting projects are characterized by ever-greater mutuality. The same tendency would hold for most other kinds of cross-regional endeavor. But the results remain uneven, in large part due to the generally limited institutional and infrastructural depth of the Latin American partners. Successful reformatting projects require not only a high-quality product, but also a broader environment that encompasses appropriate buildings and equipment, trained staff, capable management, internalized technical standards, and ongoing support. Such contexts for success depend on knowledge, persistence, and a good bit of cash.

From the Latin American perspective, these examples suggest several conclusions:

1. Local institutions need to ensure equitable arrangements and appropriate follow-up support when they engage in cooperative endeavors.
2. International norms and standards should be scrutinized with care. Compliance with one standard often invokes a cascade of complementary commitments, and a failure at any point can compromise the entire endeavor. Within the reformatting realm, for instance, specialists confidently assert preservation microfilm's half-millennial life span. But repeated local experience demonstrates that Latin American microfilm lasts for only a fraction of this term, usually due to inadequate provisions for

storage or inappropriate policies for use: the promised "permanence" is an illusion.[19] Uninformed adherence to international standards can be expensive, unsuccessful, and profoundly counterproductive.

3. The resources and experience needed to carry out projects that meet established standards and are thus technically correct can seem entirely out of reach. More flexible and economical approaches might bring greater success. The necessary adaptations, loosely categorized as "appropriate technology," are peripheral to Northern agendas. Yet modified models often require development and testing capabilities beyond those available in the South.[20] Makeshift solutions and mutual frustration are frequent results.

NEW FORCES FOR CHANGE

The dispiriting panorama described so far is one of often inert or impoverished institutions, sited within an uncertain international context, whose perceptions are shaped by a mixed historical record. Are the prospects for fruitful cooperation as limited as this analysis might suggest? Changes in at least four interrelated areas offer some grounds for hope. First, Latin America's institutions are evolving, bringing new agendas and expectations to the fore. Second, changing models of research and teaching reinforce these trends. Furthermore, new players, external as well as internal, are extending the potential depth of both cooperative programs and local capabilities. Finally, new technologies may allow fundamentally different kinds of approaches. We now turn to each of these topics.

Institutions, Their Agendas and Expectations

The image of hidebound and insistently irrelevant Latin American libraries, archives, and universities is beginning to change.[21] Some of the shifts may facilitate cooperation. Redemocratization, which in most countries dates from the 1980s, has encouraged a broad movement toward responsiveness and efficiency. Neoliberal economic doctrines, in conjunction with precarious economic situations, have provoked lean budgets that mandate effective programs and visible results. Private universities are now competing with public institutions for students and resources. International funding agencies are also ever more aware of the role of education in development. Change is slow and often bumpy, but the public institutions that are responsible for many of the region's libraries and archives are becoming more open to new possibilities.

Models of Scholarship

Traditional scholarship in the humanities and social sciences privileged great books, great men, and nation-states. Academic inquiry was organized in terms of discrete disciplines, each with its own research methodologies and preferred information sources. The written word enjoyed pride of place. These approaches have for some decades been in flux. Research agendas now favor topics like popular culture, social history, regional studies, and nuanced examinations of "subaltern" and "post-colonial" actors. Multidisciplinary perspectives are increasingly common. Film, radio, television, and digital media have expanded the array of source materials. The new models have intensified the demand for all-inclusive information services. These trends, worldwide in scope, affect both Latin American academics and the outside scholars who work within the region.

Latin America's instructional models are also changing, albeit at a perhaps slower pace. Lecture-based teaching and rote learning are giving way to more active approaches. Students are also increasingly expected to confront original sources in their studies. The eventual consequences for libraries and archives will be profound.

Finally, many Latin American universities are stimulating scholarship through new incentives, expanded publishing opportunities, and more rigorous criteria for appointment and promotion. The results once again include intensified demands for strong libraries, archives, and information services.

New Players, Outside and In

Changes in institutional expectations and the evolving modalities of scholarship and instruction, while they mandate a library response, are all rather abstract. The impetus for change is manifested more concretely through specific individuals, organizations, and agencies.

These players, internal and external, old and new, are crucial to the shifts now underway.

More and more Latin Americans are traveling abroad for basic studies or supplemental training, or to attend international seminars and conferences. More and more students and professionals from the North are spending time in the region. Increasing numbers of Latin American corporations, official agencies, and non-governmental organizations rely on sophisticated information capabilities. And the Internet provides immediate access to a host of information products, including library guides and catalogs. The contrast between what is and what could be, and direct exposure to alternate models for operations and services, are raising expectations throughout the region.

Some library organizations and institutions have moved ahead on their own. Venezuela, Chile, and Brazil, for instance, all boast (sometimes shaky) bibliographic networks. National organizations of librarians and archivists, while often preoccupied with matters of credentials and pay, can also accomplish a great deal. Argentina's ABGRA (Asociación de Bibliotecarios Graduados de la República Argentina), for instance, routinely hosts conferences that include several days of presentations by local and foreign specialists during the Buenos Aires book fair. These and many other examples demonstrate the dynamism within Latin America's library and archival communities. The pressure for change is not solely coming from without.

A number of foreign agencies are engaged in bilateral programs. Cooperation is often an explicit goal as these entities strive to leverage limited resources for the greatest possible impact. One of the most effective North American organizations is the Commission on Preservation and Access, now folded into the Council on Library and Information Resources (CLIR). The Commission has provided technical as well as financial support for efforts like the Latin American Register of Microform Masters, and has also sponsored preservation training and translation programs in Brazil, Chile, and Venezuela. The Northeast Document Conservation Center (NEDCC) has offered seminars and workshops for Cuban professionals, and is poised to add new countries as well. Organizations as diverse as the (U.S.) Library of Congress Field Office in Rio de Janeiro and OCLC have involved themselves in MARC training courses in Brazil and Argentina. The Association of American Universities/Association of Research Libraries "Latin Americanist Research Resources Project" is on the verge of a grant-funded experiment to test its distributed resources model with a few Latin American partners.[22] And the Latin American Microform Project has conducted microfilming projects with Latin American institutions throughout its twenty-five years of existence.

Some of these agencies have used their own resources to fund international activities. Since money is always in short supply, foundations and other funding agencies have played a critical role as well. The strategic investments of The Andrew W. Mellon Foundation have been particularly important. Direct foundation grants have supported a number of projects for library automation and retrospective conversion, as well as other efforts to adapt information technology to the region's needs.[23] Mellon has also supported training programs and internships, often by means of grants channeled through agencies like CLIR or NEDCC. And the Foundation has funded the "Program for Latin American Libraries and Archives," a Harvard-based re-granting initiative that finances competitive small projects to preserve or improve access to research materials in Latin American repositories.[24] By its termination date, in 2003, PLALA will have awarded about $1,000,000 through awards averaging between $5,000 and $10,000 apiece.

Bilateral efforts are by no means limited to the United States. Spain's Fundación Histórica Tavera, for instance, has conducted evaluations of Latin American archives, offered occasional small grants, and spearheaded campaigns to mobilize more inclusive programs of support. Spain's "Agencia de Cooperación Internacional" intends to expand its activities. Foreign aid programs based in other parts of Europe and Japan, as well as Canada's International Development Research Centre (IDRC), have also provided support for Latin American repositories. Finally, some Latin American foundations have funded occasional library projects. The national foundations associated with the Liechtenstein-based Lampadia Foundation (Antorchas in Argentina, VITAE in Brazil, Andes in Chile) have been especially noteworthy for the consistency, strategic purpose, and magnitude of their support.

All the agencies mentioned so far are either philanthropic organizations or non-profit entities. Commercial firms, and agencies that charge to recover their costs, are important as well. OCLC, a non-profit, fee-based service provider, has executed several catalog conversion projects, and is also recruiting Latin American library customers. Systems vendors, equipment suppliers, booksellers both local and foreign, and microfilming firms are likewise expanding their client bases. The products and services offered by these organizations usually conform to international standards, so that each sale expands the regional roster of fully contemporary installations. Commercial firms looking for business can seem like awkward bedfellows to those whose financially disinterested objectives center on improved operations and expanded cooperation. The resonance is nonetheless clear.

International organizations, both young and old, are also playing a role. Latin America's relatively new Association of Ibero-American National Libraries, ABINIA, may evolve into a forum through which the region's national libraries can become more assertive and professional.[25] The fledgling "Red de Archivos Diplomáticos Iberoamericanos," Ibero-American Network of Diplomatic Archives, hopes to foster cooperation and common programs among the region's foreign ministries.

More venerable international agencies with a regional presence include IFLA, the r International Federation of Library Associations and Institutions. UNESCO, aside from promoting Micro-ISIS bibliographic software, is spearheading the "Memory of the World" program in an effort to rescue endangered documentary heritages. The World Bank has become increasingly interested in the full range of its members' cultural patrimonies, and has sponsored several meetings of potential donor organizations to develop assistance strategies for Latin American libraries and archives. The Bank, after commissioning the four archival assessment surveys carried out by the Fundación Histórica Tavera in Argentina, Brazil, Colombia, and Mexico, has likewise sponsored intensive planning workshops within each country. The Organization of American States shares many of the same interests.[26] Some of these agencies are also involved in overlapping efforts to improve Latin America's educational systems through programs that encompass information technology and library services. Other initiatives would strengthen Latin America's contemporary archives and records management programs to the end of transparency and good government.

Libraries and archives deserve pride of place in our discussions of change. But many other individuals, organizations, and agencies are crucial as well. Our long list has only begun to suggest the depth and diversity of the actors, all of whom have roles to play in promoting change and cooperation.

Technology and Transformation

A final impetus for change centers on new technologies for information and communication. Several aspects merit note, starting with the Internet as a communications tool. Expensive and inefficient telephone services, unreliable post offices, and difficult transportation systems have in the past posed daunting obstacles to even the most straightforward exchanges. With the Internet, more and more Latin American librarians and archivists can for the first time participate in a larger world. At the simplest level, e-mail communications provide some of the contacts and connectivity that have long benefited professionals and institutions in the North.

The Internet conveys information as well as enabling communications. Library guides, automated segments of catalogs, information on standards and procedures, and basic statistics are all available online. The flip side of the coin is the capacity to provide institutional information to the world off-site. For some dispersed institutions, coordinated Web pages have allowed even more. The Universidad de Chile, for instance, is a huge, decentralized institution that has generated a newfound sense of cohesion (and also hammered out some common policies) by establishing a centrally managed Web presence. The University's site combines information from a host of its units, including almost all of its previously isolated libraries and documentation centers.[27] Thanks to the Internet, the University can now project itself in a way that may eventually affect its substance as well as its image.

Finally, digital technologies can facilitate access to bibliographic and substantive information. The World-Wide Web is dotted with online library catalogs and archival funding aids. Projects to provide scholarly "content" can be even more evocative. A Mellon-funded digitizing project by the Latin American Microform Project, for instance, has produced page images of hundreds of scarce, printed Brazilian documents from the nineteenth and early twentieth centuries, to the resounding gratitude of researchers in both Brazil and the United States.[28] Many similar examples reveal how digital products can overcome the obstacles of distance, scarcity, fragility, and dispersion.

Additional digital initiatives might have still broader impacts. The

"American Memory" effort centered at the Library of Congress, for example, is pitched to an audience that includes both schoolchildren and the general populace. Similar programs in Latin America might mobilize new constituencies of users and generate new sources of funds, while highlighting both the strengths and the needs of libraries and archives. The success of such projects, of course, is partially dependent on broad-based Internet penetration and connectivity–both less advanced in Latin America than in the United States.

Latin American libraries, universities, and research institutes are beginning to adapt or to subscribe to journal-based document delivery services. These can provide ready, albeit still only partial, solutions to the problems of incomplete serial collections, poor bibliographic access, and difficult interlibrary loan. Latin American agencies may eventually apply similar models to resources created within the region itself. As in the North, some of the copyright implications are still not clear.

All these forces for change suggest an optimistic outlook for Latin America's libraries and archives. These same elements, however, encompass only some of the preconditions for successful cooperation. The next section focuses more specifically on the needs that have not yet been resolved.

CURRENT CHANGES AND THE CONDITIONS FOR COOPERATION: A NARROWING GAP?

Institutional transformation, new models for scholarship, and the emergence of new actors are creating a broadly positive environment for improved library services. Electronic technologies that exploit the fluidity of digital information may facilitate new kinds of connections. Programs for collections cooperation require organized holdings, readily accessible bibliographic information, clear arrangements for interlibrary loan, and efficient mechanisms for document delivery. As we think about international cooperation, we need to examine all of these requisites in terms of how they will be affected by new technologies and by our other forces for change.

Organized Collections. Organized holdings distinguish libraries and archives from warehouses that merely stockpile papers and books. Almost all repositories, whatever their size or location, contain pockets of unprocessed materials. Projects to organize local holdings are usually decided within institutions, on a case-by-case basis. Broader efforts might select categories of materials or types of institutions (ecclesiastical archives, for instance) that particularly deserve attention. Nonetheless, when we think of collections cooperation, our normal starting point is repositories whose holdings have already been described. Our universe consists of libraries and archives that deserve their designation.

Shared Bibliographic Access. Broad-based resource sharing became possible with the advent of union catalogs, which in turn required organized local collections and common approaches to bibliographic control. The Library of Congress played a central role in standardizing North American cataloging through its card distribution service, which provided high quality catalog cards at minimal cost. The MARC format, whose development again owed much to the Library of Congress, has since become an international norm in the online environment. However, few Latin American libraries use MARC. The region's card catalogs need to be converted to MARC files, its nonstandard automated records need to be upgraded, and all the resulting electronic records need to be amalgamated into union catalogs. The process will be slow and costly.

Cooperative Concepts and Interlibrary Loan. The MARC format enables shared bibliographic records, one of the preconditions for collections cooperation. Sharing the books themselves is another matter. A functional, though pedestrian system for interlibrary loan is solidly in place among North American repositories. However, our mechanisms for interlibrary loan are based on undifferentiated access to one another's library holdings, pretty much regardless of subject. Most collections cooperation, by contrast, is built around precise assignments of collecting responsibilities. Librarians here at home face two main challenges as they confront this disjuncture. The characteristics of international loan transactions add some other twists as well.

The first challenge follows directly from the consortial economics and obligations that underlie most arrangements for interlibrary loan. One library within a cooperative collecting program may focus its acquisitions on a particular category of materials. Separately constructed pacts for resource sharing, however, may mean that interlibrary loan requests for those same materials in the first instance flow toward other holding institutions. Agreements for distributed collections often assume roughly equitable interlibrary loan traffic, but a balance may be difficult to achieve.

The second challenge is at once more subtle and more profound. The distributed collections model seeks to make available the broadest possible range of materials. However, contrasts between areas of cooperative collecting specialization and the varying scale of participants' acquisitions can generate cross-cutting effects. Specialist bibliographers have engineered most of these programs, which have to date arisen within limited fields like Latin American studies. Within these contexts, large libraries may from the first collect more heavily in some specific areas than the smaller repositories that claim them as a cooperative responsibility. On the other hand, almost all research libraries can point to some areas of truly exceptional collections strength–but these areas may fall outside of cooperative programs that are narrow in scope. Our cooperative results, as reflected in actual movements of material, might be more convincing if they encompassed the full rage of our collections. We don't yet really know how to join diverse institutions in topically limited programs for distributed collections.

The architects of cooperative collecting programs in fields associated with global and area studies are beginning to recruit international partners. The same issues of resolving inconsistencies between cooperative collecting pacts and interlibrary loan priorities, and of combining libraries of different sizes and collection strengths, will again come into play. There are other challenges as well. Most Latin American libraries lack access to the online bibliographic databases, like OCLC, that would permit them to precisely direct their loan requests. The diffuse organizational structure typical of many of the region's academic library systems presents another complication. A Latin American engineering or chemistry library, for example, will probably request materials pertinent to its field, but is unlikely to hold items sought by its "developed world" counterparts. Those materials are more likely to be held by libraries which correspond to (and are funded by) other university units. Successful programs will have to address internal as well as international balances between "net borrowers" and "net lenders."

The conceptual clarification that would harmoniously link interlibrary loan procedures with arrangements for collections cooperation has not yet taken place. The specific mechanisms to promote direct exchanges with Latin America are absent as well. Broad changes in the library environment will encourage progress on both fronts, though the leap from general models to concrete agreements will always be a challenge.

Delivery Mechanisms. Uncertain and expensive postal services have to date dampened interest in large-scale interlibrary loan both within Latin America and between Latin America and other parts of the world. Courier services offer speedy and secure alternatives, but at prices that are prohibitive for all but the most urgent requests. When many Latin American libraries have to stockpile their exchange materials for want of postage, finding the funds for interlibrary loan is a daunting challenge. Moving hardcopy materials remains very difficult.

Digital technologies could make a substantial difference. Specific requests for materials of limited length could be fulfilled with Ariel or similar software that relies on scanning and facsimile transmissions. A number of local and international experiments, generally combining indexing services with document delivery, are already underway. Digital solutions appear less likely for more substantial items, or as a means to provide comprehensive access to Latin America's huge holdings of retrospective materials. Effective large-scale programs would need to produce durable, high quality digital files, as opposed to the merely serviceable use copies associated with demand-driven arrangements.[29] The technical requirements and the costs would both be high.

In the absence of across-the-board digitizing projects, reformatting must focus on narrow categories or individual items. Selection is therefore crucial. A mechanism that tracked interlibrary loan requests, for example, could enable those sources enjoying the highest interest to become priority candidates for digitization. Such targeted digitization, combined with on-demand scanning for journal articles and other short pieces, could significantly facilitate collections cooperation. Most materials would nonetheless remain in their original state. How this approach could be applied to current imprints, which are protected by copyright, remains uncertain.

Latin Americans have always been alive to the possibilities of "skipping stages" in their quest for development. Economic development and technological change in the more advanced economies have often been painfully disruptive. Since many of the intermediate phases have by now been superseded, it makes good sense for developmental newcomers to leapfrog directly to the most current alternatives. Digital technology is in this sense immensely appealing. Yet on its own terms, and also in the broader context of the conditions for cooperation, the digital impact on collections cooperation is not yet clear.

CONCLUSION

North American libraries are edging toward a collections model in which "access" would replace "ownership" as the most telling marker of success. Distributed collections are taking root within a broader context of organized local holdings, online union catalogs, clear-cut procedures for interlibrary loan, and efficient delivery mechanisms. This essay has considered international collections cooperation in light of these same elements, with unsettling results. Our plans for the future will need to combine what is theoretically possible with hardheaded analysis and occasional leaps of faith.

Cooperative efforts only work when all the participants satisfy their own needs as well as contributing to common goals. Our bumper stickers enjoin us to "Think globally, act locally," but the more precise cooperative challenge is to think at once locally and globally, and to act on both planes as well.

One starting point is to understand fully the contexts for our efforts. Latin American libraries and archives have arisen in environments distinct from our own, and they reflect different conceptual frameworks. They also follow their own organizational and operating models. But libraries and archives are by no means the only players in the cooperative programs we would devise. Parent institutions, external agencies, and funding sources are crucial as well. So are bibliographic utilities, systems vendors, booksellers, library consortia, and standards organizations. And individuals–those within all these bodies and also the emerging group of those looking at cooperation and change from other perspectives–are always critical. The mutuality we seek requires a conversation among all these players.

This framework suggests several areas for action:

1. Collections cooperation is based on organized collections, union catalogs, procedures for sharing needed items, and delivery mechanisms. Many Latin American librarians and archivists remain unaware of both international standards and "best practices." They often are likewise unfamiliar with the products and

services–integrated library systems, bibliographic utilities, and the like–that build upon these standards.

Training programs, workshops, and fellowships for formal study can all foster a fuller sense of the possible. Partnerships, strategic programs of targeted support, and model or demonstration projects can be effective as well.

Providing information about norms, standards, and products need not be a one-way street. Scientific and technical support in adapting international standards to Latin American circumstances could have practical as well as psychological effects. To cite but one somewhat peripheral example, the Getty Conservation Institute has joined with several Brazilian institutions to explore new approaches to museum environments in that country's "hot and humid" Northeast. Developed-world solutions rely on prohibitively expensive climate control systems, yet local experience shows how far simpler measures might accomplish almost as much. Similar efforts might generate new alternatives in areas that are problematic for libraries and archives, including storage environments but perhaps also matters like automated bibliographic control.[30]

2. Educational programs are necessary for librarians and archivists, but they could help others as well. Administrators, academics, civic leaders, and politicians might benefit from sessions on the emerging role of information in sustainable development and civil society, what fully functional libraries and archives have to offer, and criteria with which to evaluate information services. These kinds of programs could reinforce the emerging pressures for change while also providing a solid basis for expectations and plans.
3. Most discussions of North-South library cooperation, including our own, draw heavily upon the accumulated lore of the past fifty years. Circumstances are changing, and it's time to devise new experiments and develop new perspectives. These efforts should focus on institutions, but perhaps even more on those individuals whose energy, vision, and ability make them the most likely protagonists of change.
4. North American librarians and archivists, like their Latin American counterparts, devote most of their energies to their home institutions. The complexities of cooperation have, in the United States, also generated a small group of analysts and administrators

who concern themselves with cooperative programs per se. The best of these individuals are familiar with technologies, procedures, institutions, and key individuals–and can conjure up resources to boot. Specialists in North/South cooperation could similarly strengthen the prospects for international programs. Those most visible to date have been associated with cross-national training programs and international funding agencies. Other skills, and other institutional backgrounds, may become more important in the future.

5. Electronic communications and digital technologies may offer new cooperative alternatives, particularly for document delivery. The possibilities need to be clarified and then tested through training programs, model installations, demonstration projects, and careful studies of costs, performance, and legal constraints. The conundrum of cost-effective document delivery within the context of collections cooperation likewise requires attention.

Latin America has an enduring written heritage, and the region by and large is still embedded in a print culture. Our concerns with cooperative collection development are therefore based on a format that some think is doomed to disappear before the digital onslaught. Moreover, effective cooperative programs will require electronic technologies in order to succeed. Nonetheless, both the forces affecting the region's information services and the requirements for successful collaboration go well beyond technological change. The array of actors is also far larger than many might expect. International cooperation is as complicated as it is essential.

When we propose collections cooperation, we are inviting our Latin American partners to dance with elephants. By focusing on print resources, we may be suggesting a dinosaurs' duet. The many additional players to consider reveal both a crowded dance card and an overloaded dance floor. And the band that will get us moving is fully electronic. The images are thoroughly incongruous, which may be why the prospects are so inviting.

NOTES

1. For the Farmington Plan, see Edwin E. Williams, "Farmington Plan," in *Encyclopedia of Library and Information Science* (1972) v. 8, p. 361-368; also Edwin E. Williams, *Farmington Plan Handbook: Revised to 1961 and Abridged* (n.p.: Association of Research Libraries, 1961). The Farmington Plan and the Latin America Co-

operative Acquisitions Program are both treated in Robert K. Johnson, ed., "The Acquisition of Latin American Library Materials in ARL Libraries: A Report to the ARL Foreign Acquisition Committee from the Latin American Farmington Plan Subcommittee," *Foreign Acquisition Newsletter*, no. 36 (Fall, 1972), p. 1-15; continued in no. 37 (Spring, 1973), p. 8-17. Also see Hendrik Edelman, "The Death of the Farmington Plan," *Library Journal* 98 (April 15, 1973), p. 1251-1253. For the Conspectus, see (for instance) the thee papers in the section entitled "The Conspectus Ten Years On: Achievements and Future Prospects," in *Latin American Studies into the Twenty-First Century: New Focus. New Format, New Challenges. Papers of the Thirty-Sixth Annual Meeting of the Seminar on the Acquisition of Latin American Library Materials, June 1-6, 1991* (Albuquerque, NM: SALALM Secretariat, 1993), p. 235-264.

2. See Dan Hazen, "Current Issues: The Latin Americanist Research Resources Project: A New Direction for Monographic Cooperation?" *ARL: A Bimonthly Newsletter of Research Library Issues and Actions*, no. 191 (April, 1997), p. 1-6.

3. Latin America's features are also different from those of other world areas. Some phenomena may be common to many regions, but the variations are both marked and crucial.

4. The classic bibliographies on early Mexican publishing are the separate compilations covering Mexico City, Puebla, Guadalajara, Veracruz, and Oaxaca that were prepared in the late nineteenth and early twentieth centuries by Chilean bibliophile José Toribio Medina. Recent updates have been prepared under the auspices of the Instituto de Investigaciones Bibliográficas of Mexico's Universidad Nacional Autónoma de Mexico. The Medina volumes alone document about 10,900 titles published through the year 1800.

5. A North American rhetoric of reification would emphasize terms like the "information economy" or the "knowledge society."

6. Ivan Illich, *Deschooling Society* (New York: Harper & Row, 1971). Paulo Freire, taking another tack, argues that education should serve as a vehicle for the consciousness-raising that will generate social change.

7. Some national libraries find this less troubling than others. In Argentina, for instance, full reading rooms are perceived as a sign of success. In Chile, the student-led crush is felt to divert scarce resources from the library's "patrimonial" responsibilities.

8. Many of the older Catholic universities, in particular, rank among the region's best.

9. The specific case of Argentina's Universidad de Buenos Aires is described in Philip G. Altbach, "Survival of the Fittest: The University of Buenos Aires–A Model for the Future?" in *Change* v. 31, no. 3 (May/June 1999), p. 47-48.

10. The *Chronicle of Higher Education* has covered the story in its weekly print issues dated Feb. 26, March 19, March 26, May 7, May 21, July 23, and July 30, 1999 (all in the "International" section); and in its daily online report for August 18, 1999. As of late August, the strike was still going strong.

11. Among Argentina's public universities, for instance, only about twenty percent of all holdings are currently represented with automated records. This and other Argentine figures were gathered in a survey whose results are included in Argentina,

Sistema de Información Universitaria, *Módulo de Bibliotecas Proyecto: Base de datos Unificada (BDU)* (unpublished project proposal, 1999), especially Appendix V, "Resumen del resultado de encuestas." See also E. Barber, N. Tripaldi, S. Pisano, V. Werner, "La automatización de las bibliotecas universitarias argentinas: Proyectos y perfiles de implementación" (typescript, ca. 1998).

12. The Fundación Histórica Tavera circulated preliminary draft reports on archives in Argentina, Brazil, Colombia, and Mexico in the spring of 1999. These reports, commissioned by the World Bank were the focus of subsequent planning workshops in each country.

13. The ongoing debate concerning the motives and consequences of foreign assistance programs crystallizes much of the argument. For one insider's recent overview see Linn Hammergren, "Review Essay: The Development Wars: Analyzing Foreign Assistance and Policy," *Latin American Research Review* v. 34, no. 2 (1999), p. 179-197. The debate over benefits in situations of inequality cuts both ways, with "senior partners" often concerned that they'll be tapped for an unreasonable share of the total costs.

14. Francis Fukuyama, *The End of History and the Last Man* (New York: Free Press, 1992).

15. Nestor Garcia Canclini, *Hybrid Cultures: Strategies for Entering and Leaving Modernity* (Minneapolis, MN: University of Minnesota Press, 1995) is among the works offering a more nuanced (and optimistic) view.

16. See, for example, Organization of American States, Inter-American Council for Integral Development, "Programa Interamericano de Cultura" (typescript, ca. 1997). The World Bank, among other agencies, is chewing through various internal working documents to refine its understanding and approach. See, for instance, "WBI Partnership Learning Program on Records and Archives Management in Development" (typescript "Draft Proposal [06/28/99b]"). The Bank, in particular, is constrained to devise an economic argument in favor of cultural programs. The same theme prompted a late 1998 meeting at the Getty Center. See "Meeting on the Economics of Cultural Heritage," *Conservation: The Getty Conservation Institute Newsletter* v. 14, no. 1(1999), p. 21-22. For a final example, see Jef Malliet, "Cultural Heritage and Sustainable Development: How Are They Connected," *ICCROM Newsletter*, no. 24 (September, 1998), p. 10-13. (ICCROM is the International Centre for the Study of the Preservation and Restoration of Cultural Property, headquartered in Rome.)

17. This lapse has recently been rectified, thanks to follow-up funding from the Rockefeller Foundation.

18. This phenomenon is certainly not unique to Latin America. A study of microfilm prepared in Indonesia, for the most part with Ford Foundation support, found that the overwhelming majority of the reels left in the country have suffered severe deterioration for want of proper storage and care. The microfilm prepared as a "permanent" replacement for extremely fragile originals has become unusable well before the originals themselves. See: Roger Tol, with a contribution by Timothy Behrend, "Acid Irony? Or How to Deal with Negatives Positively: An Evaluation Report of the Microfilming Projects in Indonesia Supported by The Ford Foundation" (typescript, 15 June-16 July, 1998).

19. This outcome also reinforces the widespread fascination with digitization as a means for both preservation and access. Preservation advisors drum away about evanescent electronic files, but the microfilm that they would substitute has proven equally impermanent.

20. Several Brazilian archivists, for examples, are experimenting with paper made from banana fibers as a substitute for the expensive, imported "Japan paper" commonly used in book and document repair. The initial results are promising, but the new product still needs exhaustive testing in a full-scale paper laboratory.

21. To cite but one example, the World Bank is providing substantial support to modernize public universities in several countries. In Argentina, one category of grants has enabled an electronic network that links most campuses internally and that also provides connections among the institutions. Another program has supported the "Sistema de Información Universitaria," whose seven modules (including one for libraries) cover areas including accounting and finance, personnel management, academic administration, and statistics. See Argentina, Secretaria de Politicas Universitarias, Programa SIU, *Programa SIU* (typescript and powerpoint slides, julio de 1999).

22. The grant, carrying the somewhat inelegant title "International Cooperation to Expand the Range, Accessibility, and Availability of Research Materials for Latin Americanist Students and Scholars," corresponds to a new program under the Department of Education's Title VI, Section 606, whose equally inelegant rubric is "Technological Innovation and Cooperation for Foreign Information Access Program."

23. Chile's "Alerta al Conocimiento" (*http://www.alerta.cl*) has thus received a grant to automate its document delivery operations.

24. See *http://www.fas.harvard.edu/~drclas*, under "Other Programs," for a description of this Program.

25. See the ABINIA home page: *http://rrpac.upr.clu.edu:9090/abinia/index.htm* (last updated in November, 1997, according to a visit on August 24, 1999).

26. The Argentine workshop was held in Buenos Aires on July 7 and 8, 1999. The Brazilian session followed in Rio de Janeiro on July 13-15. The Brazilian workshop was accompanied by a workbook including many of the formal presentations: see Mesa Redonda Nacional de Arquivos, *Caderno de Textos* (Rio de Janeiro, 13 a 15 de julho de 1999), as well as the compilation *Legislação Brasileira de Arquivos* (Rio de Janeiro: 1999).

27. See *http://www.uchile.cl* for the Universidad de Chile homepage, prepared by its Sistema de Servicios de Información y Bibliotecas (SISIB).

28. See *http://wwwcrl.uchicago.edu/info/brazil/* for the Center for Research Libraries/Latin American Microform Project's "Brazilian Government Document Digitization Project."

29. High profile efforts like the massive scanning project at Spain's Alchivo General de Indias may have created unrealistic early expectations for what major digitizing programs might accomplish. The fullest description in English is Pedro Gonzáles, *Computerization of the Archivo General de Indias: Strategies and Results* (Washington, DC: Council on Library and Information Resources, September, 1998).

30. The joint Getty Conservation Institute/Brazil activities were presented during the 9th congress of ABRACOR, Associação Brasileira de Conservadores-Restauradores de Bens Culturais (the Brasilian association of conservation specialists) held in Salvador, Bahia from October 25-29, 1998. See also "Project Updates: Collections in Hot and Humid Environments," *Conservation: The Getty Conservation Institute Newsletter* v. 13, no. 3 (1998), p. 21. Uruguay's Ministerio de Educación y Cultura, División de Ciencia y Tecnologia, in conjunction with the Programa Regional para el Fortalecimiento de la Cooperación entre Redes y Sistemas Nacionales de Información para América Latina y el Caribe (INFOLAC), has proposed a home-grown cooperative cataloging project as an alternative to the costly approaches now available. See "Proyecto para desarrollo de un sistema de catalogación cooperativa en Internet para América Latina y el Caribe," dated marzo, 1999, under "Proyectos" on the INFOLAC Web site: *http://infolac.ucol.mx/*.

International Information Exchange: New Configurations for Library Collaboration in South Asian Studies

James Nye
David Magier

INTRODUCTION

Over the past fifteen years U.S. research libraries have altered the ways they provide their patrons with research materials on South Asia, especially those in the regional languages of the subcontinent. Attempts to coordinate South Asia collection development at the national level have gradually given way to regional and local collaborative activities for preservation and enhanced access. Recently, the most successful of such collaborations have moved away from geographically-determined partnerships and have brought together select groupings of participating institutions based on commonalities of particular

---

James Nye is Director, South Asia Language and Area Center and Bibliographer for Southern Asia, University of Chicago.

David Magier is Director of Area Studies and South/Southeast Asian Studies Librarian, Columbia University.

This paper was prepared for the conference on "Creating New Strategies for Cooperative Collection Development" held November 12-14, 1999, at Aberdeen Woods Conference Center, Atlanta Georgia.

[Haworth co-indexing entry note]: "International Information Exchange: New Configurations for Library Collaboration in South Asian Studies." Nye, James, and David Magier. Co-published simultaneously in *Collection Management* (The Haworth Information Press, an imprint of The Haworth Press, Inc.) Vol. 24, No. 3/4, 2000, pp. 215-239; and: *Creating New Strategies for Cooperative Collection Development* (ed: Milton T. Wolf and Marjorie E. Bloss) The Haworth Information Press, an imprint of The Haworth Press, Inc., 2000, pp. 215-239. Single or multiple copies of this article are available for a fee from The Haworth Document Delivery Service [1-800-342-9678, 9:00 a.m. - 5:00 p.m. (EST). E-mail address: getinfo@haworthpressinc.com].

© 2000 by The Haworth Press, Inc. All rights reserved.

research and teaching interests. These new collaborative groups have focused their energies on special projects that have garnered more than five million dollars in support from foundations, from Federal government agencies, and from direct contributions of the institutions themselves. Increasingly these projects have begun to recruit international participation, particularly from institutions in the subcontinent itself.

This paper addresses: first, the principles underpinning those projects and their international character; second, the characteristics of programs that have been most successful; and third, future directions for further international collaborations supporting scholarship on South Asia. Special attention is given to the balance between newer and older technologies; the development of models that depart from the traditional "colonial plunder" approach to collection development by providing equal benefits both inside and outside the subcontinent; features of these models that are likely to provide long-term self-sustainability for the projects; and the potentials for leaping over intermediate technologies as digital systems are developed in the region and supported by the projects themselves.

PRINCIPLES

Several principles are foundations for the preservation and access projects described below. The principles have developed over time based on experience–sometimes painful experience. They have most often been the result of inductive reasoning. We argue that the world of deductive reasoning exhibited by Dr. Pangloss in Voltaire's *Candide* is ill suited to preservation and access.

Selection of Projects

How do we select projects to pursue?

Inherent Merit, Broadest Benefit

Projects with demonstrably great value for scholars, that produce easily accessible resources are the most beneficial to undertake. Within area studies, we have found that many of the projects meeting these basic criteria of merit and benefit involve *international* collaborations and that those collaborations are sustained because of the synergies created among participants based upon a shared sense of the value derived.

Serendipity

The role of serendipity in the evolution of our projects has been striking. While it is easy to imagine valuable projects, those that happen to present themselves (through a clustering of contacts, suggestions from scholars, and communications from unlikely sources) are often not the ones most worth pursuing. The challenge is to remain open to the unexpected while viewing the serendipitous encounters with hardheaded realism.

Source of Energy: Bottom-Up

Anyone can tell you more than you want to hear about how much effort it takes to make collaborative projects succeed. What characterizes successful projects? How do they generate the requisite energy? One renewable energy source is the motivation of the librarians who interact on a daily basis with library patrons. These are the librarians responsible for collection development, faculty liaison, bibliographic instruction, and reference and research consultation. This is particularly true among area studies librarians who are known to harbor strong personal commitment to their field well beyond what is strictly called for in their job descriptions. A South Asia librarian, for example, will be very highly motivated to preserve materials that his faculty and students require and to seek new, more efficient ways of providing access to unique South Asia research resources. If he relies strictly on local resources, however, he may not be able to meet readers' expectations. Initiatives to provide for those needs are not likely to come from library administrators themselves. The energies of area librarians can be fully engaged by library projects initiated by colleagues, responding to immediate and urgent needs of patrons. In our experience, library projects initiated by these area studies librarians are more likely to be successful because they are geared towards tangible solutions to strong local needs. With such initiatives arising from the bottom up, library administrators can then respond with appropriate support to ensure institutional participation.

Which Specific Materials and Projects Should We Work On?

Several presuppositions are at play here: (1) physical access implies preservation; (2) intellectual access implies bibliographic access; (3) broad distribution of benefits implies digital products. Taken together, these presuppositions suggest that successful projects must preserve important materials, provide appropriate bibliographic access for them, and selectively disseminate them over the Internet. Which materials are "important?" In practice, this is determined by the combination of serendipity (which opens the door to newly available materials and collections) and the strength of known information needs. Selection of materials for a project should be carried out by teams of library subject specialists working with committees of scholars. Which type of bibliographic access is "appropriate?" Again, this must be determined by subject librarians in consultation with scholars. For example, bibliographic access for journals implies article-level indexing. So the project must weigh the importance of journals for the particular subject/region/language selected. At the same time it is important to assess the quality of existing journal indexes for those journals. Likewise, selection of materials for full-text digital access will depend heavily on a detailed understanding of current usage patterns as well as feedback from scholars on how they would use such digital materials if they were made available.

The Forest or the Trees?

Both. That is, projects must be selected which are narrow enough to be feasible in the near term, but broad enough to suggest the outlines of some larger agenda of obvious merit. This means that although the individual projects are initiated on the basis of their own value across participating institutions, a clustering of such projects over time will lead to a broader benefit which is greater than the sum of its parts. Keeping such a broader vision in mind while selecting and prioritizing individual projects makes it more likely that follow-on support and participation from a variety of institutions will be possible. As more and more of the big picture is filled in, more institutions will detect the value of the larger program and will contribute their resources and energies. As a result of this broader participation, it is easier to demonstrate the contributive value of each separate piece. But it is the inherent merit of the larger vision of information access and preservation that enables each distinct project to engage its participants productively.

Selection of Partners

Area studies preservation and access projects are most likely to have broad benefit if they are both collaborative and international in scope. Selecting the particular partners with whom to work is a very important issue. In our experience, small *self-selected* groupings that are forged from common concern for the particular matter of the project are most likely to succeed, regardless of the geographic or structural distribution of the institutions involved. This is another instance of the bottom-up principle. Area librarians who are highly motivated to meet the needs of local readers will elect to participate in small groupings of specialist librarians with similar objectives. Two or three libraries with strong area studies programs in a given world area and able to invest some of the requisite human and material resources may initiate a project. Additional partners may be added later in subsequent phases. We also believe that projects are uniquely successful if they involve collaborative engagement by South Asian and foreign participants where librarians in each country take active responsibility and where there is mutual benefit to all the participants. A project that can incorporate foreign partners will have the better chance of achieving significant benefits. Specifically in South Asia, we have observed that non-governmental organizations are preferable as partners because they are more flexible and less subject to bureaucratic restrictions. They are also more likely to be engaged out of appreciation for the academic significance of the project itself. A side benefit of projects with international partnerships is that there are opportunities to test the practical limits of different techniques and technologies in a wider variety of settings.

Selection of Methodologies

Preservation and access projects involve a range of methodologies and approaches. We are often faced with choices among alternative approaches. How do we decide? First, in international collaborations it is important that planning and decision making involve all the participants. In order for our colleagues abroad to participate effectively in such planning, it is sometimes necessary for the project itself to provide training for librarians. For example, in India there are only a handful of schools that teach MARC or aspects of electronic bibliographic control. Yet such training is a prerequisite for effective and equitable partnership in a collaborative project.

Preservation

While funding agencies often favor experimental projects for access, it is still vitally important to distinguish preservation goals from access goals. Access over time implies prior preservation activity. But the preservation must be carried out through methodologies that are optimized for the long-term stability of the content. While many consider microfilm user-unfriendly and certainly old-fashioned, it is the most stable preservation medium for texts and also a bridge medium to the digital future if the microfilm is of high quality. What can be experimental about microfilming projects, however, is the international collaborative approach. For example, one traditional paradigm for foreign research material is what we call the "colonial plunder" approach. Western libraries swoop in with cash, buy local treasures, and sequester them in their rare book libraries or preserve them for themselves. In contrast, one new approach is to work with scholars, agencies, and libraries in the countries that are the original home of these publications. Institutions may be established in country to hold the resources locally while preserving them *in situ* and providing local and international bibliographic and full-text access. If a collection has been purchased and processed with support from U.S. institutions, the ownership might eventually be ceded to the in-country partner. Local ownership is the preferable long-term solution rather than indefinite stewardship, which might appear to some as implying colonial dependency. This methodology, if carefully controlled to ensure continuing engagement of all participants, enables readers in country to receive as many benefits (and contribute as much energy) as the international community of scholars. Another methodological consideration in the area of preservation is the need to enforce established international standards for reprography. (We are all aware of projects that responded to the need for transient access with "quick and dirty" microfilming, with the result that the materials are essentially lost to long-term use.)

Bibliographic Access

Books must be cataloged to international standards if project benefits are to be enjoyed broadly. While it is more expensive to implement consistently high standards, insisting on established international cataloging practices permits integration of the resulting records into OCLC, RLIN, and other international bibliographic databases. But of course, achieving this objective requires time. We have found that as an interim measure, partial or provisional records created by a number of local libraries and individual collections (or converted from handlists or card catalogs as a first step of a larger project) can be combined into regional union catalogs. These catalogs have the value of letting users know that an item exists and is physically available in a particular collection. Still, we have remained committed to the goal of access to the intellectual content via full bibliographic records. Bibliographic access for journals means that articles must be indexed. Again, labor-intensive efforts such as article indexing will only be valuable if the results can cluster with other seams of bibliographic data. To avoid permanently isolating information from its users, international bibliographic standards must be employed.

Full-Text and Document Delivery

The project should be constructed to permit the broadest possible access to full texts. Of course, bibliographic information is inherently valuable in its own right. scholars planning to do field work in India, for example, are very grateful for information on holdings in libraries within that country. It allows them to maximize the effectiveness of their limited time abroad. Still, this represents only a small portion of the *potential* value of those collections. So the bibliographic access alone is incomplete. Selective provision of full-text online and document delivery is a logical extension of such projects. Does this mean that cataloging and indexing a collection presupposes the intention to digitize the whole collection? No, but it does require that we evolve a methodology for identifying the materials that are likely to generate the widest use, as well as an infrastructure for providing such full text access or document delivery in response to unanticipated demand. Access to preserved materials should be provided without charge, if possible, or on the basis of cost recovery, if necessary. This follows the well-established practice of public library support by the Carnegie Foundation.

CONTEXT OF LIBRARY NETWORKS AND INSTITUTIONS IN NORTH AMERICA

The projects described later in this paper are possible only because they build upon the existing infrastructures of international bibliographic utilities such as OCLC and RLIN and organizational contexts such as CRL. For South Asia, in particular, the international collaborative projects described here have depended crucially upon the prior existence of several organizational entities, including:

1. *Library of Congress Field Offices* <*http://lcweb.loc.gov/acq/ovop/delhi/*>. The United States Library of Congress maintains offices in New Delhi and Islamabad with additional acquisition agents in Nepal, Bangladesh, Sri Lanka, Burma, Mongolia, China, and Iran. Among other things, LC's South Asia Cooperative Acquisitions Programs serve the function of a book vendor for approximately 30 research libraries with South Asia collections. Participating institutions complete a profile describing specific areas of interest. The Library of Congress staff based in the subcontinent then select appropriate books within those categories, purchase them, catalog the titles, and deliver them to the participants. Participation is open to both U.S. and foreign libraries. Prices for individual titles are considerably lower than from commercial dealers, reflecting the economy of scale in purchasing. Full cataloging records are provided for all titles acquired, saving technical processing expenses at participating institutions.
2. *South Asia Microform Project (SAMP)* <*http:wwwcrl.uchicago.edu/info/samp.htm*>. SAMP is a membership organization based at the Center for Research Libraries. It is dedicated to the acquisition of less-frequently-used South Asian resources in microform and delivery of those resources via inter-library loan. Twenty-four North American institutions pay membership fees of $550 per year. Membership is open to libraries worldwide. The major benefit for participants is rapid access to approximately 20,000 publications. SAMP has a solid record of raising

foundation and government support to supplement membership fees for use in its projects.

3. *Committee on South Asia Libraries and Documentation (CONSALD)* <*http://www.lib.virginia.edu/area-studies/SouthAsia/Lib/consald.html*>. Under this organization, all U.S. and Canadian libraries with major South Asia collections convene each year in conjunction with the annual meeting of the Association for Asian Studies. CONSALD discusses changes to the Library of Congress Field Office programs, as needed, and hears reports on activities in the member libraries. It also provides some continuing professional development via workshops.
4. *U.S. regional library consortia* for South Asia. South Asia Consortium East <*http://www.lib.virginia.edu/area-studies/SouthAsia/Lib/saceast.html*>, the Committee on Institutional Cooperation's South Asia Library Project <*http://www.library.wisc. edu/libraries/cic/soasia/*>, and South Asia Consortium West <*http://www.lib.utexas.edu/subject/area/sacwest/index.html*> are sub-groups of CONSALD with members focused on rationalizing acquisitions programs to maintain library strengths on South Asia in the eastern, central, and western regions, respectively.

VIGNETTES

Short vignettes follow for a few major South Asia projects. They are ordered in a rough chronological fashion, progressing from the earliest to the most recent. They are clustered according to broad headings as follows:

- Traditional bibliography,
- Preservation microfilming and archival reproduction,
- Collections purchased and maintained in South Asia,
- Digital projects, and
- Composite initiatives.

Traditional Bibliography

Official Publications of India <*http://www.lib.uchicago.edu/e/su/southasia/off-pubs.html*>

Improved access to the official publications of India is the major objective of a program by the University of Chicago Library and the British Library. The initiative includes:

- Production of a Web site with a searchable catalog and selected documents;
- Assembly of a bibliographic database including all pre-Independence official publications of India together with a description of worldwide holdings, beginning with the nearly 22,000 titles held by the British Library;
- Cataloging the titles and distributing the bibliographic records to the international bibliographic utilities OCLC and RLIN;
- Deposit of the British Library's duplicate official publications of India (roughly 20,000 volumes) at the University of Chicago;
- Creation of an international union list reflecting holdings of official publications of India; and
- Preparation of selected titles as full electronic texts under the Digital South Asia Library project.

Selected publications related to official publications of India have also been made available as fulltexts on the Web site. These include the following:

- Introductory matter in Frank Campbell's path-breaking *Index-catalogue of Indian official publications in the Library, British Museum*, providing an overview of those materials in what was the British Museum and now is the British Library collection.
- A guide to the *Official Publications* published by the British Library Reference Division, 1984.
- The text of "V class lists" at the India Office Records prepared by John Sims in the 1980s.
- An article by John Sims on "The Official Publications Collection in IOLR" from the *Newsletter of the India Office Library and Records.*

Preservation Microfilming and Archival Reproduction

Microfilming of Indian Publications Project <http://www.lib.uchicago.edu/e/su/southasia/mippweb.html>

Microfilming of Indian Publications Project (MIPP) is a joint project of the Library of Congress and the National Library of India. Its objective is to preserve and make accessible all 55,992 books listed in *The National Bibliography of Indian Literature: 1901-1953 (NBIL)* together with the pre-1954 titles in the *NBIL* supplement. These are books in the twenty-two major languages of South Asia selected by a group of Indian scholars for their central importance to humanistic understanding of India.

MIPP began in 1990 under a bi-national agreement between the U.S. and Indian governments. A multi-national Steering Committee with representatives from the U.S., India, and U.K. provides governance for the project.

The South Asia Microform Project (SAMP) at the Center for Research Libraries holds microfilm from the MIPP project for use in the U.S. Film copies are also available at the Library of Congress. More than sixty Indian libraries are now participating in the program by lending books for preservation under MIPP. In exchange for their participation, these libraries receive a microfilm copy of each book they loan for preservation and a copy of the project's database.

As of March 1999, more than 16,800 titles had been microfilmed. Virtually all of these books are fully cataloged and may be found in the Center for Research Libraries' on-line catalog as well as on the international bibliographic utilities OCLC and RLIN. Funding for the project from several sources currently totals $790,000. Additional proposals are under consideration that would yield $1,100,000 for the project over the next five years.

Chief among the project's benefits are that:

- Some of the most important books published during the first half of this century are being preserved, with determination of what is most important having been made by Indian scholars;
- Microfilm is being produced in India to international preservation standards;
- Indian project staff are being trained by Library of Congress reprographics experts and will be available for engagement in tbe public sector in India following the conclusion of the project;
- High quality cataloging records are being produced in India and distributed to the world via the two major bibliographic utilities, OCLC and RLIN;

- Expenses for microfilming and cataloging in India are approximately one-fifth of what they would be in the U.S.; and
- The project has elevated public awareness of preservation needs within India through coverage in the popular press. It has also demonstrated the value of large-scale international cooperation in the area of cultural preservation.

South Asia Reference Tools Program <http://www.lib.uchicago.edu/e/su/southasia/sart.html>

Many of the reference tools required for scholarship on South Asia are brittle and relatively rare. The South Asia Reference Tools Program seeks to improve that situation by making available high quality photoreproductions of selected reference tools on acid-free paper at reasonable prices. This program functions under the South Asia Library Project of the Committee on Institutional Cooperation.

The program began in 1996 with reproduction of nineteen early catalogs of South Asian materials in the British Museum. Simultaneously the contents of those catalogs was converted to a searchable electronic catalog and mounted as a resource on the World Wide Web. Based on the success of that first effort, we will be taking up another set of volumes for reproduction late in 1999. The next titles will include the nineteenth-century catalogs of the India Office Library.

Collections Cooperatively Purchased by U. S. Libraries and Maintained in South Asia

Roja Muthiah Research Library <http://www.lib.uchicago.edu/e/su/southasia/rmrl.html>

The Roja Muthiah Research Library (RMRL) was founded in 1994 as a joint project of the University of Chicago and MOZHI, an Indian public trust dedicated to developing resources in languages and culture. RMRL exists to provide research materials and facilities for students of Tamil studies in a variety of fields spanning the humanities, social sciences, and sciences. The Library's main objectives are to preserve, catalog, and expand the collection of Roja Muthiah, who during his lifetime amassed one of the world's finest private libraries of Tamil publications.

The Library's notable strengths are its holdings in classical and modern literature, literary criticism, medicine, cinema and the related culture of printed works (such as cinema song books), folklore, material by and about women, religion and philosophy, and numerous publications of historical value. The collection consists of more than 100,000 volumes of books, journals, and newspapers. In addition there are rich holdings of oleolithographs from Ravi Varma's workshop, nearly 30,000 journal abstracts and indexes, an enormous collection of clippings, drama notices, wedding invitations, business and family correspondence, and palm leaf manuscripts. Most of the publications date from the latter half of the nineteenth century and the first half of the twentieth.

The University of Chicago purchased the collection with the clear intention that the materials would not be removed from India, but rather would be cataloged and microfilmed in Madras. Following the completion of cataloging and preservation, the collection will be ceded by the University to MOZHI, our sister institution in the program, along with copies of all the microfilm created. The University is raising funds necessary for purchase of the collection, processing, development of a full reprographics facility in Madras, and all other expenses during the first six to seven years of the project. Slightly more than $1,000,000 has been raised for the project to date from the Committee on Southern Asian Studies at the University of Chicago, the Wellcome Institute for the History of Medicine in London, the National Endowment for the Humanities, the U.S. Department of Education, and the Ford Foundation. Subjects already under preservation treatment include:

- Classical and medieval literature, linguistics;
- History of medicine, including siddha, yoga, ayurveda, nadisastra, visatantra, and related topics such as jyotisastra, erotic literature/sexuality, botany, and animals;
- Biographies, Indian history, colonial materials, caste and caste histories; and
- Folklore, drama, cinema, musicology and music, and art

As of May 1999, more than 12,000 volumes had been filmed to exacting international standards for preservation microfilm. The reprographics facility at RMRL is already considered one of the three best in India even though it has been in existence for less than five years.

Urdu Research Library Consortium <http://www.lib.uchicago.edu/e/su/southasia/URLC.html>

A consortium of U.S. research libraries with collecting interests in the Urdu language have launched a program, based at the University of Chicago, to acquire and preserve the collection of Mr. Mohd. Abdus Samad Khan. His private library was purchased by the consortium, which was formed in April 1996 under the name Urdu Research Library Consortium (URLC). In its general contours the program of URLC resembles that at the Roja Muthiah Research Library.

Initial expenses were paid with funds from the sale of shares to member institutions. The following six libraries or consortia have joined the Consortium to date: CIC South Asia Library Project (including the Universities of Michigan, Minnesota, and Wisconsin as paying members); Columbia University; Harvard University; SAC-West (including the Universities of California-Berkeley, Texas-Austin, and Washington as paying members); University of Chicago; University of Pennsylvania.

Mr. Samad Khan's library is widely considered one of the world's finest for early Urdu periodicals and printed books. As a collector of great acumen, Mr. Samad Khan built the library with care and erudition over most of his adult life. Holdings are well rounded across all areas of Urdu publishing. Approximately 2,600 periodical titles (many in complete runs) and at least 26,500 monographs comprise the collection. Most imprints date from the nineteenth and early twentieth centuries and are unavailable at any U.S. library. Physical condition of the collection is very good, especially considering the age of the publications. While comparisons of collections are often invidious, we are convinced that this is one of the best collections of Urdu in South Asia.

Serials are one of the special strengths of the URLC collection. Periodicals in the collection from the last century and the early part of this century are undoubtedly the best that any scholar with whom we have spoken has seen anywhere in the world. There are more than 60,000 issues of journals along with newspapers, such as extensive runs of the rare *Avadh Akhbar*, published by Naval Kishore Press in Lucknow, and *Sahifah*, the first newspaper published from Hyderabad in Urdu and Persian. Many little literary magazines are also available. The journals, many uniquely found at the URLC collection, cover virtually all areas of Urdu writing in the humanities, social sciences, and sciences.

Monographs in the collection also cover an enormous array of topics. While relatively small at 26,500 titles, the monograph collection is extremely important. As examples:

1. *History*–more than 2,000 titles on such topics as the Qutb Shahi dynasty and the rule of the Nizams, including government gazettes, court records, and histories of official service; Muslims in India; and the partition of India;
2. *Language and literature*–approximately 12,000 titles on the development of the Urdu language; *tazkiras* (prose works on Urdu poets); studies in Urdu of traditional grammar and phonetics; and more than 2,500 volumes of Urdu poetry;
3. *Religious texts and studies*–more than 4,000 titles on all aspects of Islam, as well as Urdu publications on Hinduism, Christianity, and Jainism;
4. *Biography and autobiography*–approximately 2,000 titles on major and minor figures from South Asia and elsewhere in the world.

Digital Projects

CIC's South Asia Libraries Digital Dictionaries Program

The South Asia Libraries Project of the Committee on Institutional Cooperation (CIC) has purchased the electronic files corresponding to three modern Hindi and Tamil dictionaries and will mount them as on-line databases for Web access from ClC domains. Additionally, access to the dictionaries will be sold to non-CIC institutions under royalty agreements with copyright holders for the dictionaries. The paper equivalents of the three proposed dictionaries–widely adopted for courses in Hindi and Tamil–are:

- *The Oxford Hindi-English dictionary*/edited by R. S. McGregor. Oxford [England]: Oxford University Press, 1993. xx, 1083 p.; 25 cm.

- *Kriyavin tarkalat Tamil aharati: Tamil-Tamil-Ankilam*/ chief editor, P. R. Subramanian. Madras: Irriya, 1992. xxxvi, 979p.: ill.; 23 cm. [A dictionary of contemporary Tamil, Tamil-Tamil-English.]
- *Tarkalat Tamil maraputtotar aharati: Tamil-Tamil-Ankilam.* Chennai: Moli, 1997. xlii, 404 p.; 23 cm. [A dictionary of idioms and phrases in contemporary Tamil, Tamil-Tamil-English.]

These purchases are being covered by contributions of $2,000 each from CIC institutions with active South Asia programs (Chicago, Illinois, Iowa, Michigan, Minnesota, and Wisconsin-Madison) and $500 from other CIC members (Indiana, Michigan State, Northwestern, Ohio State, Pennsylvania State, and Purdue). Scholars at CIC institutions supporting South Asia studies will benefit most from these resources. However, all CIC members have students and faculty for whom the dictionaries will be valued resources.

Most of the groundwork for mounting the electronic files is already completed. Since investigations for this project began in 1995, test versions of all three dictionary files have been successfully converted to databases and preliminary versions of search engines are running at the University of Chicago. Search results are displayed in both roman transliteration and in the appropriate script over the Web. The University of Chicago Library will host the site. The Hindi and Tamil dictionaries will be available to CIC readers as Web databases before the end of 1999.

In a parallel collaborative CIC initiative, Chicago, Michigan, and Wisconsin-Madison received funding from the Department of Education under Title VI for conversion of an Urdu dictionary, John T. Platts' *A Dictionary of Urdu, Classical Hindi, and English*. First published in 1884 by Oxford University Press, the dictionary is still considered exemplary and is widely used by Urdu scholars. That dictionary was keyed by an offshore contractor and was made available on the Web winter 1999 as a worldwide resource, without charge.

Digital Dictionaries of South Asia <http://www.lib.uchicago.edu/e/su/southasia/605.html>

The University of Chicago, Columbia University, and the Triangle South Asia Consortium in North Carolina received a three-year grant of $444,000 in 1999 to expand upon the experience of the CIC Digital Dictionaries program to create and disseminate a much broader set of electronic dictionaries. A panel of language experts will identify key, established dictionaries which currently exist in print for each of the twenty-six modern literary languages of South Asia. At least one multilingual dictionary will be selected for each South Asian language; in the case of the more frequently taught languages, an additional monolingual dictionary will also be chosen. After the best extant resources have been identified, a team of project staff will then convert the dictionaries to digital formats. The results of this conversion will be available to readers through a searchable site on the World Wide Web, by means of standard file transfer protocol, or by compact disc. There will be no charge for access via the Internet and the compact discs will be available for the cost of duplication and mailing. This project will make a major contribution to the larger international lexical infrastructure while providing high quality resources for use by scholars and lay readers throughout the world. To complement the Digital Dictionaries of South Asia project, Columbia University Libraries has received a grant from the Hinduja Foundation, as a project of Columbia's Dharam Hinduja Indic Research Center, to convert a well-known dictionary of Sanskrit into an online database, for integration with the lexical database described above. The Columbia project will also produce online pedagogical tools for teaching scholars how to utilize South Asian manuscripts in their research. All of the lexical data will be provided with Unicode encoding.

Indic Manuscripts Access Project <http://www.columbia.edu/cu/dhirc/wqOnLineproj.html>

Under a large-scale grant from the Hinduja Foundation, Columbia University Libraries is now microfilming its large collection of Indic language manuscripts. These manuscripts, covering a wide range of topics especially important to the history of science and mathematics, will then be scanned from the film for production of high-resolution digital images, which are to be published on the web for global scholarly access. The full bibliographic descriptions of these items are being created as part of the project, and combine MARC-format records in RLIN and OCLC with the web version of the detailed scholarly descriptions of these works by Prof. David Pingree of the History of Mathematics Department at Brown University. An international body of Indological scholars and librarians advises the project.

Digital South Asia Library <*http://www.lib.uchicago.edu/e/su/southasia/dsal.html*>

The University of Chicago Library and Columbia University Libraries initiated a two-year pilot project on South Asia in 1998. The main objective of this project is to improve access to and delivery of international research resources. The improved access is the result of developing the infrastructure for inter-continental electronic document delivery to and from selected South Asia libraries and creating new electronic reference resources. These are comprised primarily of data entered by project participants in South Asia. In addition to the lead institutions, the Roja Muthiah Research Library and the Sundarayya Vignana Kendram are playing key roles in India. The pilot project is a part of a larger initiative titled the Global Resources Program. The Association of American Universities (AAU) and Association of Research Libraries (ARL) developed the program with support from The Andrew W. Mellon Foundation.

New project resources created under the pilot project include:

- Periodical indexes to select historical journals in Tamil and Urdu along with contribution of index entries for articles in English and other European languages to the *Bibliography of Asian Studies*.
- Union lists:
  - Library of Congress South Asia Serials <*http://efts.lib.uchicago.edu/efts/sa/search/search-main.html*> with holdings of U.S. participant libraries.
  - Irene Joshi's *A union list of South Asian newspapers and gazettes in reporting libraries and archives* will be available in 1999.
  - Tamil journals in Madras, including the Roja Muthiah Research Library, Maraimalai Adigal Library, and the Tamil Nadu State Archives.
  - Urdu journals in Hyderabad. The URLC collection, described above, and soon to include the Idara-e-Adabiyat Panjavurta e-Urdu.
- Full electronic texts of select official publications of India.

The Center for Research Libraries (CRL) received a grant of $540,000 in 1999 from the U.S. Department of Education for a three-year second phase of the Digital South Asia Library (DSAL)

<http://www.lib.uchicago.edu/e/su/southasia/606.html>. Through this project scholars, public policy officials, business leaders, and other citizens will benefit from an improved electronic information infrastructure and expeditious electronic delivery of digital research materials directly to their computers from the South Asian subcontinent and England. The DSAL project in its second phase will produce:

1. On-line information about contemporary and historical South Asia–including full-text documents, statistical data, electronic images of historical photographs, cartographic representations, and pedagogical resources for language instruction;
2. Delivery on demand of page images from South Asia, scanned from both paper and microform sources;
3. Internet-based indexes to highly select journals in the regional languages of South Asia;
4. Use of Unicode electronic character encoding for non-roman language data disseminated under the project;
5. An international cooperative venture whose contributing members will include leading universities in the U.S., Britain, and South Asia as well as libraries with a focus on South Asian studies; and
6. A detailed plan of operation for phase three of the Digital South Asia Library.

This second phase of the Digital South Asia Library project is being presented to The Andrew W. Mellon Foundation for partial funding of the required matching project support. Other matching support will be provided by cash and in-kind-contributions from the Center for Research Libraries, U.S. and overseas research libraries participating in DSAL, together with philanthropic foundations in the United Kingdom and South Asia. Proposals are also under preparation including: creation of an electronic *Guide to Pakistani Periodical Publications*, an on-line index to current English serial literature in the social sciences and humanities to be submitted to the National Endowment for the Humanities; creation of digital resources for South Asian art historical research and museology to be submitted to the Institute of Museum and Library Services, and creation of a union catalog of nineteenth-century South Asian publications to be submitted to the Ford Foundation.

The second phase of the Digital South Asia Library will dramatically increase the quantity and the range of research resources available as well as multiply the number of participants in DSAL. Following this proposed project, the third phase of DSAL will be largely self-sustaining, based on membership contributions from universities and individual scholars.

Composite Initiative

A Center for South Asian Libraries

The Center for Research Libraries is currently incorporating a tax-exempt overseas center for South Asian libraries. This center will facilitate scholarly research on South Asia in all academic disciplines through improved preservation of and access to the print, manuscript, and electronic heritage of India, Pakistan, Bangladesh, Nepal, and Sri Lanka and through support for the exchange of scholarly information. These aims will be accomplished through activities of the new center operating in conjunction with organizations and institutions holding similar objectives, such as the American Institute of Indian Studies. Membership in the center will be open to non-US. institutions as well. The range of activities will overlap with and extend those under the Digital South Asia Library Pilot Project. As a new American overseas research center, the corporation will apply for membership in the Council of American Overseas Research Centers (CAORC) to help achieve these purposes.

The Council of American Overseas Research Centers describes its purposes and activities on its web site <*http://www.caorc.org*>. There it states:

- American Overseas Research Centers foster international scholarly exchange, primarily through sponsorship of fellowship programs, which allow pre-doctoral and senior scholars to pursue independent research important to the increase of knowledge and to our understanding of foreign cultures.
- These non-governmental institutions are seen by their host countries as the official arm of American higher learning. The private structure of the centers and the unbiased research they promote make them respected foci of American academia in the countries in which they operate.
- The members of the Council of American Overseas Research Centers have centers in Bangladesh, Cyprus, Egypt, Greece, In-

> dia, Israel, Italy, Jordan, Morocco, Pakistan, Tunisia, Turkey, West Africa, and Yemen, and together represent over three hundred years of experience in facilitating research in foreign countries. The older centers have served as an operations base for virtually every American specialist undertaking research in the host countries.

Scholars will benefit enormously from the activities of the new center, tentatively called the Center for South Asian Libraries (CSAL). Current library collections in the United States are, for several reasons, ill equipped to provide scholars with early printed texts in the languages of South Asia. Because most library collections on South Asia in the States have been developed since World War II, their greatest strengths are in holdings of recent publications. Aside from recent work by the South Asia Microform Project and the Microfilming of Indian Publications Project, there has been little systematic effort to acquire early imprints in most languages of the South Asian subcontinent. In the past faculty and students exerted only slight demand for access to earlier printed texts. The need for access has changed dramatically, however, as a result of forty years of U.S. federal funding for the study of "critical languages."

The Center for Research Libraries (CRL), the home base in the U.S. for the new South Asia library center, is an institution with global interests and reach. As a consequence, it makes sense to locate the new center under the CRL umbrella. CSAL, a self-sustaining and independent corporation, will deposit copies of the resources resulting from its activities in South Asia with CRL. Additionally, CRL will be able to rely on the overseas center as a means of collecting research materials such as doctoral theses that are difficult to gather without a presence in the country of origin. The South Asia Microform Project (SAMP), based at CRL, will also find the bases of operation maintained by the new South Asia center of value as it continues to expand access to microforms from and about South Asia.

Current and proposed members of CAORC include the American Institute of Indian Studies, the American Institute of Pakistan Studies, the American Institute of Bangladesh Studies. and the American Institute of Sri Lanka Studies. Some of these institutes maintain libraries. The new CSAL will offer to assist those libraries to improve access to their collections and generally to enhance their infrastructure through collaborative engagements with the center. Starting with a base of operations in India, the center will likely expand its activities to Pakistan, Bangladesh, Nepal, and Sri Lanka. Already we have established a cooperating partnership with the Madan Puraskar Pustakalaya, a unique library in Kathmandu, Nepal with a comprehensive collection spanning the history of publishing in the Nepali language. The Madan Puraskar Pustakalaya, like the RMRL in Madras and the URLC in Hyderabad, will work with the Digital South Asia Libraries project, through the coordinating efforts of the CSAL, to catalog and preserve its collections, index its important journals, and provide bibliographic and full-text data via the internet. These new activities will be taken up after consultation with relevant CAORC centers in those countries.

FUTURE DIRECTIONS

What does the future hold? A few things seem reasonably clear. The first is that serious support for preservation microfilming of South Asian scholarly resources will dwindle. In large measure this is because foundations and government agencies are devoting more of their support to digital projects. It is important to expand electronic horizons through imaginative funding for the development of resources delivered via the Internet. Yet the needs of South Asianists are quite different from those of other scholars. Classicists working in Greek and Latin, for instance, have had years of sustained support by agencies around the world for preservation microfilming of the most important literature in that field. Further, scholars of ancient Greece can confidently state that all the major ancient Greek texts are available in electronic form along with most of the minor texts and inscriptions. In contrast, many of the most seminal publications from South Asia are in the most fragile of conditions, with relatively few copies in existence. Others have simply disappeared without a trace due to the pervasive impact of a harsh, variable climate, insects, and internal destruction due to the use of highly acidic paper.

This leads us to state that the future must hold more international initiatives for preservation and access. South Asian nations do not have adequate resources to meet the preservation needs within the region. We expect that the new center for libraries in South Asia (CSAL), which is being established by the Center for Research Libraries, will be one of those new initiatives providing external support for preservation and access activities within the subcontinent. The new center will be open to broader participation by non-US. institutions. Interconnection with other area groups is an additional future arena for international engagement. South Asians are dispersed throughout the world. They have found diasporic homes in Singapore, South Africa, the Caribbean, and China, to mention a few examples. By working in collaboration with our fellow scholars and librarians in those far-flung regions we will ensure that materials are preserved for telling the entire, worldwide story of South Asian peoples.

Our colleagues in South Asia deserve better access to scholarly resources. We need to expand the array of U.S., European, and East Asian publications about South Asia made accessible in South Asia itself. One often hears the lament of colleagues in the subcontinent over the difficulties they face in obtaining foreign journals or purchasing books printed in wealthy nations. This lack of access to the most recent writings of other scholars leaves many of them incapable of joining international scholarly discourse on an equal footing. They will contribute more effectively as colleagues if they have easier access to all publications about South Asia. More robust programs are needed for exchange of books and journals. As our institutions move toward delivery of publications over the Internet, there is a need to lobby for preferential pricing for our colleagues in South Asia. Certainly, we should strive to make the digital resources we create under our international collaborative efforts accessible to scholars in South Asia without charge, following the model of the free public library.

CONCLUDING COMMENTS

South Asia has been the focus of this paper. And yet, we see significant potential in engagements across the boundaries of world regions. Two developments hold promise for the near term. The first is a planned meeting of the Global Resources Project (GRP) participants whose projects cover materials and information resources from Africa, Germany, Japan, Latin America, South Asia, and Southeast Asia. One objective of that meeting will likely be sharing experiences of GRP's component projects so that others may understand more fully what has and has not been successful. Other probable topics include realistic assessment of impediments as we move towards self-sustaining status as programs and consideration of economies of scale we may achieve through common approaches to similar activities such as creation of periodical indexes. The second development relates to the Council of American Overseas Research Centers (CAORC) and creation of the Center for South Asian Libraries mentioned above. While that new Center will devote most of its attention to activities in the subcontinent, there are early signs that CAORC, whose broad American Overseas Digital Library project recently won a major grant under U.S. Department of Education's Title VI program, would value the sharing of expertise through consultancies with its other member centers, many of which have libraries. It may also be possible to organize workshops for training librarians from other centers in preservation, bibliographic access, and digitization.

We also believe that some of the approaches described in this paper could be generalized as models for other regions of the world. For example, the model we have discussed as a counterpoint to colonial plunder seems reasonable to consider for implementation in other areas formerly under colonial rule. We encourage the formation of an online repository for best practices related to international information exchange.

While we see many reasons for optimism regarding international library collaboration, we realize that there are many potential and actual impediments. These include:

- Government bureaucracy in foreign countries and in the U.S.;
- Suspicions by scholars and bureaucrats abroad over the motives for our activities and the repeated suggestion of imperialism as a driving force behind our engagements;
- Unevenness in the expertise brought forward by some collaborators abroad (while simultaneously recognizing that in several instances we have found greater expertise in India for our digital projects than in the U.S.); and
- The lack of international standards in certain areas (such as for microform color images) and the partial implementation of standards (such as fonts for representation of non-roman characters over the Web).

It would be valuable to discuss methods by which these and other impediments may be minimized.

Finally, we encourage candid discussion of the fit between programs considered at this conference and trajectories of support from foundations and government bodies. How do we best avoid collapse during periods of reduced funding for major projects? The projects described in the vignettes above were organized with many modest milestones and sub-units. This has permitted us to undertake activities in relatively small batches or units. With the MIPP project, the preservation activities have been undertaken either language-by-language or by preserving all the relevant titles in a single collection. We have also considered hibernation modes for projects if funding were to evaporate, although it has not been necessary to implement this approach yet. Hibernation would involve maintenance of critical staff as a nucleus from which activities could begin again when funding was once more made available. This could be achieved through use of reserve funds set aside from the several projects. Another question we would like to open for discussion is the degree of realism undergirding self-sustainability for international projects. For obvious reasons, most funding agencies encourage movement towards self-sustenance and are wary of projects that are excessively dependent upon their support. Creative thinking will produce ancillary streams of revenue from resources developed under these projects. As an example, the British Library is discussing the possibility of selling through its Web site extremely high quality photographs generated under the Digital South Asia Library project. Those images are from originals held by the British Library. They will be scanned at high enough resolution to be used in commercial publications. (Lower resolution images will be distributed without charge via the DSAL project site.) As part of this marketing arrangement, the British Library is willing to consider payment of royalties to the project. Another approach we have found useful is one of encompassing or subsuming older projects under newer ones, giving a new flavor to the older activities. For instance, as funding agencies have shown a preference for digitization projects, we have sought funds to convert selected scholarly resources created under earlier preservation projects into digital archives and to index them for easier access.

We thank the organizers and sponsors for creating this forum and look forward to continued engagement with the institutions represented at the conference.

From Farmington Plan to the Pacific Rim Digital Library Alliance: New Strategies in Developing International Collections

Phyllis Mirsky
R. Bruce Miller
Karl Lo

Eliminating Borders: What are the implications and opportunities presented to cooperative collection development by the growing unimportance of national borders and other geographical restraints? Can technologies provide new forums for cooperation? Can we grow new partnerships?

INTERNATIONAL COLLECTION DEVELOPMENT IN THE UNITED STATES

Many landmark initiatives in the development of international collections in the United States were inspired or triggered by national and international events. World War II inspired the Farmington Plan.

Phyllis Mirsky (e-mail: psmirsky@ucsd.edu) is Deputy University Librarian; R. Bruce Miller (e-mail: rbmiller@ucsd.edu) is Associate University Librarian, User Support Services; and Karl Lo (e-mail: klo@ucsd.edu) is Director, International Relations and Pacific Studies Library, University of California, San Diego.

[Haworth co-indexing entry note]: "From Farmington Plan to the Pacific Rim Digital Library Alliance: New Strategies in Developing International Collections." Mirsky, Phyllis, R. Bruce Miller, and Karl Lo. Co-published simultaneously in *Collection Management* (The Haworth Information Press, an imprint of The Haworth Press, Inc.) Vol. 24, No. 3/4, 2000, pp. 241-250; and: *Creating New Strategies for Cooperative Collection Development* (ed: Milton T. Wolf and Marjorie E. Bloss) The Haworth Information Press, an imprint of The Haworth Press, Inc., 2000, pp. 241-250. Single or multiple copies of this article are available for a fee from The Haworth Document Delivery Service [1-800-342-9678, 9:00 a.m. - 5:00 p.m. (EST). E-mail address: getinfo@ haworthpressinc.com].

© 2000 by The Haworth Press, Inc. All rights reserved.

Sputnik triggered the National Defense Education Acts. Agricultural surpluses provided funds that led to the PL-480 programs.

> Over the years, research libraries have pursued a number of strategies to build comprehensive collections through cooperation in collection development The establishment of the Farmington Plan after World War II was the most far-reaching effort to ensure that "one copy of every important foreign book" was available in the United States. The Farmington Plan exemplified the large-scale, decentralized system of specializations by voluntary agreements among American research libraries. By 1972, tensions between cooperative collection responsibilities and institutional priorities, the complexities of the subject allocations, the high costs of acquiring and processing materials, and the perceived inclusion of materials marginal to local interests all contributed to the decision to terminate the Farmington Plan.[1]

> The National Defense Education Act of 1958 was the most important federal bill related to higher education since the 1862 Morrill Act. . . . The general provisions of the act articulated the Cold War motives of Congress: "an educational emergency exists and requires action by the federal government. Assistance will come from Washington to help develop as rapidly as possible those skills essential to the national security." Federal expenditures for education more than doubled. For higher education, this included funding . . . for curriculum development in the sciences, math, and foreign languages. [I]ts greatest impact was within the realm of an evolving and expanding network of research universities.[2]

PL-480 was a . . .

> 1958 amendment to the Agricultural Trade and Assistance Act of 1954 which permitted the U.S. to accept foreign currency in exchange for agricultural products and to spend the foreign currency in that country, for such materials as books and periodicals. PL-480 allowed selected research libraries in the United States to acquire current publications from some developing countries.[3]

These were unilateral endeavors of the United States, mostly from government agencies. As the significance of the events faded, the related programs were forgotten, leaving neglected and orphan collections scattered around the country.

Of course, credit must also be given for direct initiatives within the research library community.

> Among these is the National Program of Acquisitions and Cataloging at the Library of Congress, which supports acquisition and cataloging of research materials published throughout the world. The collecting programs of the Center for Research Libraries have enriched access to specialized foreign materials, especially to foreign newspapers, foreign dissertations, and foreign government publications. The Shared Resources Program of the Research Libraries Group is another important effort. Central to the RLG program is the assignment of primary collecting responsibility for certain categories of materials. Still another example is the Seminar on the Acquisition of Latin American Library Materials (SALALM), which has concentrated on improving support for and access to Latin American research resources. In addition to these highly visible cooperative efforts, many regional, state, and local cooperative arrangements have been carried out over the years.

Additionally, private foundations such as Ford, Luce, Mellon, and Rockefeller have fostered coordination and collaboration for the acquisition of foreign materials.

> All of these efforts, both past and ongoing, provide valuable experience in coordinated collection development and help to define the limitations. They underscore the fact that libraries have achieved significant progress through collective action, but they also bring into sharp focus the fact that current efforts are quite limited. While some areas of the world receive needed attention, many others are without cooperative programs. Many of the questions that past cooperative efforts tried to address remain, but technology provides a new framework and new opportunities to address the issues.[1]

NEW OPPORTUNITIES FOR INTERNATIONAL COOPERATION

The increasing ubiquity of the internet and ease of access via the world wide web have opened the door to new opportunities for delivering information resources to our faculty and students. In the past, research libraries in the United States have tried to coordinate collection development in order to use finite financial resources to physically acquire at least one copy of scarce publications that could then be shared. These scarce publications were kept together in physical collections that enabled scholars to identify where to seek selected materials. Interlibrary loan or individual travel to the holding library provided access. Within the United States, we pride ourselves on our interlibrary loan structure and our willingness to share our collections.

Interestingly, interlibrary loan is not yet well developed among Asian libraries. There are complex and myriad reasons, but one factor is the strong cultural bias toward self reliance: "My library should have the best collection possible for my faculty and students." Before you judge this environment, stop and think about the pride that U.S. libraries have for our interlibrary loan structure. We proudly loan to each other, but our library materials only cross our national border under exceptional circumstances. Granted, time and cost factors are significant issues for international interlibrary loan. Nonetheless, consider the cultural bias that is implicit. Could it be argued that U.S. libraries have a history of acquiring foreign library materials through coordinated collection development in order to be self reliant within our borders?

National identity is inherent in who we are. Instead of trying to overcome cultural bias in relationships among libraries in different countries, we should seek ways to capitalize on these differences. "Eliminating Borders" is one of the themes of this conference. We don't need to eliminate borders. Borders help define us. We need to make them easier to cross. Ultimately, the scholar doesn't care which library owns an item as long as he can quickly put his hands on the information inside it. Can we develop means that truly facilitate international sharing of limited information resources? Can we make it as easy to deliver from across the Pacific Ocean as it is to retrieve an item from our local off campus storage?

With these thoughts in mind, we pose that it is time to move beyond nationally focused coordinated collection development. However, knowing the inherent limitations of the coordination model, it is clear that simply transplanting that strategy into an international venue is not a useful venture. Instead, it is time to shift our focus to international *cooperation*.

Recent economic prosperity and technological advancement around the Pacific Rim region have given rise to a new kind of cooperation to provide widespread access to diverse information resources. The body of information produced about and throughout the Pacific Rim during the last few decades has been increasing at a rate far in excess of what a single library can acquire and provide for its users. The development of comprehensive collections of foreign publications is particularly challenging. More and more, libraries have come to rely on borrowing from each other to meet the needs of their users. This principle of resource sharing via interlibrary loans is sound, but there are significant obstacles that manifest due to political, language, geographic, and technical issues.

The *Pacific Rim Digital Library Alliance* was formed in an effort to overcome these obstacles using the strategy of practical projects and agreements to improve scholarly access to the collections held by its members. Through this cooperation, we believe that over time the Alliance will profoundly affect intellectual exchange and mutual understanding between East and West.

HISTORY OF THE PACIFIC RIM DIGITAL LIBRARY ALLIANCE

In 1995, the University of California, San Diego Libraries received a two year grant from the National Security Education Program to develop a multilingual computer server to provide international access via the internet to online information in Chinese, Japanese, and Korean scripts. As part of the NSEP grant, the UCSD Libraries hosted a seminar in December 1995 and invited technical specialists from Pacific Rim countries to provide input into the development of the multilingual server. Further developing these relationships, the UCSD Libraries initiated bilateral arrangements with key participants to use the internet to expand traditional library exchange arrangements. One of the first agreements enabled the provision of scientific information from UCSD in exchange for access to Chinese language databases from Academia Sinica in Taiwan. This unprecedented electronic exchange of diverse scholarly information across academic disciplines and national boundaries has been highly successful and is greatly valued by scholars at both institutions. Since then, similar exchanges have been launched with Peking University, Hong Kong University, and the Australian National University.

The success of these initial bilateral exchanges inspired the concept of a multilateral partnership among libraries from major academic institutions around the Pacific Rim. In June 1997, UCSD hosted a conference during which the Pacific Rim Digital Library Alliance was conceptualised. Invitees to the conference included senior management from institutions that were represented at the December 1995 seminar and from other institutions with whom close personal working relationships had been established. The Alliance was formally ratified by its members in October 1997.

The Pacific Rim Digital Library Alliance is a consortium of thirteen prestigious academic libraries in Australia, Canada, China, Japan, Korea, Mexico, Singapore, Taiwan, and the United States. The goal of the Alliance is to facilitate improved access to scholarly research materials throughout the Pacific Rim. Resource sharing, document delivery, cooperative collection development, personnel exchange, and the use of technology are seen as key cost effective strategies for overcoming budgetary constraints and the barriers of distance, language, and culture.

The charter members of the Alliance include:

- Academia Sinica, Taipei
- Australian National University Library, Canberra
- El Colegio de Mexico Library, Mexico City
- Keio University Library, Tokyo
- National University of Singapore Library
- Peking University Library, Beijing
- Seoul National University Library
- University of British Columbia Library, Vancouver
- University of California, Berkeley Library
- University of California, San Diego Libraries
- University of Hong Kong Libraries
- University of Washington Libraries, Seattle
- Zhongshan University Library, Guangzhou

The National Institute of Japanese Literature, Tokyo, is an associate member. The Alliance also has technical partners in support of the complex issues that are found in creating and managing digital library resources:

- Council on Library and Information Resources, Washington, D.C.
- Digital Library Federation, Washington, D.C.
- San Diego Supercomputer Center and Center for Advanced Computational Science and Engineering

Significant infrastructure funding for the Alliance has been provided by the Henry Luce Foundation. The Alliance has also received private individual financial support and a software contribution from Innovative Interfaces.

PACIFIC RIM DIGITAL LIBRARY

We are creating a Pacific Rim digital library that will directly serve Alliance students and faculty. Construction is underway for a virtual "building": *http://www.prdla.org*. The catalogs for Alliance libraries are now available from this site. Work has begun to mount the first exhibit: a digital Pacific Explorations Archive which will include books, diaries, ships' logs, atlases, manuscripts, sketches, photographs, etc. The Chinese Digital Library will comprise another very large "wing." The Chinese Digital Library project charts new territory that requires the integration of varied technologies across operating systems, character codes, proprietary software, mass data storage, and cultural boundaries. In addition to the international academic partners. we are working closely with four companies that have exceptional multilingual capabilities: Superstar (Beijing), Star+Globe (Singapore), Digital Heritage (Hong Kong), and Innovative Interfaces (Emeryville, CA).

As this paper is being written, we are finalising the acquisition of a server at the San Diego Supercomputer Center to provide the technical support for internet access to some of the collections in the Chinese Digital Library. These are databases of fully digitized Chinese language books including the Qing Dynastic Lid and a large corpus of recent acquisitions by the national Library of China. These digital libraries are of significant importance to scholars, but they also contain works that are of interest to the general public, e.g., literature and history. The initial implementation in the early fall of 1999 will require 200 gigabytes of active disk. Plans are being formalized for the Chinese Digital Library to provide a mirror site for major databases in Beijing, Hong Kong, and Taipei within the next twelve months, possibly creating the largest Chinese digital library site in the world. Growth is expected to be in the terabyte range within a few years. The UCSD Libraries and SDSC will use the composite database as a test bed to conduct research and development in the scaling issues inherent with managing very large library databases. Additionally, the Libraries will develop emerging technologies for the creation of digital images and for the management of multiple-byte character sets. Within copyright constraints, all data will be accessible free of charge to anyone who has a web connection.

It should be noted that the Alliance is not predicated upon Chinese studies or even a broader Asian studies focus. Chinese language materials are not the motive; they are the opportunity. The readily available Chinese language materials form the corpus of an early venture into full text online, but don't forget the earlier reference to scientific information supplied by UCSD. For example, we have faxed thousands of pages of photocopied science and engineering articles to our Alliance partners in Taiwan and Hong Kong in exchange for online access to their proprietary databases. The Alliance institutions support all disciplines in a multilingual environment that includes users who natively speak Chinese, English, French, Japanese, Korean, and Spanish.

The potential resources are enormous. A conservative estimate concludes that there are more than 50 million printed volumes among the combined holdings of the Alliance libraries. An important byproduct of this effort is that access to many Alliance resources will become available to anyone who can connect to the internet, whether or not they are associated with Alliance universities. Electronic document delivery and interlibrary loan will provide access to materials that are not available online.

Networked digital technology provides the focus for tangible products of Alliance cooperation. However, equally important is the effort to create a sustainable organizational infrastructure. To be successful, it is imperative that we understand our cultural strengths and weaknesses, and that can be done only through long term personal relationships. To that end, we have begun a series of long term personnel exchanges. We also have supported numerous site visits among the Alliance members. It is possible to accomplish international business by using email, but it is orders of magnitude more effective to meet face to face when planning and implementing complex technical projects. Along the way we become friends and colleagues and establish trust that helps us use our cultural differences in positive ways. This is a long term investment that will be enjoyed by future generations.

The Pacific Rim Digital Library Alliance is unique in that it is directly driven by leadership from university libraries and those who are most knowledgeable about and committed to the services that can be provided. Administrative bureaucracy has been minimized, pilot projects with rapid results are preferred over "grand schemes," and cooperative ventures among subsets of the membership are encouraged. Successful pilot projects quickly deliver needed information resources to scholars and, at the same time, provide the foundations and test beds for the development of even more substantial resources. Each successful bilateral arrangement opens the door to include additional partners in the future. Each personnel exchange is an investment that will be repaid many times through long term relationships that will ultimately benefit our users.

CONCLUSION

The traditional role of the library to acquire, organize, and deliver information is an enduring one. However, rapid changes in both the quantity and the formats of information resources have combined with budgetary limitations to undermine the viability of the classic library founded on large, comprehensive collections. We seek to overcome these constraints through aggressive resource sharing and the use of technology in support of document delivery. The Pacific Rim Digital Library Alliance seeks to overcome associated political, language, geographic, and technical obstacles through a variety of practical projects and agreements. The Alliance members believe that this strategy is an opportunity to profoundly affect intellectual exchange and mutual understanding between East and West.

NOTES

1. "Research Libraries in a Global Context: An Exploratory Paper–Cooperative Collection Development Programs" *(http://www.arl.org/aau/Global.html)*. This paper was originally prepared by ARL Staff for the ARL Board of Directors and the ARL Committee on Collection Development. Prepared December 1989, Revised October 1992. In *Report of the AAU Task Force on Acquisition and Distribution of Foreign Language and Area Studies Materials (http://www.arl.org/aau/FATOC.html)*. Submitted to the AAU Presidents Steering Committee April 4, 1994, Washington, DC. Endorsed by the AAU Presidents April 18, 1994, Washington, DC.

2. "The Historical Importance of the NDEA and the Establishment of NASA" *(http://ishi.lib.berkeley.edu/cshe/ndea/info.html)*

3. Alma Dawson. "Resource Sharing" *http://adam.slis.lsu.edu/courses/7003/default.htm* (handout: LIS 7003: Principles of Collection Management Spring 1999) School of Library and Information Science, Louisiana State University.

Co-operative Collection Development: A UK National Library Perspective

Geoff Smith

The British Library is one of the one of world's great library collections. As an institution, however, it has only existed since 1973, when it was created as the national library of the United Kingdom, taking over the library functions and collections of a number of separate precursor institutions, each with separate collecting aims and traditions. I will describe some of the difficulties and challenges the Library has faced over recent years in relation to its collection development, and bow, following a Strategic Review in 1998, it now wishes further to develop co-operative and partnership approaches to collection development and related activities with other organizations both nationally and internationally. Given the nature of the British Library's existing collections and current collecting, this paper concentrates primarily, but not exclusively, on issues relating to the collection development of printed publications.

The Library's collection covers many centuries of recorded knowledge. It contains material in all major and many minor languages, from all countries and in all disciplines. For over two hundred years the Library and its predecessor, the British Museum, have collected systematically UK printed publications through legal deposit. At the

---

Geoff Smith is Director, Co-operation and Partnership Programme, The British Library.

This paper was produced for the conference "Creating new strategies for cooperative collection development," November 1999.

[Haworth co-indexing entry note]: "Co-operative Collection Development: A UK National Library Perspective." Smith, Geoff. Co-published simultaneously in *Collection Management* (The Haworth Information Press, an imprint of The Haworth Press, Inc.) Vol. 24, No. 3/4, 2000, pp. 251-262; and: *Creating New Strategies for Cooperative Collection Development* (ed: Milton T. Wolf and Marjorie E. Bloss) The Haworth Information Press, an imprint of The Haworth Press, Inc., 2000, pp. 251-262. Single or multiple copies of this article are available for a fee from The Haworth Document Delivery Service [1-800-342-9678, 9:00 a.m. - 5:00 p.m. (EST). E-mail address: getinfo@haworthpressinc.com].

© 2000 by The Haworth Press, Inc. All rights reserved.

same time as building the national archive of UK printed publications, the Library and its predecessors have assembled and developed one of the world's greatest research library collections. It is renowned for having incomparable holdings of manuscripts, maps and music, one of the world's largest archives of sound recordings, the world's largest collection of patent specifications and of conference proceedings, and rich and vast holdings of early and modern books and periodicals from the UK and overseas.

Increasingly, the Library is taking in or accessing elsewhere publications in electronic form and, at the same time, continues to collect publications in those more traditional forms which are the historic basis of its collections.

The Library provides access to its collections within its reading rooms in London to scholars and researchers from the UK and all over the world on the basis of their need to use the collections, and as a back up and extension to the resources they have available to them in their own institutions. At the same time, its document supply and interlending services, based at Boston Spa in the North of England, deal with over four million requests a year from both UK and foreign users for copies of articles and other texts, and for interlibrary loans of items from the Library's collection. This allows other libraries to concentrate on building their own core collections secure in the knowledge that material outside of that core will remain accessible systematically to their researchers through remote supply.

Until the mid 1990s the component parts of the Library brought with them traditions of acquisition for reference and for remote supply which were largely sustained, funded and staffed independently of one another. This resulted in considerable duplication in different parts of the collection, particularly of UK publications, of serials in both humanities and science held separately for document supply and reference purposes, and of English language monographs held both at Boston Spa and in London. Following a review in the mid 1990s, the Library brought together in 1996 its collection development functions and staffing under a single department to assist in the shaping of a corporate collection development policy and to move towards the development and use of a Library-wide "single collection." This has aimed to minimize duplication as far as possible, and to use where practicable a single copy of an item to support both reading room access and remote document supply. However, some level of duplication continues to be required on either policy or service grounds. Items belonging to the national published archive, which have been deposited by publishers under legal deposit arrangements, are only available to readers who visit the Library's reading rooms, and are not used for remote supply. Duplicate copies of UK publications, both serials and monographs, continue therefore to be purchased for document supply purposes and interlending. Other items, particularly some scientific journals, are in such heavy demand by both readers and remote users that reference and document supply services cannot both be provided adequately from a single printed copy. And so duplication has continued, initially of print copies, but increasingly using electronic versions where publishers are willing to license these for both reading room and document supply use.

In 1998 the British Library carried out a Strategic Review to help it define its role and plan its activities for the future. This included a wide-raging consultation exercise to seek the views of stakeholders, particularly users and other UK libraries and related organizations. Responses to the consultation exercise emphasized the importance of the Library's collection in underpinning its services to support scholarship and research. Responses recommended that the Library should play a leading role in creating a national strategy for national library and information provision, to lead to an efficient and effective library infrastructure. It should ensure that its strategy is informed by and compatible with the development of parallel arrangements in other parts of the world. It should ensure that the Library's new direction is firmly set in the context of the United Kingdom library and information network and that its role is clearly understood by all. It should conduct proper and timely consultation with the library and information community before changes are introduced.

In relation to collection development the Strategic Review recommended that:

- building the collections should continue to be a top priority, with a wish to spend substantially more on acquisitions than 1998/99 in each of the next 3 years;
- digital works should form an integral part of the Library's collection, with efforts continuing to extend legal deposit to cover non-print publications;

- it should be recognized formally that collecting in all subjects, in all languages and from all nations cannot be sustained;
- there should he particular emphasis on material which is most used, or most likely to be much used in the future;
- co-operation on the collecting of legal deposit material should continue and develop further with the other UK legal deposit libraries;
- there should be increased cooperation with UK public libraries on the collection of and provision of access to local newspapers and other categories of local publications;
- there should be continuing emphasis on the extensive collecting of works published world-wide relating to the UK and the UK experience, and of English language materials of research level significance;
- material should be collected which interprets and illuminates the non-UK material in the Library's foundation and historic printed collections, and in the Library's great special collections of manuscripts, maps and music;
- material in foreign languages should be collected which adds value or meaning to the existing collection, subject to expectation of need and use.

The Library's Board endorsed the main recommendations of the Strategic Review, in particular that the Library should seek to develop partnership arrangements with other institutions that would enable a more distributed approach within the UK to collection development and other activities. Co-operation on collection development would form one strand of the Library's wider program of increasing cooperation with other UK libraries and institutions, expected to cover co-operation also on access, preservation, digitization, record creation and bibliographic services.

To help take forward these recommendations and the outcomes of the Strategic Review, the Library has set up a small team of staff to develop and co-ordinate a cooperation and partnership program, and has established a new fund to support practical co-operative activities and projects in the UK. The program is headed by Geoff Smith. The purposes of the team are to define and develop the program of co-operation and partnership in the key areas mentioned, to co-ordinate existing and new BL cooperative activities, working with colleagues in the relevant operational areas, and to provide an external focus and point of contact relating to co-operation.

Discussions have begun with a number of institutions, and a number of projects have been initiated to take forward this co-operation program. Examples of these are given below.

COLLECTING OF UK PUBLICATIONS

Several initiatives are under way in relation to the collecting of United Kingdom publications. Within the UK legal deposit system, consisting of the British Library, the university libraries of Oxford and Cambridge, the national libraries of Scotland and Wales, and Trinity College Dublin, there is increasing co-operation on collecting and preservation responsibilities for particular materials, starting with leisure journals and local newspapers, but expected to extend in the future to further types of material.

In pursuit of a long standing joint aim the UK legal deposit libraries are seeking to extend legal deposit arrangements to cover non-print publications in both microform and electronic form and to bring these into the national published archive. In December 1998, following the report of a working party of library and publisher representatives, the Secretary of State for Culture, Media and Sport, announced his intention to move towards legislation for this once further work on definitions and impact on business had been completed. The legal deposit libraries are currently working with publishers' representatives to agree to a code of practice for the voluntary deposit of non-print publications to fill the gaps in collecting until legislation comes into force. It is expected that this code of practice will be agreed upon before the end of 1999, with a voluntary scheme to be implemented from early 2000, while it is hoped that the legislative process will begin within the next eighteen months. It is the view of the deposit libraries that, as for printed publications, deposited electronic items should be available to researchers within each of the deposit libraries, either through deposit of multiple copies, or through limited access across networks between the libraries. Planning for management procedures and for the network mechanisms is currently under way between the libraries.

Discussions have begun with the public library sector to improve collecting of and access to UK local publications. A research project is being carried out at Loughborough University on a case study of local publications from Leicestershire and from the city of Leicester. The main aims of this research are to identify and develop models which will facilitate co-operative initiatives and partnership arrangements at local, regional and national levels, intended to improve the coverage of collecting of local publications and to ensure their recording in the British National Bibliography.

FOREIGN COLLECTING

It is in the area of collecting foreign materials, particularly those in foreign languages, that the greatest changes in the British Library's collection development policies and practices are likely to occur. The 'universal' model of collecting was established in the British Museum by its great Keeper of Printed Books, Antonio Panizzi, in the middle of the 19th century. In 1861 his deputy, Thomas Watts, wrote:

> the object . . . has been to bring together from all quarters the useful, the elegant and the curious literature of every language; to unite with the best English library in England or the world, the best Russian library out of Russia, the best German, out of Germany the best Spanish out of Spain, and so for every language, from Italian to Icelandic, from Polish to Portuguese.

This ideal, though affected over time by budget fluctuations and by external political circumstances, remained since then the basis of the British Museum's, and subsequently the British Library's collecting policies and practices, with collecting organized on the basis of language and country of publication rather than on the subject basis more common in academic libraries.

As stated earlier, the 1998 Strategic Review recommended that 'it should be recognized formally that collecting in all subjects, all languages and from all nations cannot be sustained.' One of the factors influencing this conclusion was the financial pressure arising from escalating costs of materials, the associated collecting activity, and the long-term life cycle costs of processing, storage and preservation. In addition, however, analysis of British Library usage data, and external developments in publishing, technical structures, researcher expectation and library provision, all point to the need for the British Library's foreign collecting to be better coordinated with that of other major collections in the UK and elsewhere to ensure overall optimization of the use of limited resources, and best overall provision to meet research needs.

Significant factors include the high overlap in user communities with academic libraries in the UK. In many areas the Library's current collecting overlaps significantly with that of other academic and specialist institutions. At the same time there is relatively little use of current foreign language materials (as compared to foreign language materials in the Library's historic collections). Reader use of recent (post 1990) foreign language humanities and social sciences material is low, suggesting that researchers' first resort needs for access to such material are being met elsewhere. Purchasing of foreign language monographs in science, technology and medicine has virtually ceased, with little apparent impact on services or users. At the same time, demand for items for document supply shows a continuing diminution of the proportion of foreign language requests, with, in the most recent survey carried out, 96% of items requested being in the English language.

There appears to be general consensus that in principle there should be increased and improved co-operation on collection development. The difficulties lie in establishing effective and economic ways to achieve this, and in finding overall a systematic way forward that is to the benefit of both libraries and researchers.

A number of projects are under way to collect and analyze data on current collecting patterns and usage, to examine models and to identify appropriate solutions based on collaborative and partnership approaches. Some of these have been initiated by the British Library as pilot projects. Examples include investigation of the collecting of German language humanities and social science materials (with Cambridge University Library); history of medicine materials (with the Wellcome Institute); natural history materials (with the Natural History Museum); oriental materials (with the School of Oriental and African Studies at London University). Work so far suggests in each case that there is scope and likely benefit in closer collaboration on collection development and access.

At the same time the Library has been invited to be a participant in a number of initiatives within the UK higher education sector as part of the higher education funded Research Support Libraries Program

(RSLP). The Library is involved in ten separate projects, including collaborative collection development and collection management projects relating to Russian and East European studies, Asian materials, foreign legal materials, official publications, music, archaeology, Icelandic materials, and resources for Caribbean Studies and the history of Black and Asian people in Britain. These projects will take place over the next three years and are intended to map existing provisions, establish models, and provide a framework for agreeing upon responsibilities and mechanisms for the future for improved collecting and access arrangements on a distributed basis.

The challenges to be faced in achieving successful co-operation should not be underestimated. It will not be successful without the support of specialist staff in the British Library and elsewhere, who need to understand and believe in the mutual benefits and to be committed to establishing effective ways of working together. Equally important is the understanding and acceptance of users of the rationale and the overall benefits. A number of difficult issues will have to be addressed. Some of these issues are described below, together with suggestions for how they might be approached.

There is concern at the prospect that for non-UK materials the range of languages and/or disciplines collected by the British Library, and the level of its duplication of current collecting with other institutions, will be reduced through co-operative agreements, and thereby leading to a reduction in the quality of its collections and its value to current and future users. It will be important to ensure that material no longer taken by the British Library will be collected by and accessible in or from other institutions. It will be equally important that in addition to appropriate rationalization of collecting, co-operation should also aim for and be able to demonstrate overall improvement in the rage of material available to researchers where there is an identifiable need for this extended rage.

There is likely to be a conflict between usage as a key driver of collecting policy in all institutions and the need to ensure systematic overall availability of lower use material as institutions move from a holding to an access strategy. There is a tendency for all institutions under budget pressure to retreat to a common core of collecting of material most in demand. The British Library intends to continue systematic collecting on a centralized basis of materials for document supply, particularly of serials and English language materials. It will collect both materials in high demand from its services, and other materials, for which the cost in relation to local levels of use are uneconomic to individual libraries outside of their core areas of collecting, but for which there is sufficient aggregate level of use at the national level.

There is an expectation in the UK that the British Library should continue to be the last resort systematic collector of some categories of material, particularly foreign language, of which it may be the only significant holder in the country–even where there is little evidence of either their use for reading room reference or remote supply. It needs to be examined and debated whether last resort, low-use material in individual disciplines or languages is best held centrally or whether it would be better held in the specialist institutions or academic collections, where first resort use is also most likely by researchers in the field concerned. In some cases it should be considered whether categories of last resort 'just-in-case-material' in particular disciplines or languages need to be held within the UK at all; or whether reliance on remote supply services or even reference access in other countries, including the country of origin, would be sufficient in the event of future research need.

There is likely to be resistance of users to the concept of more distributed collecting, in particular if its implementation were to mean they would have to travel significant distances to use material they would previously have found in their home institution or in the British Library. This argues that printed material in high use and demand should continue to be held locally, even where it duplicates material elsewhere, with distributed approaches being more appropriate for lower use material, for material for which there is an imbalance in use (high in one institution but low in another) or for electronic resources which can be accessed locally regardless of where they are physically held. In a more distributed collecting environment efforts will need to be made to ensure wherever possible that material held elsewhere is accessible via interlending or remote supply copying rather than solely by on site reference access. It may be possible, if wished by users and the libraries concerned, to extend the backup arrangements currently operated by the British Library's Document Supply Centre so that requests can still be routed via a single point, even if the request is subsequently filled by lending or copying from another institution.

There is a fear among libraries, and possibly among funding agencies, that co-operation may in fact result in either an increase in overall costs, or in an unequal redistribution of costs, with savings in one institution resulting in an increase in costs in others. This points to the need to examine and discuss openly the economics of cooperation, and to develop models able to identify in financial terms the success or failure of co-operation.

Changes in collecting policy and responsibility are likely to impact on staffing needs and organization, leading some staff to view co-operation as a threat to the status quo. In the British Library this is reinforced by a belief in some staff that the centralized 'universal' model of collecting remains valid, and is still the most appropriate method of provision at the national level for meeting current and long-term research needs, particularly for onsite reference use. To overcome this attitude, staff need to be encouraged to become more outwardly focused on user needs and external developments rather than internally focused on their own collections. They need to see the establishment of effective co-operation in their field, in order to improve overall provision for researchers, as an important professional opportunity and challenge, and to be become actively involved in the detailed investigation of and planning for co-operation.

Future research needs are unpredictable, given an assumption that research libraries collect material as much for future generations of research use as for the present. That this assumption has validity can be seen from the evidence of the continuing high levels of use of the British Library's historic humanities and social science collections. The diversity of this use suggests that it would have been impossible a hundred or two hundred years ago to identify selectively only that material then being published which would be of interest to the researchers of the end of the twentieth century, and that the greatest legacy of those collectors was in the range and depth of their collecting. Similar considerations are argued in terms of what of current output will be of long-term value to the researchers of the future. For UK material it is accepted that the purposes of current legal deposit collecting are both to support current use and to build and preserve systematically and comprehensively the national published archive for future generations of researchers. However it can no longer be realistic for an individual national library to carry out this same dual role for the published output of the whole of the rest of the world, particularly when electronic publications are added to the still growing print output. Here it will be essential for libraries to collaborate both nationally and internationally, to ensure that the material needed to support current research is collected and held where current use and demand are likely to be highest, whether in national libraries, specialist collections or academic institutions. Responsibilities for long-term preservation, retention and access provision to support future research also need to be agreed upon, either between the same libraries, or, increasingly with institutions abroad, including national libraries and major collections in the country of origin.

These, then, are some of the barriers to co-operation that will need to be overcome if it is to be effective and successful. The need to work together effectively has never been greater. Most libraries in the UK, and almost certainly in other countries, including the USA, have been subject to budget pressures and have seen collecting budgets shrink in real terms as the rise in cost of materials, particularly serials, outstrips general inflation and any increase in institutional funding. In the UK all public institutions have experienced pressure on their staffing, while user numbers and demand continue to grow, stimulated by the government's learning and education agendas.

At the same time, the opportunities to work together more effectively, and the enabling technologies and mechanisms to allow us to do so, have never been better. Electronic mail and list servers offer our staff improved communication to assist their working together. Our major library catalogues are now mostly in computer form, and are accessible to each other across the World Wide Web, though many of us still have valuable but underused resources in material still needing to be catalogued, or catalogues still needing to be converted to computer form. In the UK significant amounts of funding continue to be allocated to major retrospective conversion projects, and the British Library is involved in support for the development, promulgation and quest for funding of a national strategy on retrospective catalogue conversion. At the same time, there are significant developments in inter-availability of library catalogues, with the development of Z39.50 capabilities, giving users the capacity to search seamlessly and at the same time the catalogues not only of their home institution but also those of other institutions with related holdings.

The development of subject gateways and other resource discovery tools offer the librarian powerful ways to guide users to the relevant electronic and physical resources to meet their needs; while the World

Wide Web, with its vast and rapidly growing electronic content, increases massively the range of materials accessible to our users, whether direct or while in our reading rooms. At the same time it provides us with a mechanism for delivering to users the content of our own collections, once converted into digital form.

In the UK there are significant new funding initiatives to ensure that the capabilities of the Internet are made widely available to the general population through greatly improved provision in public libraries, and there are major opportunities for collaboration between library sectors in the provision of digital content for this 'New Library Network.'

The British Library believes the time has never been better to explore and implement shared approaches to our common concerns, and to build a framework of agreements and a network of collaborations to lead to an improved, coordinated, and increasingly distributed national and international library resource that will meet the needs of current and future generations of researchers.

Specialized Cooperative Efforts in Collection Development: An Analysis of Three Slavic Programs

Bradley L. Schaffner

The ever-increasing cost of acquiring publications and providing access to scholarly information has driven academic and research libraries to search for ways to maximize collection development resources. Cooperative efforts increasingly appear to be the only viable way for libraries to provide their patrons with access to the broadest amount of published research and information currently available. As Richard M. Dougherty succinctly states, "No research library is self-sufficient."[1] Similarly, Joseph A. Boissé recently wrote: "The phrase 'library cooperation' has become something of a mantra in the library world in the late 20th century. . . . In our Herculean efforts to overcome many of the enormous obstacles which we face, we look to 'library cooperation' as a panacea."[2] Boissé is correct in his assertion that cooperation will help, but it is not an all-inclusive cure for collection development financial woes.

Although not a panacea, there is certainly room in this age of both "traditional" paper and electronic resources for many types of cooperative collection development activities among academic libraries. Some of the most successful cooperative programs, such as the Online

---

Bradley L. Schaffner is Head of the Slavic Department and Coordinator for International Programs at the University of Kansas Libraries (E-mail: bschaffn@ukans.edu).

[Haworth co-indexing entry note]: "Specialized Cooperative Efforts in Collection Development: An Analysis of Three Slavic Programs." Schaffner, Bradley L. Co-published simultaneously in *Collection Management* (The Haworth Information Press, an imprint of The Haworth Press, Inc.) Vol. 24, No. 3/4, 2000, pp. 263-280; and: *Creating New Strategies for Cooperative Collection Development* (ed: Milton T. Wolf and Marjorie E. Bloss) The Haworth Information Press, an imprint of The Haworth Press, Inc., 2000, pp. 263-280. Single or multiple copies of this article are available for a fee from The Haworth Document Delivery Service [1-800-342-9678, 9:00 a.m. - 5:00 p.m. (EST). E-mail address: getinfo@haworthpressinc.com].

© 2000 by The Haworth Press, Inc. All rights reserved.

Computer Library Center, Inc. (OCLC), the Research Libraries Information Network (RLN), and the Center for Research Libraries (CRL), have a national and international focus. In addition to national and international cooperatives, there is also a need for small-scale efforts to solve specific or local collection development challenges. If they are to succeed, these specialized cooperative ventures must not only be carefully planned and implemented, but librarians must begin to understand their importance and offer them the same level of consideration as the larger programs.

Donald B. Simpson, President of the Center for Research Libraries, warns against librarians duplicating cooperative programs simply to acquire local control over a project. Such actions result in scarce resources being spread too thin as "overhead and management and governance structures (of cooperative ventures) are needlessly replicated again and again."[3] According to Simpson, the one exception to this caution is the creation of statewide consortia that are more in touch with local needs and priorities.[4] Although not the same as statewide consortiums, the programs examined in this paper are similar because they are focused cooperative efforts enacted to solve specific needs. This paper will examine three such efforts in the field of Slavic collection development.

The programs include a Slavic duplicate book exchange arrangement; *Slavcopy*, a cooperative program to preserve brittle Slavic books at reduced costs; and, finally, a consortial arrangement between five university libraries to acquire a Slavic electronic database. These cooperative ventures, which have experienced varying degrees of success, range from informal to very formal arrangements. The University of Kansas (KU) Libraries' Slavic Department plays a leading role in all of these ventures. After briefly reviewing these programs, the paper will examine the challenges of operating these programs and outline some of the conditions that need to exist in library institutional culture to better facilitate cooperative programs between libraries.

SLAVIC DUPLICATE BOOK EXCHANGE

Since 1989 the KU Libraries' Slavic Department has worked with North American libraries to exchange duplicate Slavic publications. There are a number of reasons why libraries tend to acquire duplicate publications. To explain briefly, during the Soviet period and even in the post-Soviet period, libraries used and continue to use a variety of sources to acquire publications from East Central Europe. The two primary sources are Slavic book vendors and library book and serial exchange partners.[5] Many libraries have established approval plans with both vendors and exchange partners so the duplication of titles occasionally occurs. Slavic books tend to be priced in a range where it is often cheaper to keep the duplicate book than to go to the expense of returning it. This, combined with donations which also generate duplicates, means that most Slavic collections have at least a small number of duplicate titles. Fortunately, these duplicate titles can be put to good use. The Slavic publishing market is such that once a book is published it is only available for a relatively short period of time–perhaps a month or two. Once the printing of a title is sold out, there is very little chance that a library will be able to acquire the book unless a vendor that still holds a copy is located. Therefore, duplicate Slavic books exchanged between academic libraries are a valuable commodity because they are often no longer available on the open market. In addition, the exchange allows libraries to acquire specialized materials that are on the periphery of the institution's collection development parameters. For example, Romanian publications are not a high priority for KU. However, the library is interested in some reference and literature materials and is able to acquire them through its duplicate exchange program.

The KU Libraries' Slavic Department exchanges its duplicate Slavic books with about twelve other libraries in the United States and Canada. Reciprocal arrangements are established individually between each institution. For example, KU has established an individual arrangement with Indiana University; it also has a similar arrangement with the University of Chicago, and so forth. This is an uncomplicated system that allows each library freedom to negotiate arrangements. So although KU exchanges with twelve partners, its partners may exchange books with more or fewer libraries. An effort is made to maintain exchange equity between partners. However, libraries are free to be as active or inactive as they choose; the level of participation is often based on both the numbers of duplicate books on hand for exchange and staff time available to work on the program.

Title pages of each book are photocopied and sent to an exchange partner. (Some libraries use variants of this procedure, such as creating electronic lists that include all bibliographic information. Regardless of format, the program continues to operate on the same principles.) That partner selects needed titles and returns all of the photocopies. The requested books are sent to the partner and the unclaimed titles are offered to the next partner. KU covers the cost of shipping duplicates to the partner; in return, the partner will do the same. This simplifies the process because there is no need to bill partner libraries for this expense. Each participant is encouraged to keep track of the titles that are sent and received from each partner to ensure that there is a fairly equitable exchange of materials in order to justify shipping costs.

In 1997, KU acquired 462 titles on this exchange program and sent out 541 titles on exchange. The following year KU received 1,182 titles and sent out 867 titles. As a result of this program, 1,644 Slavic titles that could not be acquired in any other way were added to the KU collections from 1997 through 1998. In addition 1,408 volumes were sent to other libraries to benefit students and researchers at these institutions. This program plays an integral role in the collection development strategy for KU Slavic studies.

SLAVCOPY

Slavcopy is a cooperative effort established and administered at the KU Libraries to facilitate the acquisition of archival-quality preservation photocopies of brittle Slavic materials at reduced prices.[6] The focus of this program is the preservation of Slavic and other East Central European language publications. Currently there are over 20 libraries that participate in *Slavcopy*. The program operates through an electronic listserve to which participating libraries post the bibliographic data of titles they wish to preserve. If additional libraries wish to acquire preservation copies of a listed title, the price for that title is reduced. Titles submitted to *Slavcopy* must be old enough that their reproduction will not violate copyright laws.

Citations and orders are listed on *Slavcopy* for one month. The list is updated and sent out to subscribers on a regular basis. This allows participating libraries to see which other libraries are ordering a copy of a specific title. Librarians can then make an informed decision about acquiring the title based on their collection development needs, which can include a consideration of the expected use of the title. If the book falls outside of the institution's collection development parameters and other libraries are ordering the title, it is probable that the book will be available to patrons through interlibrary loan. Therefore, not every library needs to purchase a copy of each book listed on *Slavcopy*.

After the book is posted on *Slavcopy* for one month, it is sent to KU Libraries' Preservation Department for processing. Prep work includes erasing marks in the text, mending tears, and checking for and replacing missing text. Once the book is ready, it is sent to National Bridgeport Bindery in Agawam, Massachusetts, for processing. After the reproduction is completed, National Bridgeport Bindery sends a copy and an invoice directly to each library that requested the title. The institution that submits the book will also receive the original volume, which is taken apart during the copy process to ensure that the sharpest reproduction of each page is produced.

There are a number of benefits for participating in *Slavcopy*. First and foremost are the substantial savings on the cost of these photo reproductions. The savings can be as much as 50 percent off the listed catalog price for similar services offered by some vendors. All books are prepared for copying by the staff of the KU Libraries' Preservation Department, therefore, libraries participating in *Slavcopy* further reduce their preservation costs because KU bears the labor costs of preparing and processing the materials for reformatting. Another benefit is the ability to create a completed copy from incomplete texts. For example, many of the works submitted for preservation are in very poor physical shape–with some volumes missing text.[7] On a number of occasions, *Slavcopy* has orchestrated the reproduction of a single title by using copies of the book held by two or more libraries. In some cases, these books were in such poor physical condition that they were only one use away from destruction. Finally, unlike many other preservation projects, *Slavcopy* allows librarians to identify and preserve publications on a title-by-title basis. A library can submit as many as twenty titles or more, or as few as a single title and still receive savings through this program.

CONSORTIA ACCESS TO THE RUSSIAN ACADEMY OF SCIENCES (INION) DATABASE

In May 1996, the KU Center for Russian and East European Studies and the KU Libraries hosted a meeting of Slavic Librarians from five schools to discuss possible cooperative ventures. This meeting was funded as part of the Center's US/ED (United States Department of Education) Title VI Comprehensive National Resource Center Program grant. The National Resource Center Program has long encouraged linkages and collaboration between institutions. The KU Libraries provided additional funds for the meeting. Slavic Librarians from Indiana University, the Ohio State University, the University of Michigan, and the University of Texas, Austin, met with the KU librarians for three days to discuss possible cooperative ventures in the field of Slavic studies. These institutions were invited to participate because their Slavic collections and programs were similar in size and scope to the program and collections at KU. One of the firm proposals that came out of these meetings was to work together to purchase access to the Russian Academy of Sciences (INION) Database which is offered through the Research Libraries Group (RLG).

The primary reason for establishing consortial access to the Russian Academy of Sciences database was financial. Currently, RLG charges $1,500 for access to the database for one library. Additional users in a consortium can be added at $500 per site. Therefore, five libraries subscribing as a consortium can acquire the database for $700 per library, rather than $1,500 for a single library subscription. While consortial access does provide substantial savings, one limitation is that the consortium libraries can only have five simultaneous users accessing the database at a given time. However, after one year of consortium access, this limit has posed no problems to the users. In fact the KU group voted to expand the group to include a sixth library. If the limit of five simultaneous users is insufficient, RLG will upgrade access to allow ten users–of course, this would result in a price increase for the consortium.

Savings of $800 for access to the database may sound insignificant, particularly when the savings are seen in light of academic library acquisition budgets that can run three million dollars or more per year. However, if an academic library could save over fifty percent on each of its electronic subscriptions through consortial access with no noticeable deterioration in service for its patrons, these savings would be substantial indeed!

EVALUATION OF THE PROGRAMS

Other than their focus on Slavic collection development and preservation activities, the three projects described above are very different from each other. They range from an informal arrangement for the exchange of duplicate Slavic books; to the semi-formal *Slavcopy* program (semi-formal because libraries do need to sign up to participate in *Slavcopy*);[8] to the formal consortium arrangement to subscribe to an electronic database. One project is focused on preservation while the other two deal with collection development issues. All of the programs have had varying degrees of success. The common thread in these Slavic programs is that the KU Libraries and the author have played a leading role in their organization and operation. As such, the author has gained experience in dealing with a number of issues and challenges in the operation of specialized cooperative ventures. A discussion of these issues and challenges may assist other librarians as they work on focused cooperative ventures.

Numerous library scholars have published articles that examine issues related to library cooperation. Many of the authors have listed a number of characteristics or basic principles that must be met in order for cooperative ventures to be successful. Joseph A. Boissé published eleven postulates that should be considered when initiating a cooperative project. These postulates are:

1. Library cooperation is easy when money is plentiful.
2. Library cooperation is easier to launch with someone else's money.
3. The more meaningful it is, the more difficult it will be to implement.
4. Library cooperation is easier to establish in a hitherto unexplored area.
5. The more democratic the organization you create is, the more difficult the decision making.
6. Your own library will never be the same.
7. Be prepared to lose some autonomy.
8. Success will be dependent on the effectiveness of delivery systems.
9. Once established, a library cooperative never ceases to exist.
10. Don't boast too much about success of cooperatives.
11. The proof is in the implementation.[9]

Most of Boissé's postulates are self-explanatory and self-evident, although, one must question his first postulate because if money is plentiful, the incentive for libraries to cooperate diminishes. However, the other postulates are agreeable. Any type of program, cooperative or not, is easier to establish when outside funding is available. In addition, it is also simpler to create new programs, rather than attempting to convert existing library programs into cooperative ventures. The establishment of the *Slavcopy* programs provides a good example of this concept. While many libraries preserve Slavic materials in their collections, few, if any, were participating in cooperative ventures that allowed each institution to preserve books on a title-by-title basis before *Slavcopy* was established.

Frederick C. Lynden argues that real resource sharing must meet a number of characteristics in order to be considered a success. Such characteristics include, but are not limited to the following. First, requirements of the users must be satisfied and resources available when needed. Second, local programs will result in more resources being available locally; national programs will result in resources being shared nationally. Third, these projects allow libraries to realize savings and reduce costs. Finally, real resource sharing projects will receive the support of library administrators.[10]

Donald B. Simpson adds five key questions, regarding the sharing of electronic resources, that are similar to Lynden's key characteristics needed for success. Basically, these five questions are most applicable to the discussion of the Russian Academy of Sciences database. Although these questions are aimed at electronic resources, they do have some relevance to other cooperative ventures and should be considered when cooperative programs are in the planning stage. The five questions are:

1. What are the expectations of students and faculty in relation to the availability, accessibility, and their use of electronic resources?
2. What criteria will the library use to make decisions about what electronic resources it holds locally versus what it obtains through resource sharing mechanisms?
3. What kinds of resource sharing mechanisms for electronic resources are most likely to be effective for an individual library?
4. What impact will sharing electronic resources have on cooperating libraries and the library cooperative?
5. What are the costs of sharing electronic resources and are there cost advantages in doing so?[11]

The characteristics, postulates and questions discussed by these authors, as well as others, are important ideas to consider when establishing cooperative collection development projects. Based on the author's experiences of organizing and operating the above-mentioned Slavic projects, there are also a number of other issues that must be resolved and conditions that must be met for the successful operation of cooperative programs.

Library administrators and other staff must be willing to make accommodations in local procedures to assist employees who are working to establish and/or participate in consortia. Consortial access to the Russian Academy of Sciences database did not come easy. It took almost two years to negotiate the contract and to have all of the schools agree to its terms. The KU Libraries took the role of lead institution in this undertaking. As such, KU signed the contract with RLG and paid for the full subscription. Each of the other consortium libraries signed a letter of participation stating that they would follow the terms of the contract, reimburse KU for their share of the subscription price, and notify the other libraries in a timely fashion if they planned to leave the group. It was necessary for each library to review the contract since each was asked to adhere to it. Lawyers from each institution made suggested changes to the wording. Each time this took place all of the other schools reviewed the contract once again. Also, the electronic resources committee in each library reviewed and then re-reviewed the documentation, further slowing the process. Not surprisingly, this took an inordinate amount of time to complete. With much persistence the consortium libraries, which now comprised Indiana University, the University of Michigan, the University of Pittsburgh, the Ohio State University and the University of Kansas, finally offered patron access to the database at the start of the 1998-1999 academic year. The project's success has led the consortium to expand to include George Washington University at the group's second meeting at KU in June 1999.

As mentioned above, it took almost two years to establish consortium access to the Russian Academy of Sciences database. Under different conditions the project would not have taken so long. Before other institutions were asked to review the documents, KU lawyers reviewed and revised the contract in coordination with the database vendor to meet the requirements of KU, the signatory institution. Upon review of the revised contract, lawyers at most of the other institutions suggested changes. These revisions dealt with editorial minutiae that did not change the underlining meaning or basis of the document. Since the contract was only signed by KU, the lawyers at the other institutions could have streamlined the process by avoiding simple editorial changes and suggesting only revisions that actually impacted the contract.

Furthermore, the process was slowed by each institution's electronic resources committee that reviewed each change made by the lawyers. Unfortunately, several committees were unwilling to give priority consideration to the consortium documents, so paper work often sat at a library for months without being considered. This of course, forced every other participant to wait.

For one member of the consortium, the problems did not end when the contract was finally signed and the database purchased. It was an easy and quick procedure to mount and make available the web-based database at the other institutions. However, after one year, the database was still not accessible to the patrons of one library because the electronic resources committee at this library did not undertake the implementation of the database. This institution already offers many other RLG products, so their reluctance to add this database is not due to any technical reasons. The committee has simply not made the effort to add the Russian database to the public catalog. This is unfortunate because the library paid for this resource that it has yet to make available to its patrons. Because of this, the Slavic librarian at this institution may drop out of the consortium because he rightly can not justify paying for an item that his patrons can not use. He also believes that this database is a resource that his library should offer to its patrons; and, ironically he fears that he will eventually be forced to purchase the database individually for $1,500 simply because the appropriate officials in his library refuse to add the database in a timely fashion.

If the staff and administration in the participating libraries were more accommodating in instituting consortium access to electronic resources, the implementation would have gone more smoothly and quickly. Unfortunately, because this did not take place, KU, as lead institution, had to invest an extraordinary amount of staff time in order to shepherd this process to a successful conclusion.

A lack of accommodation by administrators or staff has not hindered the other programs outlined in this paper as much. In many ways, the Slavic duplicate exchange program is the most successful program that needs the least accommodation by library staff for its implementation. On occasion, libraries have withdrawn from the exchange. Each time this has happened over the last five years it was because the library administration at the withdrawing institution decided that the exchange was labor intensive and therefore not worth participating in. It usually appeared that the decision was made without an understanding of the Slavic book trade. And in all cases, after the value of this program was explained to the library administration, the institution was again allowed to participate in the exchange. This illustrates the importance of librarians taking the time to explain and justify reasons for participation in a specialized consortium to their administration. Such efforts will prevent any misunderstanding regarding the value of the program in the future and promote more accommodating efforts by administrators.

Regarding accommodation by library staff, *Slavcopy* falls somewhere between the two other programs. As mentioned above, *Slavcopy* is a new title-by-title approach to the cooperative preservation of Slavic publications. As such, many libraries have added the *Slavcopy* service to their library's preservation program. However, the Slavic librarians at some non-participating institutions have told the author that although they would like to work with *Slavcopy* they are unable to participate. The preservation librarians at these institutions do not see the need to participate in a cooperative project, even if the materials can be preserved in a more cost-effective manner through the program. It is unknown whether these librarians are refusing to participate because they fear losing local control over some preservation activities.

Cooperative collection development projects will succeed only if all of the participants are flexible and willing to compromise in order to implement and participate in a program. Many cooperative programs generate lower prices by using standardized procedures to acquire materials or to access information. Unfortunately, these procedures may not precisely mirror established routines at each participating library. If librarians are really committed to successfully implementing cooperative programs, they will make every effort to make local procedures flexible to accommodate these programs.

The operation of *Slavcopy* illustrates the need for local institutional procedural flexibility. In order to lower costs, each volume preserved on *Slavcopy* is produced and bound identically with each step of the process, meeting or exceeding established preservation standards. To facilitate the copy process, the book is taken apart to ensure the best reproduction of each page. When this is completed, every copy of the book is identically bound. Because every step is standardized, it is impossible to entertain specific requests, such as not taking the book apart for copying or producing each title with a different color binding. These types of requests defeat the standardization process that the cooperative implemented to lower costs. Therefore, when participating in cooperative ventures, libraries must be flexible. Being flexible does not mean that a library needs to accept a lower quality resource through cooperative programs. However, it may mean that the institution may have to compromise on how the resources are produced and/or offered to its patrons.

The cooperative implementation of the Russian Academy of Sciences database demonstrates how libraries can compromise. Five libraries now share access to a database that allows only five simultaneous users. This means that it is possible that a patron may not be allowed into the database on their first attempt to access the resource. They would have to wait until one of the five users signs off. While this is not as convenient as immediate access that some electronic resources provide, the members of the consortium decided that in order to save money, the group would only offer access to five simultaneous users rather than upgrading to ten users. This decision was based on the idea that most libraries generally purchase a single copy of a monograph and only one person at a time can use the item. Only recently, with the widespread implementation of electronic resources, have libraries begun to offer immediate, remote access to information for multiple simultaneous users. In order to save money, libraries and consortia need to consider limiting simultaneous users to specific products such as the Russian Academy of Sciences database which is generally used for quick subject searches to identify journal articles. It should be noted that in the first year of consortial access to this database, not a single complaint regarding access was made to any of the participating librarians. By limiting simultaneous access to five users the consortium is able to save money and still provide access to this important and highly specialized resource.

Successful cooperative projects must receive the support of the library administration and the commitment of the other participants in the group. This is particularly true during the organization and implementation stages of a project.[12] Specialized projects, such as those outlined in this paper, are developed with little or no additional staff assistance or financial support. Librarians who organize these projects do so in the belief that their efforts will ultimately make a difference in helping participants to provide better service to their patrons. Library staff, administrators, and other project participants can help by simply supporting the efforts of the project leader. An institution's willingness to be flexible can provide an important display of support to a burgeoning cooperative program. In addition, library and university administrators can provide support by recognizing the efforts of staff in their performance evaluations. "Such incentives are likely to reinforce positive, committed attitudes towards the projects and other participants."[13]

Along with recognition by administrators, there is also a need for the participants to acknowledge the efforts made to initiate and run a program. Specialized cooperative programs are generally conceived and established by one person. Upon implementation, other institutions are then invited to participate. The other participants need to be aware that the leader of the project is often organizing the initiative in addition to all other responsibilities. Therefore, participants need to *understand* that because there is often no extra help provided to work on these projects, it occasionally takes a little longer than usual to process or acquire materials cooperatively. Once again, *Slavcopy* provides a good example. Upon joining the list, new members are informed that it usually takes at least 12 weeks or more from the time that a title is posted until the book is processed and sent to the ordering library. (Books generally stay on the electronic list for four weeks; it then takes at least eight weeks for the titles to be prepared and processed.) Sometimes it takes longer than 12 weeks to process books for a number of reasons. First, the KU Preservation Department, which prepares all books for processing, also deals with institutional preservation projects. Therefore, the books may not always be prepared in the outlined timeframe. Also, because *Slavcopy* contracts its reproduction services with an outside vendor, it often takes longer than the outlined time because the vendor has other commitments. Unfortunately, the facilitator of *Slavcopy* has no influence over the vendor's production schedule. Although this situation is made clear to all participants when they join the listserve, there are often complaints that the process takes too long. Generally, a library's acquisition staff makes these complaints because their acquisition system automatically claims materials that are not received in a short period of time–for example, within eight weeks of creating the order in the acquisition system. Such complaints can be demoralizing for the project staff who work very hard to keep this program afloat. In addition, responding to these inquiries places additional demands on the staff, who often have limited time to work on cooperative projects.

Similarly, several of the participants in the consortium to access the Russian Academy of Sciences database complained when the database was not immediately available. Although it took the participants almost two years to sign the letter of participation, patience was lost when the KU staff could not provide immediate access to the database for only one week after the contract was signed. An impending price hike prompted KU to sign the contract early, before the details of providing consortium access to the product were fully worked out. By signing the contract early, each consortium member saved about $90 on the subscription price. Even after this situation was explained to the members, one institution went so far as to complain about the fact that it took a week to establish web access and requested a refund for the week that the database was not available. While no institution should pay for a resource that it does not receive, in this case, the contract was signed early to save money. The only alternative was to work out the access issues before signing the contract and then pay the higher subscription rate, which did not seem logical. Once again it was a demoralizing situation for the leader of the consortium who worked hard to establish this arrangement. In light of this type of interaction, one must be committed to the idea of library cooperation to play a leadership role in specialized consortium arrangements.

It is also important that all members understand that cooperative programs are established as on-going projects. Unfortunately, as Christy Hightower and George Soete write:

> Some participants however, will view pilot collaborative projects as not serious–perhaps as a momentary diversion from the real business of acquiring and building local collections. Such misunderstandings can lead to broken agreements and feelings of betrayal.[14]

Such an incident happened as this paper was being written. On June 3-6, 1999 members of the Russian Academy of Sciences database consortium met at KU for their second biannual meeting. During this meeting, the group voted to expand the consortium to include George Washington University. A week after the meeting one of the Slavic librarians informed the group that his institution would be withdrawing from our consortium access to the database because his library was now working with a statewide consortium to acquire the same database. His administration simply made this decision without his input, and they did not inform him of the decision even though they knew that KU was sponsoring his trip to Lawrence for the consortium meeting. Such actions by library administrators belittle the work of specialized consortia and show a lack of respect for the librarians and libraries involved in this project. It also means that the other members of the consortia will have to seriously consider not working with this institution on other projects if they are not committed to previously established groups to which they have signed formal letters of participation.

It should be noted that the library that withdrew from the KU Russian Academy of Sciences database consortium remains committed to cooperative collection development. However, the institution has prioritized the cooperative ventures in which it will participate. In this case, the statewide consortium negotiated the purchase of a number of RLG products that included the Russian Academy of Sciences database. It is understandable that the institution would choose to obtain this database at no cost. However, the actions of the library's administration in withdrawing from the established cooperative are reason for concern. When they joined the specialized consortium to access the Russian Academy of Sciences database, they should have informed the other members that their membership in this group was a lower priority than the statewide consortium and that they would drop out of the specialized consortium if the statewide group ever acquired the product. More important, they should have followed the letter of agreement that they signed which stated that they would provide advanced notice of their intention to back out of the consortium. It is very likely that this statewide consortium spent time negotiating with RLG for the acquisition of the database, so there is no just reason for their late notice to withdraw. Furthermore, the institution's administrators knew that KU was paying to have their Slavic librarian travel to

Lawrence to attend a consortium meeting, yet they said nothing. Rather, they waited until the meeting was over to announce their withdrawal from the group. This is an unacceptable way to treat the other members of the consortium and illustrates the lack of support and respect some library administrators have for specialized cooperative efforts. To avoid these setbacks, librarians who establish specialized consortiums must ask potential members what their library's priority is for membership in the group. If the priority is low, the leader of the consortium should seriously consider not including the institution in the project.

A similar situation regarding the possible withdrawal from the consortium occurred earlier with another library. In this case, the library administration was considering acquiring the Russian database by other means when the Slavic librarian reminded them that they already received the database through an established consortium. As a result, the administrators decided to continue to acquire the database through the established consortium.

CONCLUSIONS

Given all of the problems of small cooperative efforts, one may ask why institutions like the University of Kansas Libraries bother with establishing and participating in such arrangements. For programs like the Slavic duplicate book exchange, the answer is simple. KU benefits through participation. KU acquires important Slavic publications through this program that could not be acquired in any other way. This program is very informal and the only effort involved is to exchange information on what books are available and then to ship the books to the requesting institution. The benefits of operating *Slavcopy* are also fairly easy to explain. The preservation work accomplished through *Slavcopy* needs to take place, whether it is done cooperatively or not. Thanks to electronic mail, it is rather easy to establish a cooperative program. Furthermore, by running *Slavcopy* KU can negotiate very good pricing structures with the vendor who does the photo-reproduction work. So while KU staff do all of the work to prepare materials for *Slavcopy*, all KU preservation photocopying, whether it is listed on the cooperative programs or not, receives the favorably negotiated prices.

In the case of the Russian Academy of Sciences Database, the answer to why we do it is not so evident. Money spent on KU staff time to implement the program far exceeds the $800 per year it saves on the annual subscription cost. However, the organizer hopes that this consortium arrangement can be expanded to include other resources, both electronic and more traditional forms of publishing; thus allowing the consortium to work together to offer a wider range of materials to its patrons.

For this reason, the KU Libraries' Slavic Department staff, with the support of the administration and other staff continue to work on specialized cooperative ventures. Although there are many challenges in establishing and operating specialized cooperative ventures, the value of these programs far outweigh all of the problems encountered during their implementation.

Unfortunately, until librarians and library administrators are truly committed to all forms of cooperation, the smaller specialized programs will be difficult to establish and continue to struggle in their operation. If cooperatives are to succeed, librarians and administrators must do more than simply profess a readiness to cooperate. They must actually be willing to:

- Be flexible and willing to make accommodations and compromises in local procedures for consortial participation.
- Be supportive and committed to the idea of local or specialized cooperative collection development programs.

Until library culture changes so that these criteria are met, it will continue to be difficult, or even impossible to establish and implement specialized cooperative programs that can be used to address many of the collection development challenges academic and research libraries are currently facing.

NOTES

1. Richard M. Dougherty, "Resource Sharing Among Research Libraries: How It Ought to Work," *Collection Management* 9, Number 2/3 (1987): 79.

2. Joseph A. Boissé, "Library Cooperation: A Remedy But Not a Panacea," *IFLA Journal*, 21 (1995) No. 2: 89.

3. Donald B. Simpson, "Solving the Challenges Presented by Electronic Resources: Creating Opportunities Through Inter-Institutional Collaboration," *Journal of Library Administration* 24, number 4 (1997): 55.

4. Simpson, "Solving the Challenges," 55.

5. For a good summary and description of Slavic book and serial exchanges see: Tatjana Lorkovic and Eric A. Johnson, "Serial and Book Exchanges with the Former Soviet Union," *The Serials Librarian* 31, no. 4(1997): 59-87; Margaret S. Olsen, "The More Things Change, the More They Stay the Same: East-West Exchanges 1960-1993," *Library Resources & Technical Services*, 39, no. 1 (January 1995): 5-21; and, Bradley L. Schaffner, "Slavic Book and Serial Exchanges," chapter in *Libraries: Global Reach–Local Touch*, edited by Kathleen de la Peña McCook, Barbara J. Ford and Kate Lippincott (Chicago: American Library Association, 1998): 144-149.

6. For a more detailed account of *Slavcopy* and its sister program *Brittle* (for the cooperative preservation of all other materials) see Brian J. Baird and Bradley L. Schaffner, "Extinguishing Slow Fires: Cooperative Preservation Efforts," chapter in *Racing Toward Tomorrow: Proceedings of the Ninth National Conference of the Association of College and Research Libraries, April 8-11, 1999*, edited by Hugh A. Thompson (Chicago: Association of College and Research Libraries, a division of the American Library Association, 1999): 228-233. ACRL is also planning to post the corrected version of the paper (which should include the footnotes which were inadvertently left out of the paper publication) at: *http://www.ala.org/acrl/detroit.html*

7. For a discussion of the condition of Slavic publications see: Bradley L. Schaffner and Brian J. Baird, "Into the Dustbin of History? The Evaluation and Preservation of Slavic Materials," *College & Research Libraries* 60, number 2 (March 1999): 144-151.

8. Libraries can participate in *Slavcopy* by sending an e-mail request to: *Slavcopy@ukans.edu*

9. Boissé, "Library Cooperation": 90-93.

10. Frederick C. Lynden, "Will Electronic Information Finally result in Real Resource Sharing?" *Journal of Library Administration* 24, numbers 1/2 (1996): 63-64.

11. Donald B. Simpson, "Electronic Resources: A New Set of Questions for Resource Sharing Efforts," *Collection Management* 21, number 1 (1996): 61-62.

12. For a good discussion of the implementation of cooperative collection development programs see: Christy Hightower and George Soete, "The Consortium as Learning Organization: Twelve Steps to Success in Collaborative Collection Projects," *The Journal of Academic Librarianship* 21, number 2 (March 1995): 87-91.

13. Hightower and Soete, "The Consortium . . . ," p. 90.

14. Hightower and Soete, "The Consortium . . . ," p. 90.

Libraries of One World: Librarians Look Across the Oceans

Frederick J. Friend

Perhaps the single most important feature in shaping British history is that Britain is separated from Continental Europe by twenty-one miles of water. It does not sound like very much, but it has had a profound effect in preventing cultural invasion as well as armed invasion. As a boy, I grew up in Dover, and I used to stand on the White Cliffs looking across at a foreign land that I could see but which I did not visit until I was 15 years of age. This paper is about looking out across more than twenty-one miles of the English Channel. We must look across thousands of miles of ocean. The world has changed a great deal since my childhood, on the whole for the better, and one of the improvements is that we are more aware of other cultures. Cultural differences are important in demonstrating both our common humanity and our unique identities. They illustrate what we have in common and also what we can offer to others as our contribution to the human race. The ancient world and the medieval world were harsh environments for mankind, but in Europe those harsh environments produced a sense of cohesion in the form of a common language and a common spirituality. That cohesion was lost as the cultural pendulum swung towards national identities, but in the electronic environment we may have a new opportunity to create a new sense of common identity which does not over-ride local culture.

Frederick J. Friend is Director, Scholarly Communication, University College, London (e-mail: f.friend@ucl.ac.uk) (website: www.ucl.ac.uk/scholarly-communication/).

[Haworth co-indexing entry note]: "Libraries of One World: Librarians Look Across the Oceans." Friend, Frederick J. Co-published simultaneously in *Collection Management* (The Haworth Information Press, an imprint of The Haworth Press, Inc.) Vol. 24, No. 3/4, 2000, pp. 281-287; and: *Creating New Strategies for Cooperative Collection Development* (ed: Milton T. Wolf and Marjorie E. Bloss) The Haworth Information Press, an imprint of The Haworth Press, Inc., 2000, pp. 281-287. Single or multiple copies of this article are available for a fee from The Haworth Document Delivery Service [1-800-342-9678, 9:00 a.m. - 5:00 p.m. (EST). E-mail address: getinfo@haworthpressinc.com].

© 2000 by The Haworth Press, Inc. All rights reserved.

Our life in the world of information is part of that mix of unity and diversity, of common features and variety. In the past our ignorance of other cultures was matched by our ignorance of other people's information and other people's information needs. I generalise of course, and you may correct my generalization by pointing to examples of women and men who had a world-view of information long before the age of the aeroplane or the computer. But it is nevertheless true that geographical barriers such as twenty-one miles of sea have had a profound influence upon the development of information services. The way in which academic library services have developed, for example, is very different in the various countries of Europe, and we need to understand and respect those differences if we are to achieve international collaboration. The question I shall address in this paper is this: now that the geographical barriers to the flow of information are breaking down or disappearing, how can we use the new internationalism to provide users of information with a better service? This is not a question of technology but of structures. Our co-operative structures were shaped in the age of geographical barriers to information. Should they or can they be reshaped in a truly international way?

Some publishers, libraries and other information intermediaries are still acting as though the geographical barriers to information were still in place. Others recognise the importance of the international electronic world but cannot adapt their structures to take full advantage of the new opportunities. The cooperative organizations we have in the UK do an excellent job within the UK but we are not finding it easy to absorb the implications of the international electronic world into our structures. This is not due to any lack of awareness of the international dimension to information. Librarians in the UK are very aware that the problems they face, such as the escalating price of journals, are faced by librarians across the world. Librarians in the UK are also very aware of the vast range of information sources now available globally. The difficulty comes in turning awareness into programmes, incorporating the work of individuals into corporate plans and structures.

Let me illustrate what I mean by describing the work of three UK organizations: JISC, SCONUL and CURL. JISC is the Joint Information Systems Committee of the four Funding Councils which channel taxpayers' money into UK universities, and JISC is the agency which looks after national information issues in networking or in content. It is JISC that has developed services such as NESLI, the National Electronic Site Licence, and JISC is the right organization to promote collective purchasing within the UK. JISC is certainly aware of the potential benefits of international collaboration in its work and has negotiated deals for UK-wide access to databases such as JSTOR. However, the way JISC has to approach a purchase is from the UK looking out, looking outside the UK for a product or a service which it cannot supply from within the UK. That is understandable given the structure and funding of JISC, and I am not being critical, merely pointing out that it is difficult for even an excellent organization like JISC to think or act in a truly international way. Where JISC has been able to act in a truly international way is in the development of document delivery software, as the development of the new version of the RLG Ariel software has been a true collaboration between people in Australia, the U.S. and the UK.

SCONUL promotes collaboration between academic libraries in the UK and the Republic of Ireland, and SCONUL has a Scholarly Communication Committee which is very concerned with international developments. Nevertheless SCONUL's mission statement and strategic plan is that of a UK and Irish organization, not that of an international organization. The international dimension is, again perhaps understandably, one of SCONUL participating in the international world of information only at points at which that world touches UK and Irish interests. CURL, which represents the large research libraries, took a very bold international step in joining RLG "en bloc." This was in recognition that research libraries in particular have to be fully-immersed in the global information world. There are some in CURL who would wish to choose only those RLG services which are relevant to their local needs, and when budgets are under so much pressure I can understand that wish, but there is a big difference between selecting information resources from another country and a truly international perspective, looking at the situation in one's own country from a global perspective. It is like the difference between seeing the world from where we are, thus seeing only part of the world, and seeing the world from outer space, thereby seeing the *whole* world.

Having been both complimentary and critical of UK organizations, let me be both complimentary and critical of three U.S.-based organizations: OCLC, RLG and ARL. Perhaps the U.S. organization best-known outside the U.S. is OCLC. As one who helped Fred Kilgour to bring OCLC to Europe twenty years ago, I pay tribute to his vision. A truly international action by OCLC at the time was that Fred agreed to supply the University of Essex, where I was Librarian, with sheaf slips for its catalogue instead of the catalogue cards all the other OCLC libraries were using. Adapting OCLC's procedures presented a big challenge but this was the action of a man who did not limit his offer to what the organization already had. Fred started by thinking that this international development was right, and did whatever was necessary to make it work. I have to say that the more recent perception of OCLC in the UK, where its services are still used heavily, is that this is not a truly international organization but a U.S.-based organization which is offering services internationally as a by-product of its U.S. services. By contrast RLG has made real efforts to become a truly international organization, working with partners outside the U.S. to develop its services, although RLG has a huge gap in its portfolio from an international perspective, and that is its lack of any serious effort in the STM area. Perhaps RLG's international role is as a support for research in certain specific areas rather than providing a comprehensive support for research. ARL has not avoided the STM area, and its SPARC programme in particular could have a big influence upon global information provision in science and medicine, helping both directly and indirectly to reduce the price burden for libraries throughout the world. And ARL has set up SPARC as an international initiative, finding academic and library support across the globe. ARL, however, faces the same problem as SCONUL and CURL in the UK, that apart from initiatives like SPARC its main activities have to be US-centred because that is where its roots lie.

One very interesting organization from the perspective of global information is ICOLC, the International Coalition of Library Consortia. There are times when ICOLC acts as a U.S.-based organization which has decided to include some members outside the U.S. You will understand from what I have said so that I do not believe this kind of approach is right in the new international electronic world. However, ICOLC at its best is adopting a truly international approach, its policies shaped not by the needs of one country alone but by the needs of libraries world-wide. The interesting lesson from ICOLC is that this international approach has been possible because ICOLC is a virtual organization. It does not have premises. It does not have a subscription. It does not have staff, as everybody who works for ICOLC does that work as part of their normal job. I would like to suggest that it is the physical structures associated with traditional co-operative organizations that restrict their movements in this new international electronic world. If an organization has buildings and paid staff, that inevitably anchors the organization within a particular country and subjects it to the priorities of that country. Perhaps we need more virtual organizations to meet the needs of the new virtual world. The difficulty, of course, is that a virtual organization like ICOLC is totally dependent upon the good-will of the individuals who work for it and the organizations they represent. Can the kind of organizations we need to be effective in the international electronic world depend upon such voluntary help? The key may lie in the attitude of our existing co-operative organizations towards using their own staff resources in a new way, devoting their time less towards internal objectives and more towards objectives which set their organization in an international context.

In some respects the need to adapt to the new international world has become an imperative, a matter of survival, and in other respects it can be described as a vision, a view of the future which offers users of information a service vastly superior to the service they now have. The threats are certainly very real in this new world. Many commercial organizations have adapted to the new environment more quickly than libraries. The corporate strategy of many publishers is now truly an international strategy, whereas the strategy of many libraries is understandably focussed very locally. The threat in that situation could be offers by publishers to supply local services from their international store-house, bypassing local information-providers like libraries. Commercial organizations are also seizing the opportunities provided by the electronic medium in a more determined way than libraries. Of course we have had electronic information services in libraries for many years, and at one time we were persuading reluctant commercial interests to enter the new electronic world. Now commercial interests have entered that world with a vengeance and are determined to control it. The only way we can defend the public good interest we represent is by organizing ourselves in a way that is equally-determined and equally-efficient.

The vision lies in the opportunities in the new international electronic world. The world of global information really is here. I do not see it as a village. The word "village" carries connotations for me more of the old world, the world constrained by space and time. We are now in a world in which information has no constraints of space or time. Instantaneous transfer of information across the world is now a reality. The barrier of cost is certainly there, particularly in countries which cannot afford the infrastructure, let alone the content of information. But overcoming that barrier is part of the vision for rich and poor countries alike. The importance of information to world development, national development and individual development makes it essential that we should have a global vision of electronic information, and if librarians cannot help to shape that vision and turn it into reality, who can? Underlying our policies should be the thought that our libraries are libraries of one world.

How can we adapt our organizational structures to take advantage of the international electronic world? The situation in Europe has demonstrated both the difficulties and the advantages in such an approach. The vision behind the creation of the European Union is exactly the kind of vision we need, respecting national cultures and yet cooperating across national borders. And yet translating that vision into co-operative structures has proved controversial, and some would say ineffective. In respect of access to libraries, for example, it is difficult to point to any way in which access to libraries for citizens of Europe is any easier now than it was before the formation of the European Union. Indeed, in one respect, the European Commission threatens to make access more difficult through its attempt to change copyright legislation in the interests of publishers rather than the interests of library users. The Commission has devoted large amounts of money to a Libraries Programme which has sponsored many projects, but no Europe-wide policy on access to information has emerged from that work. No common purchasing policy has been developed. Some library organizations have begun to act in a European way. LIBER, for example, has developed licensing principles from a European perspective. EAHIL, the European Association for Health Information and Libraries, was founded specifically to improve access to health information across Europe. As the EAHIL web site says, "Health and illness know no frontiers," and they could equally say the same about information. This example of European collaboration has come in a subject area in which information is very important, literally "vital." It will be interesting to see if this proves to be a model for wider international collaboration. Can a global approach to information come through the formation of new groups in specific subject areas or with a very specific remit?

I believe it can. It will be difficult for many existing library organizations to re-shape their strategies to start from the global and apply the global perspective in a national situation. But such an approach will be possible for a few existing organizations and for any new organizations that are formed. Their remit will have to be defined very clearly if they are to be effective. *One* global library organization attempting to cover *all* aspects of library services cannot be effective, as we have seen for many years with IFLA. Too wide a role can render an organization ineffective. Some have thought that ICOLC might purchase databases on behalf of consortia throughout the world, but such a wide role would render ICOLC ineffective in its true remit, which is to provide a forum for collaboration between consortia continuing to make their own purchases. In this particular role ICOLC is effective in a truly international way. I believe that there is a strong case for the development of subject-specific virtual organizations which could be effective in their own particular areas in improving the flow of information to users across the globe. Perhaps such virtual organizations will grow out of the listserve groups which already correspond on a global basis. If such groups begin with an initiative in a particular country, I hope that they will quickly become, like ICOLC, truly international. Librarians across the world are working together more closely than they were when I began my career, and a new internationalism in information provision is developing, but the time has past when we could only take an interest in what happens across the oceans in a superficial way. As those who provide access to information we have to think global in the same way as those who are creating information are thinking globally. The research teams in our universities are often collaborating across oceans, the publishers are publishing globally, and we cannot continue to live within a restricted world. The world has opened up since I stood on the White Cliffs of Dover 50 years ago, opened up in an exciting and a challenging way. Our collaborative organizations face the same exciting challenge that we face as individuals. We *are* librarians of one world.

The Politics of Information Institutions, or I Am Not a Luddite, But . . .

Martha Gould

First let me make very clear that I am speaking today from a personal point of view, and my comments are not to be construed as those of the National Commission on Libraries. I am delighted to be here, and the subject of this conference is of great interest to me from policy and political points of view. Understand, I am not an academic librarian, even though some 50 years ago I started my career at the Baker Memorial Library, Dartmouth College.

Basically I am a retired director of a small urban county library system, a former library lobbyist for my state library association and county government, and much of my career has been in management and administration of public libraries. Somehow I managed to become a presidential appointee to the National Commission. I mention the latter, as it has much to do with political acumen. I am and have always been a political animal.

This is a skill that everyone here should acquire. Not just in terms of university or association politics, but to influence funding authorities and legislative bodies. Testimony is the only part of the political process. Being a member of your institution's legislative committee in determining priorities and working one-on-one with elected officials is very important for both private and publicly funded institutions. I am curious as to how many here, after reading an ALAWON, or even

---

Martha Gould is Vice-Chair, National Commission on Libraries and Information Science.

[Haworth co-indexing entry note]: "The Politics of Information Institutions, or I Am Not A Luddite, But . . ." Gould, Martha. Co-published simultaneously in *Collection Management* (The Haworth Information Press, an imprint of The Haworth Press, Inc.) Vol. 24, No. 3/4, 2000, pp. 289-295; and: *Creating New Strategies for Cooperative Collection Development* (ed: Milton T. Wolf and Marjorie E. Bloss) The Haworth Information Press, an imprint of The Haworth Press, Inc., 2000, pp. 289-295. Single or multiple copies of this article are available for a fee from The Haworth Document Delivery Service [1-800-342-9678, 9:00 a.m. - 5:00 p.m. (EST). E-mail address: getinfo@haworthpressinc.com].

© 2000 by The Haworth Press, Inc. All rights reserved.

testifying before Congress on, say, intellectual property, have followed up with a letter or visit to your Senator or Congressman? Not an e-mail, but an actual letter hand-delivered to their local office with a request that it is sent to the Senator or Congressman. And the same can be said for dealing with state funding authorities, and your own academic hierarchy.

PREACHING TO THE CONVERTED

I have read with great fascination the papers for this conference. They are interesting, scholarly, and would probably bore finance directors and politicians to death. While you may be making sense, and I happen to think in many instances you are, you are still only talking to each other. Certainly, based on the rationale for this conference, you are not talking to those who control funding, those in Congress who control legislation, and lastly, the publishers. In addition I do not see where you are in negotiation with scholarly and scientific associations whose journals have been bought up by or sold to publishers.

From my reading of the conference papers, you all are still talking to yourselves, good ideas, good examples of cooperative programs, but somehow no one has really taken that leap from talk to a strategic plan and then to implementation.

In looking over the list of participants today, I see only one university president and one professor. No representatives of scholarly or scientific associations and no representatives of the scientific publishing field. Before you all rise up and stone me in the market place, please remember that I am a view from the outside, a voice not of the choir, and if my impressions are incorrect, then you have failed to make your case outside of your own peer group.

Information has become a valuable commodity. Until you begin to think like the private sector in how to address the issue of collection development and management in the digital era, you will never get beyond the talking stage. Not everyone can be king of the mountain. Once you are willing to compromise, establishing cooperative and collaborative endeavors can be achieved.

Several suggestions: Develop partnerships. Whoever said it is the sole responsibility of librarians to save the world of scientific research and publishing? So you are going to have to learn to think out of the box. The problem facing research libraries is not just a library problem; it is a societal problem. To address this you must look at the issue from the other side of the table, hone your negotiating skills, and learn how to write contracts. You may well want to remember that publishers have to sell products, and if you go beyond just talk, give up territorial imperatives, and are willing to develop partnerships with non-academic organizations, maybe, just maybe you will be on your way to solving your problems of increasing costs and decreasing funding. Publishing in the digital age can and will make for some strange bedfellows.

Many years ago, I had a very young and arrogant budget analyst who told me that he had lost much respect for me because I was willing to get down into the muck and the mire of politics in budget fights. First of all, I resent and will always resent the comment about the muck and the mire of politics because the majority of elected officials really want to do what is best for their constituents, sometimes under very difficult conditions. But they cannot if you, as a constituent, cannot make your case. Speaking in platitudes about societal good, public good, etc., is just so much verbiage. On the other hand, if you can tie your needs to economic development or quality of life issues, you will have a stronger justification.

To do this you also will have to know the priorities of your institutions. If you cannot make a case that the library's need for additional funding will benefit both "town and gown," or that your need for additional funding will benefit the mission of the institution, you're dead in the water.

THE HINGE PERIOD

We are at what I call the hinge period, the hinge swinging between how we have done collection development in the past, and how we must do collection development and management in an electronic future. At this point I want to digress for a moment. In what I see as our mad rush to technology, we seem to have forgotten that the vast majority of the world's collective knowledge is maintained in print and will probably never be digitized. And the techniques for permanent access, preservation, and archiving are still wedded to the printed word. Who is going to be responsible for maintaining permanent access, and for the archiving of information? What is the cost? Where is the strategic planning for orderly migration to as-yet-unknown technologies? Are our institutions spending scarce dollars for hardware and wiring when wireless is around the corner as a viable technology?

If we as librarians are morphing ourselves into information specialists, what is happening to such basics as reference advisory services and content knowledge? In fact, what is happening to our profession as a whole? Librarians bring the ability to evaluate information sources, print or electronic, and to direct the user to that which meets a specific need. If we just collect information in electronic format without the human interface between information and the user, we will go the way of the dodo bird. Considering the number of library schools that have disappeared, we may well be an endangered species.

Is it possible that the very specialized scientific or academic journals exist because of the need to publish or perish? What would happen if, in being considered for tenure, publication of papers for conferences, etc., were given the same stature as publication in a peer reviewed journal? For that matter, adapt peer review to electronic publications. If faculty were your allies, could you not begin to change your institution's tenure policies? Instead of associations doing the peer reviews, have it done within the author's own institution by his or her peers and published by that institution either in print or online, bypassing the need to go to a for-profit publisher.

If the policies of an institution change, then how researchers publish electronically will also change and, of course, how peer review is done in the digital environment. You talk about it, but as yet I do not see anyone taking a leadership role in starting to implement needed changes.

I would like you to think about natural allies: faculty, students, and other types of libraries. Why have collection development or management librarians from public libraries not been invited? They also have the same concerns in terms of cost of online periodicals, and many collect and maintain the same journals as the academic research libraries.

IMPORTANCE OF STRATEGIC PLANNING

A number of papers at this conference talk about cooperation, and there are some specific examples, but not one of the papers has gone into the strategic planning that created the contracts that established such cooperative programs, nor has there been any substantive description of organizational structures. We learn of the what and the why but not of the how.

For that matter, is it time that the Center for Research Libraries takes the lead in establishing a national archive for electronically published materials, both monographs and journals, as well as print materials? University of Kansas Provost David E. Shulenburger stated, and I quote, "It is time we . . . focus on panaceas, for this crisis is growing to the point that scholarship and education will be damaged significantly if we do nothing." This statement prefaced his proposal for a National Electronic Article Repository. Is this possibly the new role for CRL? Also, has anyone thought about the future role of OCLC, aside from OCLC?

In looking to the future, it is necessary to evaluate what is the most cost-beneficial way to archive collection materials. Last week, the National Commission met with ASIS and after one of the sessions, I overheard a participant say never has microfilm looked better. In terms of permanent access, high tech may not be the best answer or the most economically feasible. For your institution, will the mad rush to technology provide better service to both faculty and students?

INITIATING CHANGE

I teach a certification class, distance education class, on library administration. I devote three sessions to the politics of budgets. Understanding how your institution functions, who sets the priorities, and the revenue and funding base for the institution is vital in any strategic planning. I also have my students read two books, *The Art of War* by Sun Tzu and *The Prince* by Machiavelli.

In *The Prince* Machiavelli states, "It should be borne in mind that there is nothing more difficult to handle, more doubtful of success, and more dangerous to carry through than initiating changes in a state's constitution. The innovator makes enemies of all those who prospered under the old order and only lukewarm support is forthcoming from those who would prosper under the new. . . . To discuss this subject thoroughly, we must distinguish between innovators who stand alone and those who depend on others, that is between those who achieve their purposes can force the issue and those who must use persuasion. In the second case, they always come to grief, having achieved nothing; when, howsoever, they depend on their own resources and can force the issue, then they are seldom endangered."

In *The Art of War* there are five essentials for victory.

1. You will win when you know when to fight and when not to fight.
2. You will win when you know how to handle both superior and inferior forces.
3. You will win if your forces are animated by the same spirit throughout all ranks.
4. You will win if prepared, and wait to take your enemy unprepared.
5. If you know your enemy and know yourself, you need not fear the result of the battle. If you know yourself and not the enemy for every victory there will be a defeat. If you know neither the enemy nor yourself, you will succumb in every battle.

These are elements of the art of war and also of the art of politics.

I am sure that the reading I did for this short talk, as someone who is not a member of the choir, consists of the same articles you have either produced or read. It is just that, as a neo-Luddite, I am not necessarily wedded to technology. Technology is only a new tool we can use to do our business, but it is a tool that has forever changed how we will do our business, provide our services, and preserve our history. That is why you must be wedded to the absolute need to plan, develop new ways of doing business, reach out to non-traditional allies, and take a long and careful examination of what your mission really is, and then implement the necessary changes. Please, less talk and a little more action.

I would like to suggest an action plan template.

1. What is it you really want to accomplish?
2. How can you best achieve your goal?
3. What other organizations are working toward this same goal, and can you cooperate?
4. Who will benefit?
5. What funding and resources are required? Are they available and, if not, where can you obtain them?
6. How can you determine when you have accomplished your goal?

While my comments are personal, I plan on learning from this conference and will take back to the National Commission's Committee on Journal Pricing my notes and suggestions for possible future policy recommendations.

In looking at the assembled group, I believe I may be the oldest, and my career of more than 50 years predates technology and predates the MLS and/or the MIS. So I will leave you on a cautionary note. Technology is just fine and dandy until the power goes out. Therefore, I suggest you go to your library and borrow a book titled *Alas Babylon.*

Index

© 2000 by The Haworth Press, Inc. All rights reserved.